Science and Faith

Science and Faith

Understanding Meaning, Method, and Truth

William H. Chalker

Westminster John Knox Press
LOUISVILLE • LONDON

Book design by Sharon Adams
Cover design by Lisa Buckley

First edition
Published by Westminster John Knox Press
Louisville, Kentucky

This book is printed on acid-free paper that meets the American National Standards Institute Z39.48 standard. ♾

PRINTED IN THE UNITED STATES OF AMERICA

06 07 08 09 10 11 12 13 14 15—10 9 8 7 6 5 4 3 2 1

Library of Congress Cataloging-in-Publication Data is on file at the Library of Congress, Washington, D.C.

ISBN-13: 978-0-664-22753-1

ISBN-10: 0-664-22753-8

Contents

Preface

The aim of this book is to present and defend a thesis about how to understand scientific and biblical knowledge-claims—and their apparent incompatibility. Therefore it is organized as a sustained argument and not as a reference work or compendium of key ideas by writers on the subject. It is especially not a compendium of my own opinions on such key ideas. It would be a serious misuse of this book to scan it in order to learn if I "believed in" evolution or miracles. In science, facts are theory laden and cannot be understood as having a meaning or truth apart from the theory to which they belong; similarly, in this work my beliefs about such topics are "thesis laden" and have no meaning apart from the thesis of this book, in which they are embedded.

To make the structure and progression of the argument as clear as possible I have tried to keep footnotes and side discussions to a minimum, using them only when I think they are essential to the understanding of some critical turn or point in the argument. But the shortage of such notes should not be taken to indicate that the ideas incorporated in the argument are original. Indeed, I am not aware of saying anything here that is new or original. Most of it has long been in the public domain, and all of it is part of the received tradition to which most current writers are indebted. If every idea were annotated, most sentences could have several footnotes, the size of the volume would be easily multiplied, and its readability, diminished. Any originality in the thesis stems from the way various well-known ideas about science and biblical theology have been brought to bear on the question of the compatibility of scientific and theological knowledge-claims.

In place of numerous footnotes, I offer this brief chronological account of how I first became acquainted with the now-familiar ideas that are the essential parts of the thesis:

The first event in my life of which I have any clear remembrance was an experience of paradigm shift, although at the time, of course, I did not call it that. At the age of five or six I had just explained to my mother that the world could not be round, because if it were, people on the other side would fall up instead of down. She explained to me that because of gravity, the world was like a large magnet (one of my favorite toys) that made every thing move toward it. I must have understood that the concepts "up" and "down" are theory laden, because I never again worried that Chinese children might fall up.

I was first nurtured in the biblical faith in my family, and later as an early adolescent in the Ensley Highland Presbyterian Church in Birmingham, Alabama, where Frank M. Cross Sr. was pastor. That faith, which is mine today, did not begin with the fear of going to hell and then move on to the search for a sure way to escape it. Instead, it was solidly centered in the confession "We love others because God first loved us." To this day I am still momentarily taken aback when I realize that someone else is using the Bible as if it were a how-to book on hell avoidance.

My abiding appreciation for the humane face of *system* came in my late teen years. I had enlisted in the Navy when I was seventeen years old to become an electronics technician specializing in aviation radar. When our training course began, all that those of us in the class knew about radar was that it was important and secret. Otherwise, it was a mysterious black box. We began with a thorough grounding in Ohm's law. Twelve months later we knew what all parts in the box were for, why their values were what they were, and what the symptoms would be if any part of the system were faulty. Most important, we knew it to be our responsibility to see that before a plane took off, every part of the system was functioning properly. If we failed to know the system and to keep it in working order, some pilot who might have made it safely home could die; some battle strategic to our effort could end in disaster; and the Allied cause, so important for the survival of humane civilization, could be lost. Fortunately the war ended before my systematic knowledge and skill had to be put to the test; but to this day when I hear speakers complain that *scientific system* is the antithesis of all that is *humane*—and I hear it all too often—I think, "They do not know what they are talking about."

When I was a sophomore at Maryville College in Maryville, Tennessee, I took my first course in philosophy. There I came to realize that if Democritus were correct about *metaphysical reality* being made up of atoms moving in accord with deterministic laws, then neither he nor I could ever know that he was right. If he *was* right, it had to be about something *other* than metaphysical reality. In the second half of the course I realized that the important contribution of Francis Bacon was not his precise account of the scientific method; it was his dictum that knowledge is power or utility to ameliorate the human condition. Later in the same course I learned that you cannot refute Berkeley by kicking a stone. *Scientific* experiments do not lead to *metaphys-*

ical truth. And in the same course David Hume made me realize that it was possible to be right about individual causal laws but to be completely wrong about *causation* itself.

In my first year at McCormick Theological Seminary in Chicago, George Ernest Wright enabled me to see that although much of Israel's cultic life imitated that of the Canaanites, it expressed a faith that was almost diametrically opposed to the Canaanite faith. Scripture is itself theory laden, and to suppose that you can get to its literal meaning without theological theory is just as erroneous as it is to suppose that you can understand the literal meaning of the word *atom* without the theory in which it is used.

Also at McCormick I learned from Joseph Haroutunian what predestination is about and, equally important, what it is not about. In his senior seminar, when Esther Cornelius Stine read a paper on the subject "God does not exist to solve our problems," I saw with indelible clarity why scientific knowledge-claims and theological knowledge-claims are not about the same thing. The former are about how to get what we want; the latter are about the ultimate purpose of human life.

In graduate school at Duke University, when I read A. J. Ayer's *Language, Truth, and Logic* for the first time, I became quite excited, not because he had relegated theological knowledge-claims to the realm of the emotive, but because he had so forcefully stated that whatever theology is, it certainly is not the same thing as science. From that time I have believed it to be important to clarify the difference by study of each on its *own* terms.

In my early days of teaching at Albertson College of Idaho I found Ernest Nagel's *The Structure of Science* to be most helpful to me and to students in understanding the scientific method and the foundations on which it rested. Especially important to me was his discussion of the instrumental view of theories. At the time I was using Nagel's work as a text, Thomas Kuhn published *The Structure of Scientific Revolutions,* and in so doing provided the whole field of the philosophy of science with a new vocabulary for discussing and questioning the truth of scientific theories. His view of scientific revolutions, it seemed to me, made it impossible to think of scientific truth as correspondence to metaphysical reality and made it all the easier to see that Bacon's dictum provided the scientific method with all the foundation it needed. Soon after reading Kuhn I began to use the picture in Figure 1 (p. 11) as an analogy for interpreting all experience under either the rubric of utility or the rubric of ultimate purpose of human life, and not as an analogy simply for understanding different paradigms within science.

In more recent years the writings of Richard Rorty have alerted me to the danger of thinking that theology creates truth-claims about the metaphysical reality of God. The correspondence theory of truth is no more appropriate in theology than it is in science.

These, then, are the essential ideas that I have freely taken from the received tradition and woven together into the thesis of this book. I gladly acknowledge my indebtedness to those who knowingly or unknowingly provided me with them.

The theological truth-claims considered in formulating the thesis of the book are limited to those of the biblical faith for three reasons. First, the controversy that gave rise to the book is specific to the biblical book of Genesis and its alleged incompatibility with scientific evolution. Therefore, the thesis presented here may or may not be appropriate for truth-claims of other religious faiths. Second, my quite limited knowledge of other faiths is secondhand and thus disqualifies me from speaking about them responsibly. I hope that those who do profess other faiths as their own are doing for them what I have attempted to do for the biblical faith here. And finally, I am not at all convinced that the term *religion*, as it is commonly used today in discussions such as this one, is an appropriate or useful one. Many of the practices that are commonly called "religious" today are significantly more akin to science than they are to the biblical faith, so the thesis of this book would not pertain to them at all. To undertake a study such as this with the assumption that there is a generic "religion" would be in my opinion a serious intellectual mistake. If there is justification for such a category, it should emerge at the end of many studies such as this one.

In the United States today the debate concerning the relationship between science and religion—and specifically biblical religion—is being conducted more vigorously and more earnestly than it has been in many years. Much of the debate is focused on the apparent, basic incompatibility of the scientific theory of evolution, on the one hand, and the account of creation in the book of Genesis, on the other. Proponents of what they call "creation science," an allegedly biblically based narrative of human origins, want that account substituted for evolutionary science in public schools or taught as a scientifically supportable alternative. Despite setbacks on the national and state level, the proponents of creation science are determined to win at the grass roots.

The debate as it is now being waged, especially on the issue of origins, has serious implications that reach to the very foundations of our society. If the creation scientists should win in legislatures, school boards, and courts, then one very important area of the separation of church and state would be abolished and the freedom of inquiry in public educational institutions would be drastically curtailed. A public debate with implications of this magnitude calls for a serious examination of the foundations of *both* scientific and theological truth-claims in order to assess the nature and extent of the alleged conflict.

As we are often reminded, there are many adherents of a biblical faith, both Jews and Christians, who have no vested interest in creation science either inside or outside the public schools. Many of them are either professional scientists in the widely accepted understanding of that term or educated people who accept the method of science and its findings. For them the manner in which their religious beliefs and their scientific beliefs are to be related to each other is a matter of deep concern. No doubt a similar observation could be made about many adherents of other religious faiths. And there are many scientists and supporters of science who, while not professing a religious faith, nevertheless strongly hold to ethical standards that, although not substantiated by the scientific method, are not thought to be shattered by their scientific views. They, too, no doubt seek an understanding of how their scientific beliefs and their ethical beliefs might be related. On the grassroots level these are the people whose support the creation scientists are trying to win with appeals to "fairness" and "balanced treatment." Many of these people have heard the appeals of the creation scientists, and they are seeking a deeper understanding not only of the scientific issues but also of the theological and ethical issues before they decide which side to support. It is my hope that this book will provide such a deeper understanding by examining the foundations of the scientific method and the theological method that have produced the documents that are at issue.

Although this book is prompted by the evolution versus creation science debate, it does not focus primarily on that debate, and it is not written with the intent of coming to a conclusion in the final chapter about throwing out either Darwinian science or the book of Genesis. Clearly, if the accounts of human origins as given by evolutionary scientists and by the Genesis writers were alternative claims *about the same issue,* as many people on both sides of the debate seem to think or to assume, then those accounts *would* be incompatible, and at least one of them would necessarily be false. In that case we *should* debate simply about the truth or falsity of each. Unfortunately, too much of the debate today is waged on this assumption, with too much heat and too little light. But it should be equally clear that if the two are distinct claims about *different issues,* the one scientific and the other theological, then our first task should be to come to some understanding of the difference between scientific truth-claims and theological truth-claims in general.

It is the claim and thesis of this book that science and theology are human intellectual activities that produce knowledge- or truth-claims of two distinct kinds. It follows from this thesis that the two accounts of origins, scientific and theological, *are* about different issues—so different, in fact, that construing the Genesis account of creation to be science is not only bad science, as many scientists have asserted, but also bad theology, as many theologians have asserted. To construe these two accounts to be about the same concern is to do the very opposite of what the biblical writers were urging their readers to do. To use a common metaphor, to construe Genesis as science is to keep the bathwater but to throw out the baby. To treat Genesis as a source of scientific truth is not to honor Genesis; it is—when one understands what a scientific truth-claim is and what a theological truth-claim is—to deny the central truth-claim that Genesis makes. But it is equally the case that when *in the name of science* it is maintained that the truth-claims of religious "myths" have been refuted or demonstrated to be nonsense, then the very foundational principle of science has been violated, and in doing so, the proper understanding of science has been jeopardized. Both science and religious faith are too important for the proponents of either side to rejoice in some spurious victory over the other.

To appreciate the difference between scientific and theological truth-claims we must turn our attention away from a debate about the truth of the particulars in each account and concentrate instead on coming to an understanding of science as a human intellectual activity for producing truth-claims of one type and of theology in the biblical mode as a human intellectual activity for producing truth-claims of a different type. Doing this will require us immediately to face the question of why we seek knowledge at all. Does our knowledge arise from mere curiosity and awe, or does it arise from more specific promptings? Do scientific knowledge-claims and theological knowledge-claims arise from the same concern, or from quite different concerns? If the concerns are different, how does the method of scientific inquiry differ from the method of theological inquiry so that each uniquely satisfies its own concern? And since both scientists and theologians write creation stories or stories of origins, how do these stories satisfy the concerns of each? In the course of dealing with these and similar questions we also must ask, In what sense is the claim "All truth is one" appropriate and in what sense is it not?

This path of investigation will, I believe, lead us to the conclusion that the question concerning which account is true, the evolutionist's or the creationist's, is the wrong question to ask. It is a classical *loaded question,* because it rests on and therefore accepts the truth of unexpressed presuppositions about science and about theology that will not stand up under examination.

In accordance with this path of investigation, the book proceeds in this way:

Chapter 1 is the explication of the thesis of the book. Here the claim is made that all knowledge arises out of experience, since in a very important way *experience* is all that we have. But knowledge is not the mere recording of experience. We ask ourselves, "What must a world be like for us to have the experiences that we do have?" But we ask that question under two quite distinct concerns, which here are called *rubrics:* the rubric of *utility* and the rubric of the *ultimate purpose of human life.*

Chapter 2 is a justification for the choice of our thesis by showing that the two concerns underlying the two rubrics are pervasive in our intellectual history.

Part 2, comprising chapters 3 through 6, is the analysis of the scientific method, a method that employs the rubric of utility in a sustained attempt to satisfy our desire for knowledge that is useful. This attempt results in what I call the *putative world of science,* the world that is the object of all scientific knowledge. In this section we especially note those aspects of the scientific method that are relevant for comparing and contrasting it with the biblical theological method. Part 2 is structured as a test of the first half of our thesis: that science is a human intellectual activity whose aim is to produce knowledge-claims that will maximize utility.

Part 3, comprising chapters 7 through 9, is the examination of the biblical-theological method, which employs the rubric of ultimate purpose of human life. The result of employing this method is the *putative world of theology,* all of the features of which point to the ultimate human purpose of *imaging* the biblical God, YHWH, whose character is understood to be faithful lovingkindness. In this section we will especially note the sustained insistence in the biblical material that the biblical God is *not* to be understood under the rubric of utility. Part 3 is structured as a test of the second half of our thesis: that theology is a human intellectual activity whose aim is to produce knowledge-claims about ultimate human purpose.

Part 4, comprising chapter 10, is a discussion of three of the most vexing topics that arise when science and the biblical faith are compared: creation, miracles, and authoritative canon. This discussion relies on the understanding of the scientific and biblical-theological methods developed in Parts 2 and 3.

PART 1 The Thesis

Chapter 1

The Primacy of Experience
and the Two Rubrics

The Primacy of Experience

All of my knowledge arises out of experience. I say this because in a very important, basic sense, experience is all that I ever have. When I say this, immediately the experiences of the senses come to mind: colors, tastes, sounds, smells, touches. But on reflection it is clear that I have many other types of experience. My experiences of pain, hunger, pleasure, sadness, elation, and the like are just as surely experiences as are those of blue, red, and yellow. I may think of some experiences as passive, such as the experience of blue, and some as active, such as the experience of proving a theorem. Even now, my dividing experiences into passive and active ones is itself an experience. I sometimes divide experiences into those that are called "objective" and others that are called "subjective." I have experiences of loving, hating, being attracted to, being repulsed by, desiring, being loved, being hated, choosing, being obligated, being humiliated, humiliating others, feeling shame or pride, enjoying, being bored, anticipating, being disappointed, being surprised, doubting, feeling certain, and so on.

The total content of my consciousness is simply experience, and the experience given in consciousness is *all that I ever have*. Yet even here I should be careful not to suggest that consciousness is *one* thing within which experience, which is quite *another* thing, occurs. *Consciousness* perhaps is better thought of as a collective term for all occurring experience. (Unfortunately, the word *consciousness,* like so many other words, is used with different meanings, sometimes making me think that a question is about a fact when it is really about a definition. Hence the question of whether or not I am conscious when I am dreaming is really a question of the definition of the word. In my definition, I am conscious when I am dreaming; otherwise I would not be aware that I had been dreaming. I do not distinguish dreaming from being

3

awake by noticing that I am not conscious when I am dreaming but by noticing in retrospect some differences between certain experiences.

Although I often speak of *having* such things as food, clothing, an automobile, and even a body, my justification for saying that I *have* these things
is only through experience. If I should cease to have experience, I would have
nothing, not even myself. I can never step outside of experience to check to
"see" if the food, the clothing, the automobile, and my body are "really" there
and have some status in "being" that is independent of experience and can be
known to be independent of experience, and being independent of experience,
can be said to correspond to it. I can never compare an experience to something that is not an experience. I can only compare one experience to another
experience, and such comparing is itself an experience. I cannot imagine having food, clothing, automobiles, and a body in a way that is other than—or
more than—having a collection of experiences, including certain experiences
of expected patterns, arrangements, and lack of surprises. I distinguish between
dreaming and being awake only by experiences, not by something that is not
experience.

I take this primacy of experience to be the significance of Descartes's
Cogito, ergo sum, "I think, therefore I am." I can, for example, doubt that the
computer before me "exists" in the ordinary sense. I may be dreaming and in
an hour will awaken and decide that it was only a dream. But I cannot doubt
that the experience occurred. The one thing that I can surely assert is that *experience is occurring.*

I shall try to use consistently the verb *occur* when I speak of experience. I
shall try not to speak of experience as "real" or "true" or "existing." Those
words will be used in another context for a different purpose. Experience simply occurs; as to its occurrence, it is unproblematic. To doubt the occurrence
of experience is self-contradictory; doubting is itself an experience.

Although all my knowledge arises from experience, it does not consist in
a mere record of experiences. I organize them into groups or categories to give
meaning to what would otherwise be a meaningless, inchoate string of experiences. Not content with just having experiences, I ask myself what a "world"
must be like for these experiences to occur as they do. In response to this question, I formulate words, concepts, and generalizing laws to organize my experiences and thus envision a world in which other people and objects *exist* along
with me—a world in which many, but not all, of my experiences are taken to
be of objects in that world. It is a world in which other people are said to have
experiences in the same way that I do. This is the ordinary, everyday world of
our experience. When speaking of this world and the objects in it, I no longer
confine myself to the first-person-singular pronoun, and I no longer restrict

my discussion to the occurrence of experiences. Now I can begin to speak of the *existence* of objects and make knowledge-claims about these objects. Nevertheless, all my knowledge of myself, of objects, and of other people has arisen from my experience, and all the knowledge-claims that I make are checked by it. Indeed, in almost every moment, in important and in trivial ways, I am revising my knowledge of myself, of objects, and of other people by new experience. *As long as experience continues to occur, my present knowledge-claims are subject to revision.*

A few examples may be of help here.

Example 1: Suppose that I am color-blind. How do I come to the conclusion that I *am* color-blind? Certainly *not* by having some nonexperiential knowledge of what colors are, and then noticing that I cannot *experience* these colors. No; I come to the conclusion by the many experiences that I *do* have. I experience many other people using such words as *red*, *blue*, and *yellow* apparently to make visual discriminations that I cannot make. Furthermore, they generally agree on which of these words to use in any given situation. Then in the physics laboratory I encounter pieces of optical equipment that under certain circumstances give numerical readouts or other results (which I *can* see) that correlate with other people's use of the color terms. I also notice that a few other people attest to their inability to make the same apparent discriminations that I cannot make.

What must the world be like for me to have all these experiences? I could perhaps conclude that there is a grand conspiracy of these so-called non-color-blind people to perpetrate a hoax on the few of us who are outside their circle. But the preponderance of my experience makes such a conclusion highly unsatisfactory. So I conclude that most other people see what I do not see, and I am content to call those things "colors." I even learn to use color words correctly in some circumstances. For example, I learn to answer correctly if someone asks me at a busy intersection if the green light is on, because I can discriminate between the top light's being on and the bottom light's being on. And if I am a scientist in the field of genetics, I may propose a research project to see if there is some genetic condition that distinguishes me from "normal" people. And, of course, the results of such research would be based on experience. In short, concluding that I am color-blind makes everything (all my experiences) fall into place in a much more satisfactory way than does any other explanation thus far.

Example 2: How do I know that there was a world before I was born? Again, certainly not by some nonexperiential knowledge that I mysteriously possess. Rather, it is by *all* of the experiences that I do have: hearing the stories that my mother told me about her childhood, observing that babies are being born during my life, reading historical accounts, studying fossils, and millions of others. I never experience the world that existed before I was born, but concluding that such a world did exist is the simplest satisfactory way I know of to make sense of the totality of the experiences that I do have.

Example 3: On a visit to a museum of science and industry I see an exhibit, a black box about the size of a bread box, with a peephole in the front and a larger hole in the side. The sign above it asks, "What is in the box?" I look in through the peephole, and I conclude without a doubt that a dimly glowing lightbulb is in the box. But when I put my hand into the box through the hole in the side, much to my surprise I feel nothing. On the basis of this additional experience I must revise the previous knowledge-claim that I had made with such youthful certainty. When I read the explanation of the optical illusion, then the presence of the optical experience but the absence of the expected tactile experience begin to fit together into a coherent whole and bafflement disappears.

Example 4: Last night I dreamed that I sat before my computer composing a document by typing with my fingers. While I was dreaming, I had no doubt that both the computer and my hands were really present. Today I am awake, sitting before my computer composing a document by typing with my fingers. Now I have no doubt that both this computer and my fingers are really present and that last night's computer and fingers were only a dream. On what basis do I make this revision in my knowledge-claim? Only on the basis of all my experiences, including the new experiences of today. The concepts "dreaming" and "awake" enable me to make sense of what would otherwise be a most baffling set of experiences. But is my current assurance unshakable that the computer before me and my fingers are really present? Suppose that I should soon have the experience of waking up again. I would have to make another revision. After all, I have on rare occasions had what I call a dream within a dream. And although I have never had a dream within a dream within a dream, I cannot rule out even that possibility. As long as experience continues to occur, all my knowledge-claims about fingers and computers, regardless of how strongly they might be held, are subject to revision.

Example 5: What is my justification for claiming that the sharp pain in my tooth is a subjective experience that other people cannot share with me, while my experience of red as I look at an apple is a public or objective experience that many others do indeed share? When someone else says to me, "I too see a red apple," is it possible for me ever to know if that person's experience is anything like mine? No, for all experience is private. The justification for my making the subjective-objective distinction is that such a distinction enables me to organize the totality of my experiences into a coherent world.

These examples have been given here for the sole purpose of emphasizing the primacy of experience in our knowledge of the world. That my experiences occur is indubitable and unproblematic. But the world that I envision on the basis of experience is always subject to revision. Therefore, my knowledge-claims about that world are also subject to revision.

It might be useful to make a distinction between what we could call *practical* doubt and *principled* doubt. Much of our knowledge about the world is reliable, having stood the test of time. Such knowledge is the best we have, and it would be foolish for us not to act on it on the grounds that it is subject to revision. About such knowledge we should not have practical doubts. If we did, our lives would grind to a halt by indecision. On the other hand, we should take seriously the principle that even our most tested and reliable knowledge of the world can be doubted and that future experience may make it advisable to discard it. This is principled, but not practical, doubt. If we overlook this principled doubt, we will fail to recognize one of the most important aspects of both the scientific and the theological method. To ignore it is to invite bigotry and tragedy in both areas. We will discuss this topic in more detail later.

The Two Rubrics

The commonly held knowledge of our ordinary world of experience is rudimentary and at this stage hardly qualifies as either scientific or theological knowledge. To understand the foundations of these two branches of knowledge we need to examine the reasons for our seeking knowledge in the first place. Sometimes it is claimed that science springs from curiosity about the world or from the disinterested love of knowing, whereas theology springs from the feeling of awe. Although many people experience curiosity, awe, and the yen-to-know, they hardly serve to distinguish science from theology. Many scientists have mentioned their feeling of awe at the magnificence of the universe or at the elegance of natural law as one of the reasons for their taking up a scientific career. But the method on which modern science is founded and by which it is practiced is anything but one of disinterest, and the "interest" behind the method does not allow any amount of curiosity or love of truth to ignore that interest. On the other hand, many theologians have indeed mentioned their feelings of awe at some aspect of the world as a reason for their pursuit of theological knowledge; yet their method, while different from the scientists' method, is also anything but disinterested, and it requires them to seek truth and to direct their curiosity, awe, and sheer love of learning by the dictates of theology's particular interest.

What, then, are the pertinent reasons for our seeking scientific and theological knowledge? From the earliest times we have asked two different but fundamental questions that have arisen from two different sorts of experience. Neither of these questions should be thought of as the right one or the wrong one. Both have been deemed to be so important that much of Western intellectual activity has been focused on formulating answers to them. For the purposes of distinguishing science from theology, let us call them (1) the question of *utility* and (2) the question of *the ultimate purpose of human life,* and discuss them in that order.

The Question of Utility

The question of utility arises from the fact that as human beings in our ordinary everyday world we experience wants, wishes, hopes, desires, aspirations, longings, and ambitions that this ordinary world as we confront it does not seem to be particularly anxious to satisfy. To simplify terminology, let us lump all such experiences together as *wants*. Some of the things we want, such as food and protection from the elements, are so important that we call them "needs." Unless we satisfy them our experience has led us to believe that we will not long survive. Therefore we seek the kind of knowledge that will help us cope with a world that often seems indifferent to our wants if not downright hostile to them. Such knowledge will serve as a prediction device, letting us know beforehand the consequences of our possible acts so that we can choose to do those that will have the results we want and avoid doing those that will have the results we do not want. Knowledge of this type ranges from the extremely informal to the highly organized. All of us act on some form of it thousands of times a day. It is hard to imagine living a life at all, much less an effective life, without it. In virtually all of our intentional acts we employ knowledge of this type.

The question of utility, thus, provides us with this rubric: *Thou shalt seek to maximize knowledge that has utility*. I take this to be the import of Francis Bacon's often-repeated dictum that knowledge is power or utility for the betterment of humanity. (Rubrics are authoritative rules for the performance of some activity, such as a religious rite, and are so called because they were often written in red. I broaden the term here to refer to the authoritative rules for producing scientific or theological knowledge-claims. It is appropriate to think of them as red flags to remind us not to confuse the "rites" of the scientific method with the "rites" of the theological method.) Modern science is only one of several human intellectual activities that produce knowledge-claims best understood under this rubric, but since it is science in which we are particularly interested, we shall concentrate our attention on it in part 2. Yet we should examine briefly some of the common nonscientific knowledge-claims produced under this rubric to get a sense of the pervasiveness of it in our lives, and we shall do so later in chapter 3. Before we do so, however, let us consider the second main question by which we organize our experience into knowledge.

The Question of Ultimate Purpose

The question of the ultimate purpose of human life arises from the fact that many human beings, just as surely as they have experiences of wants, also in their ordinary lives have experiences of right and wrong, good and evil, obligations, responsibilities, guilt, and the like. These give rise to the question, What kind of world do we live in if these are experiences of the world? Let us for convenience organize all of these experiences into an overarching question: What is the ultimate purpose of human life? Sometimes this is called the question of the meaning of life, but the phrase "meaning of life" is highly ambiguous. The ambiguity has led to countless arguments in which participants on each side have not understood how the participants on the other are using the phrase, with the result that important issues are obscured. It would be better if we did not use it here and settled instead on the phrase "ultimate purpose of human life." Vast numbers of people make some claim about the answer to this question, even if their answer is, Life has no ultimate purpose. Virtually all of our intentional acts are implicitly or explicitly guided by some answer to this question.

This question, then, provides us with a different rubric: *Thou shalt seek to make knowledge-claims that point to the ultimate purpose of human life.* Since theology in the biblical mode is carried out under this rubric, it should act as a red flag, warning us that all biblical material should be read under its guidance and all subsequent formulation of doctrine should be under its control. It is the claim of this book that the ignoring of this rubric, and hence the reading of biblical-theological material under the scientific rubric of utility, is at the heart of the debate about science and religion, and that no resolution of the debate will emerge until the difference between these two rubrics is understood. Because theology in the biblical mode is not the only intellectual activity that is carried on under this rubric, before we focus attention on it in part 3 we shall consider some others that do so also, in order to get a sense of the pervasiveness of this rubric in our lives.

Therefore, we shall turn our attention shortly to several common human intellectual activities that are, for our purposes, best understood under one or the other of these two rubrics. But before we do so, let us study Figure 1 as an analogy to clarify the notions of (1) the primacy of experience and of (2) organizing experience under one rubric or the other. I emphasize that we will use Figure 1 only as an analogy, not as an illustration of what the two rubrics are. Like all analogies, this one will have features that are helpful and some that are not. Therefore, we shall try not to apply this analogy beyond its helpfulness.

In its sheer givenness Figure 1 is just an inchoate jumble of black and white patches. But the question beneath it invites us to "look" at it in two ways, and to see it first as a picture of an older woman and second as a picture of a younger woman. Study the figure until you can see it in both ways (though not at the same time!). Get help from someone else if you need to before you proceed.

Once we can see it as both a younger woman and an older woman, it should be clear that it is inappropriate to ask of the figure in its sheer givenness, "Is it *really* a picture of a younger woman, or is it *really* a picture of an older woman?" No answer could be given, and it would be pointless to debate the question. But let us look at it as one of a younger woman. Now we can begin to ask some questions that we can answer at least tentatively and about which there might be some disagreement and debate. For example, (1) "Does she have an ornament on her left ear?" or (2) "Is her left eye open or closed?" or (3) "Is her necklace a ribbon or a piece of enameled metal?" or (4) "Is her fur collar real or fake?" These are now *factual* questions, the answers to which are tentatively *true* or *false*.

If someone else were looking at the picture as one of an older woman, how would that person understand these same questions? Questions 1 and 3 would be strange indeed, because neither the older woman's left ear nor her neck is visible and therefore there is no evidence on which to make even a tentative answer. Question 2 would make sense, but the answer given would rest on a completely different set of data, for the older woman's left eye is the younger woman's left ear, and the older woman's right eyelash is all that we can see of the younger woman's left eye. Question 4 would seem to be the same question for either way of looking at the picture, but the answers could differ on the basis of indirect evidence. Because the younger woman seems to be quite elegant, we might argue on the basis of inconclusive evidence that the fur must surely be real, since such a woman would not wear fake fur. But because the older woman seems perhaps to be a peasant, someone looking at the picture as one of an older woman might argue on the basis of inconclusive evidence that the collar is frayed cloth and not fur at all.

Similarly, if we should look at Figure 1 as a picture of an older woman, we could ask a number of factual questions, the answers to which we might have disagreements about. But in that case someone seeing it as a picture of a

Figure 1: Older Woman or Younger Woman?
Other writers have used this figure to illustrate two paradigms within science. I use it to illustrate two rubrics.

younger woman might be perplexed by some of our questions and wonder why in the "world" we asked them in the first place and how in the world we came to our answers, different though they might be, since for these questions there was no evidence for any answer whatsoever. Furthermore, such a person might attempt to answer some of our other questions that seem meaningful, but would understand them in a completely different way and answer them on a completely different set of data.

The important point for us to understand is that (1) a group of people who all see the picture as one of a younger woman may have differences among themselves about the facts of the case and (2) one group of people who see the picture as one of a younger woman and another group of people who see the picture as one of an older woman may (and indeed will) have differences between themselves, *but these two sets of differences are of quite different kinds.*

To make this point in a slightly different way, if you and I each see Figure 1 in a different way, *and if neither of us realizes that this is the case,* there is very little chance of our having any fruitful dialogue. We will probably end up shouting at each other. Only when we both acknowledge that there are two possible ways of seeing the figure, and only when we agree on which way we will look at it, will our differences become understandable, and only then can we begin to try to work out our differences.

Let us make one final point about the analogy. Suppose that I see Figure 1 as an older woman. It could be the case that by habit or by constant instruction I am (or become) oblivious to the possibility of seeing it as a younger woman. I would then *implicitly* claim that my way of seeing the picture is the only way to see it, and that it is *really* a picture of an older woman (except that I would not state it this way since it does not even occur to me that there might be an alternative). I would say simply that I observe *reality* and that reality is an older woman. Furthermore, my way of seeing the picture becomes for me the standard of *rationality.* Anyone who makes a knowledge-claim about the picture based on a different way of seeing it is *irrational.*

It should be clear that the two ways of seeing the picture are not examples of using the two rubrics that we have discussed above. But from this analogy we can make several important points to keep in mind when we think about employing the rubrics as ways of construing a world in science and in theology:

Point 1: We are not likely to make serious systematic knowledge-claims about experience as it occurs in its sheer givenness. We make such knowledge-claims only about a *world* that results from *experience comprehended under a rubric.*

Point 2: It is conceivable that we could comprehend or interpret all of our experiences under the rubric of utility at one time and all of our experiences under the rubric of ultimate purpose at another time. It is the employment of such rubrics that generates significant systematic knowledge-claims. The word *holistic* is commonly used today to refer to the ideal—never actually attained—of systematic knowledge-claims comprehending all experience. It is these worlds resulting from our comprehending experience under rubrics that we will call "putative" worlds later.

Point 3: Two systems of knowledge-claims, each formulated under the same rubric, can possibly be incompatible with each other. In such a case, the conflict must be dealt with according to the rules and methods appropriate to that rubric. And in such a case we are figuratively driven to resolve any incompatibility that is apparent, and we do not rest easy until it has been resolved. It is here that it is appropriate to claim as an ideal, "All knowledge is one."

Point 4: Two systems of knowledge-claims, one formulated under one rubric and the other formulated under the other, will *appear* to be incompatible, and one or both could be self-contradictory. But in this case, each must be evaluated under the rules and methods appropriate to its own rubric. One rubric cannot be used to judge knowledge-claims formulated under the other as true or false. Here it is inappropriate to claim that all knowledge must be one and therefore must be the result of the employment of only one rubric.

Point 5: The differences in points 3 and 4 are of two quite different types and should not be confused.

Point 6: Neither rubric in its own rules and methods contains the universal standard of rationality. There can be rational and irrational thinking in both theology and science.

Chapter 2

Justification for Choosing
the Two Rubrics

*T*he next major step in the orderly development of the thesis of this book is to examine the method of science under the rubric of utility and the method of theology under the rubric of ultimate purpose of human life, which we shall do in parts 2 and 3. Before we do so, however, it is appropriate to provide some justification for the choice of these rubrics, since the presentation of them thus far has been primarily stipulative or dogmatic. This excursus, then, does not attempt to develop further the thesis of the book. The goal instead is to acquaint us sufficiently with the implicit or explicit pervasiveness of these two rubrics in intellectual life to assure us that the use of these rubrics is reasonable or prudent before we go further.

How should such a justification proceed? Certainly not by attempting to construct a proof that the two rubrics are the true or correct ones, in obedience to which the two disciplines must be carried out. The terms *proof* and *prove* have quite specific meanings in formal logic, which we will discuss in part 2. Moreover, no valid proof of the correctness of the rubrics could be constructed in accordance with those meanings. Formal logical proofs do have an important, though limited, role to play in the construction of both scientific theories and theological doctrine, but that role is quite different from the one often ascribed to it. For example, the proper use of the scientific method does not prove by logically valid arguments that scientific laws or theories are true or that entities such as protons or electrons exist, nor do theological arguments prove the ultimate purpose of human life or the existence of God. Here is not the place to deal with this matter, but we should note it now lest we carry around with us the unexamined and hidden assumption that science and theology are in the business of logically proving their truth-claims.

To repeat our question: How then should a justification of the choice of the rubrics proceed? Since the justification of the rubrics is somewhat like the justification for defining words the way we do, let us consider that latter process briefly.

One of the most important tasks in constructing any serious intellectual system is that of defining the words to be used in that system. Words do not in themselves have indelible, unchangeable meanings. We are constantly inventing new words and defining them, or changing the meanings of words that we have inherited as a part of our culture. Words, or concepts, are intellectual devices by which we organize our experiences into a coherent world with its distinct entities (or objects) and relationships. Recall how the phrases "younger woman" and "older woman" told us what to look for in Figure 1 and how the definitions that we associate with them made it possible to discriminate between the two pictures that then emerged.

But why are we constantly redefining words? Not, as some people seem to think, just to annoy our elders and to drive linguistic purists to distraction, although that may be part of the reason. A more important reason is that as experience continues to occur, words or concepts are no longer capable of making the discriminations necessary to make a coherent world under one or the other of our rubrics. In the practice of science, when the world that has emerged under one set of definitions can no longer easily be subsumed or described by any set of laws that we can postulate, one way to get out of the impasse is to redefine some of the old words so that in effect a world of different objects emerges from the same experiences. In science, redefining words is one of the important operations by which our knowledge is advanced. Think for a moment how many times the term *atom* has been redefined and how significantly the utility of scientific knowledge has been increased by the employment of those redefinitions.

Are there any constraints on this practice of giving new definitions to words? Yes, there are, and they arise from the tasks that we want language to perform. First, if we want language to continue to communicate knowledge, then changes in definitions cannot be so widespread or so radical that an entirely new language must be learned before communication can resume. Therefore the new definitions need to be sufficiently close to the old ones for us to be able to explain just where the definitions have changed, using in that explanation many words whose definitions have *not* changed. Second, if we want language under the first rubric to be capable of being formulated into useful knowledge, then the new definitions must increase that utility, not diminish it. The use of any new set of definitions for words in science, then, is justified by these two restraints: these definitions must bear some minimum similarity to the definitions of the words in common usage; and these new definitions must be sufficiently different to be fruitful in useful knowledge.

Our two rubrics, to be reasonable and prudent intellectual tools for elucidating science and biblical theology, and not to be regarded as simple arbitrary gimmicks, must be controlled by similar restraints. First, it must be shown that *past practice* in our intellectual history has been governed significantly by these rubrics, even though it may not have been common to refer to them as such. The remainder of this excursus will attempt to show this by three sets of examples: examples taken from everyday life, fairly well-known definitive knowledge- or truth-claims that fall under one of our rubrics or the other, and examples from what is more specifically recognized as the history of philosophy. No attempt has been made to make the examples mutually exclusive and totally exhaustive. In fact most, if not all, of the examples exhibit the varying degree of imprecision that characterizes all our human efforts.

After we have evaluated our use of the rubrics by the first restraint, we must turn our attention to the second. There we will attempt to justify our use of them by showing that their explicit application for differentiating between science and theology does indeed enhance our understanding of the two disciplines and makes many of their vexing problems more tractable. Parts 2, 3, and 4 will focus on this task.

First Set of Examples: Ordinary Life

Let us turn now to evidence from our intellectual history to show the pervasive, if implicit, use of these rubrics. The first examples are of characteristic ways of thinking, analyzing, explaining, and evaluating in everyday life.

Means and Ends

One of the most common sets of concepts by which we understand, analyze, and evaluate human activities is the one of means and ends. On the level of the individual, it is seen in literature aimed at self-improvement. The advice often falls into this pattern: first formulate your goals clearly, then pursue those goals, choosing the means that are clearly capable of bringing them about. The implication is that an aimless life is not fully human and not optimally satisfactory. To follow this advice I must analyze my life to see that I have clear goals; then I must plan my activities to help develop the skills necessary for attaining those goals (and perhaps not waste my resources on extraneous activities). To be sure, the goals in this context are not usually considered to be the ultimate purpose of human life, but the pattern is definitely related to our two rubrics.

Many religious sermons or talks follow this pattern, with two distinct variations. The first goes something like this: First, decide what you most dearly want out of the life that God has given you (choose your goal). Then by your religious devotion, appropriate the power of the loving God as the means to attain this goal (or this *bliss*, as I heard it called recently, using Joseph Campbell's term). God's power is the means to attain your goal. The other variant, which you will recognize as the one I prefer, goes like this: God's character of love gives our life its ultimate purpose, for we are created in God's image. Knowing your purpose by faith, now follow this purpose with fear and trembling (i.e., with utmost seriousness), using all your talents and resources (including scientific knowledge) in pursuit of it. Here the goal or end *is* understood to be ultimate. It is on the difference between these two variants that much of the argument of this book focuses.

Moving from the individual level to the institutional level, we find the means-end classification becoming more explicitly used, although I am sure that it has hardly ever been completely ignored. In recent years the expression "management by objective" has been increasingly used. The minimal meaning of this phrase surely is that the good manager has clearly in mind what end or goal or objective his or her unit is to achieve, and then he or she deploys the human and physical resources available to achieve this objective. Again, the objective is not often thought of as the ultimate purpose, but the means-end structure is evident. And it is also evident that the means-end classification provides the context in which a manager's performance is to be evaluated.

The use of mission statements in all sorts of institutions has become so popular that it is the butt of many jokes. A few years back my Internet server each week sent out by e-mail to its subscribers a bulletin that contained two items. The first in importance was the corporate mission statement, and the second was a discussion of the various things that the corporation had done in the past week to improve fulfilling its mission. I have noticed that several national corporations have printed their mission statements in full-page advertisements. The implication is that customers are to evaluate corporations on how well they use their means to achieve their avowed ends. But still there is no claim that their corporate mission is in harmony with some ultimate purpose.

In the field of higher education in the United States the use of the mission statement has long been vital in the accreditation process. As it prepares for accreditation, an institution must first develop its mission statement, making clear its purpose—a mission statement that should be borne in mind when major institutional decisions are made. After this, and in light of it, the institution is to conduct a self-study to evaluate its performance in curriculum, faculty recruitment and policies, student recruitment and affairs, libraries, physical facilities, budgeting decisions, financial stability, and the like. The implication is that an institution with excellent means to accomplish educational tasks but with no clear purpose or mission to direct it is a rudderless ship doomed to be sunk like the *Bismarck;* it should not be accredited. Likewise, an institution with a clear and admirable mission but without the means to accomplish what its mission statement promises should not be accredited. Means and ends should be characteristics of an accredited college.

In the examples given here, the ends are not always thought of as being determined or justified by theology, but the very postulation of ends—for one's life, for a business, for a college—does raise the question of whether or not there is some ultimate end by which they are justified. Likewise, the means appropriate to attaining the ends are not always thought of as being determined or confirmed by the scientific method, but in many areas of life this is increasingly the case. We more and more look to science for the knowledge necessary for selecting appropriate means to accomplish our objectives. For example, I recently heard of a controlled scientific study being made to ascertain whether or not prayer works as an effective means to bring about the ends sought! (Do good guys really finish first? Do families that pray together really stay together?)

Humanities and Sciences

Given this widespread employment of means and ends as concepts for analyzing and evaluating human situations, we should expect to find a great deal of our intellectual energy focused on them. Indeed this is the case. In our culture, liberal arts colleges have been thought of as the institutions in which the kinds of knowledge essential to truly human life are sought, cherished, and taught. In such colleges the curriculum typically has been divided into the sciences and the humanities, the sciences being concerned with systematic generalized knowledge of means and the humanities being concerned with claims about what, if anything, is the ultimate purpose of human life. Although faculties continue to debate the question of the nature of the liberal arts institution, the abiding division of studies into these two main groups is evidence of the pervasiveness of means and ends in our thinking.

Mechanistic and Teleological Explanations

Closely related to the means-ends pattern in our thinking is the ease and regularity with which we answer the question "Why?" in two quite distinct ways when it is asked about some event in the everyday world. When the event (the *explanandum*) is one in the nonhuman world, the explanation of "Why did it happen?" consists of statements about previous events (the *explanans*) and laws of nature. This type of explanation is usually called *mechanistic*, and ideally, its statements of events and laws of nature will be in the same conceptual language; for example, mental processes will not cause objects to move, nor will moving objects cause thoughts to occur. Explanations of this type are the stock-in-trade of modern science. On the other hand, when the event to be explained is an action for which a human being could be held morally responsible, the explanation is most often given as statements of motives, purposes, or ends that the person had in mind. This type of explanation is usually called *teleological* (from the Greek word *telos,* meaning "end") and seldom contains the statement of a natural law. It is the stock-in-trade of the humanities. History, biography, and fiction, for example, abound with teleological explanations.

Few of us, however, deal in only one type of explanation. Many scientists who would totally repudiate teleological explanations as nonscientific when they are in the laboratory or lecture hall "doing" science—even human science—will explain their colleagues' and their own conduct teleologically when they are in faculty meetings discussing curricular or budgetary matters. And most humanities faculty members, when choosing their own health-care professionals, certainly do not want physicians who explain all diseases teleologically. Most of us can switch back and forth between mechanistic and teleological explanations just as easily as we can switch from seeing Figure 1 as an older woman to seeing it as a younger woman. And we seem to know when it is appropriate to do so.

Since the beginning of the scientific era there has been a concerted effort to eliminate teleological explanations from scientific discourse, but it has become more difficult to do as human beings themselves have become the object of scientific inquiry. One can scarcely read the almost-daily news reports of developments in the field of genetics without sensing that the effort to retain teleological explanations in scientific discussion of human conduct is a losing battle. Even in the social sciences, when human intentions are used to explain human conduct, they are explained by antecedent factors that are hereditary or environmental but ideally do not include intentions. A scientist who disdained attempts to give nonintentional explanations for human intentions would probably be thought of as not doing serious *science.*

Much of the discussion—indeed argument—about the relation of science and religion in the last century and a half has centered on the question of whether or not teleological explanations are "real" explanations. When we turn our attention to the two rubrics, we can appreciate the importance of this argument. If science is to be faithful to its rubric of producing useful knowledge, it then must eschew teleological explanations for the simple reason that such explanations do not purport to be based on the kind of knowledge that is about *means* to ends. Likewise, if theology is to remain faithful to its rubric of producing knowledge-claims about ultimate purpose, it must not depend on mechanistic explanations, since such explanations do not account for or rely on purposes. We will discuss these types of explanations further in parts 2 and 3. All we need to note here is that the pervasiveness of them in everyday discourse adds support to our claim that the two rubrics are not just arbitrary gimmicks.

Facts and Values

The terms *facts* and *values* are commonly used to distinguish between the major concerns of science, on the one hand, and religion, on the other. The choice of these two terms, however, is unfortunate, for it prejudices any further discussion. The term *facts* connotes "objective," "true," and "real." But if "values" are contrasted with "facts," are we to conclude that values are merely subjective, having no status in reality and truth? The choice of these two terms is a classic example of the logical fallacy of "begging the question," that is, of already assuming the truth of the very question that is under discussion. Nevertheless, the use of the terms does suggest a broad conviction that science and religion deal with two distinct areas of human concern that ought not to be confused and that both of them deserve serious intellectual respect and consideration. The claim of this book is that the use of our two rubrics provides a way of analyzing this conviction without begging the question. The pervasive use of *fact* and *value* in this context also adds support to our claim that the use of the two rubrics is not an arbitrary gimmick.

Second Set of Examples: Common Knowledge-Claims about the World

Scientific knowledge-claims are not the only ones that, either explicitly or implicitly, fall under the rubric of utility, nor are theological knowledge-claims the only ones that fall under the rubric of ultimate purpose. We will therefore look at several of these other knowledge-claims about the world and ask if our two rubrics, *when explicitly applied to them,* help us to understand them.

Common Sense

From earliest times human beings have accumulated a store of knowledge about how to get along in the world. They had wants and felt needs for food, shelter, and clothing, and they developed techniques for satisfying them. They learned when to plant and when not to. They developed knowledge about which plants to eat and which ones to avoid. They learned when and where to hunt and when and where not to hunt. They developed techniques to produce shelter and clothing adapted to their needs. Much of their knowledge seems to have arisen from a process of observation, trial, and error—a rudimentary scientific method. Indeed, it is hard to imagine any society's surviving without having developed this kind of common-sense knowledge. Most societies that we condescendingly call primitive survived very well indeed by such knowledge, and many items of their knowledge have been incorporated into the present corpus of scientific knowledge.

If we understand this development of common-sense knowledge under the rubric of utility, it is not difficult to grasp why so much of it has stood the test of time. What has not stood the test of time, by scientific standards, is the conceptual framework in which it was sometimes expressed. One of the distinctive features of the scientific method, as we shall see later, is a critical attitude toward *all* conceptual frameworks, even its own, and it is this critical attitude that, in part, has made modern science more fruitful than common sense in producing useful knowledge. For our purposes now, however, all we need to note is that a great deal of knowledge that we refer to as common sense has arisen implicitly under the rubric of utility.

Magic

The practice of magic was a feature of many early societies, and is still common in some cultures today. In them magicians or shamans are, of course, not entertainers; they are important people whose knowledge and ability are thought to contribute to the safety and welfare of the community. Because the natural world so often seems to behave capriciously, it is conceived to be occupied and controlled by entities who, as living spirits, account for that capricious behavior. The magician or shaman is thought to possess the knowledge of what to do and say in order to protect the society from baleful influences of those spirits and to inflict them on their own enemies. These knowledge-claims are implicitly understood under the rubric of utility; knowledge of the spirits does not entail an answer to the question of the ultimate purpose of life. The spirits are powers that can be controlled to satisfy the wants of the community, and the shaman or magician is thought to have the knowledge of how to control those powers. Incidentally, in this example the word *spirits* does not give us a clue as to the rubric under which this knowledge-claim is to be subsumed. The words *spirit, spiritual, spirituality, god, religion,* and the like sometimes appear in knowledge-claims that are best understood under the rubric of utility, but at other times they appear in knowledge-claims that are best understood under the rubric of the ultimate purpose of human life. To assume that all religions are the same is to ignore this important question of rubric.

Astrology

Astrology as commonly understood is based on a conceptualization of the world in which the heavenly bodies are associated with powers that exert significant influence on the day-to-day affairs of human life. An astrologer is one who is thought to possess the knowledge of how these powers operate and who is therefore deemed qualified to give individuals advice about what they should do and not do at particular times to get those powers to help them rather than hinder them in achieving their wishes, aspirations, and ambitions. Astrology, then, is for our purposes best understood under the rubric of utility. For this reason it is potentially and actually in conflict with science and is opposed by the scientific community, as that term is commonly understood.

Prudence

Sometimes ethical or moral precepts are deemed to be practical advice about how to get along in the world in a manner that will satisfy our desires. When ethics is so understood it is organized under the rubric of utility and is usually called *prudence*. Prudence, therefore, should be carefully distinguished from ethics organized under the rubric of purpose, which is usually called normative ethics. Examples of prudence are "Honesty is the best policy" and "If you practice the Golden Rule in business, your profits will increase." We will say more about normative ethics later.

Wisdom

Closely related to prudence is a heterogeneous collection of knowledge-claims that go under the name of wisdom. In recent years much attention has been given to wisdom literature, from motives that are as diverse as the sorts of knowledge-claims that can be found in it. In certain circles I frequently hear the assertion made that science is concerned with *knowledge*, but religion is concerned with *wisdom*. However, when we look at the specific knowledge-claims that are in the world's wisdom literature, there is little there to give that assertion any meaning. For our purposes, therefore, it is best not to attempt to give any *one* definition of *wisdom,* but to look at each knowledge-claim individually. When we do this, most of them are simply examples of prudence, whether or not the source for them is said to be a god. On the other hand, some wisdom writings—the book of Job for example—seem to have been written to counter the very idea that God's wisdom is to be thought of as prudence and to make the assertion that one who knows the wisdom of God lives from a motive quite different from the desire to satisfy one's wants. If this is the case, we can thus say that some of the knowledge-claims in wisdom literature are to be understood under the rubric of utility and others under the rubric of purpose. The thesis of this book is that the rubrics of utility and purpose serve to distinguish the significant features of science and the biblical faith, and they do so in a way that the terms *knowledge* and *wisdom* cannot do.

Closely associated with the term *wisdom* is the idea that wisdom is the peculiar possession of the elders, since it is attained only after a long life of observation about what brings long-lasting contentment and what does not. Therefore wisdom is often cast as advice from the elders to the youth, and it has a low expectation that the young will produce valuable additions to the store of knowledge until they have first learned the accumulated lore from the elders. We might merely note here, without drawing any unwarranted conclusions, that in both the history of biblical theology and the history of scientific theories it is often the young who confound the elders with revolutionary insights.

Some Religions—Idolatry

A great number of religions in the world make knowledge-claims that are based implicitly on a conceptualization of the world formed under the rubric of utility. In such a religion the god (or gods) is conceived as a power within the world that can be influenced, manipulated, or controlled by the worshiper's religious activity to get that power to work in behalf of the worshiper's wishes. Sometimes the requisite religious activities are thought of as essentially cultic or ritualistic, such as performing sacrifices, keeping feasts, avoiding the unclean, fasting, praying in a prescribed manner, observing sacraments; sometimes they are thought of as essentially legal, such as observing laws of personal purity, of social justice and compassion, or of blood vengeance and ethnic cleansing; and sometimes they are thought of as essentially intellectual, such accepting personally and publicly certain essential doctrines to be true. Although the required duties may vary from religion to religion, the desired outcome is the fulfillment of the worshiper's wants here and/or hereafter. The god's will is thought of as pertaining to the duties one must perform in order to get what one wants; it is not thought of as pertaining to some ultimate purpose that might require the worshiper to surrender his or her own wants to it. If a belief in a hereafter is a part of such a religion, it is a hereafter in which the worshiper's wants are ultimately fulfilled, not a hereafter in which the god's purpose is actualized or triumphs in the worshiper's life.

Many earlier religions of this type were polytheistic, probably because the powers, which were believed to lurk behind the visible world and capriciously cause the natural events to happen as they did, seemed to be unrelated to each other in any orderly way. Each god was more or less the personification of one power in one location. But the situation was always somewhat fluid, with gods from different locations being identified with each other, and all powers being combined into one god. Thus some monotheisms appear to be the natural outgrowth of polytheisms that implicitly belong under the rubric of power.

In the Bible, Israel's prominent prophets called such religions, whether polytheistic or monotheistic, *idolatry,* and spoke out vehemently against them, not only in the nations around Israel but most particularly in Israel itself. The prophets understood the idols to be personifications of natural powers, most notably the power of fertility, which exerted such a great influence on the fulfillment of human wants but which was so unpredictable. Since idolatry was conceived as the means to get these unpredictable gods ultimately to do human will, whenever Israel began to think of its God Yahweh in this way (and according to the prophets it often did) these prophets condemned Israel's own worship as sheer idolatry, worse than that of the other nations because Israel should have known better. According to the prophets, Israel's faith is to be understood under what we have been calling the rubric of the ultimate purpose of human life. Therefore, all the features of Israel's faith—the centrality of the exodus, the conquest of the promised land, laws, sacrifices, prayers, miracles, healings, acts of obedience, piety, worship, compassion, and social justice—even though they sometimes resembled outwardly the features of idolatry—had to be understood in a completely different way. (Here the two ways of looking at Figure 1 should come to mind.) We will discuss these matters in detail in part 3 when we consider the biblical faith as a religion under the rubric of the ultimate purpose of human life.

Normative Ethics

One of the most widely held beliefs in the world is that there are universal objective ethical or moral standards. All who hold this belief do not agree

about the content of these standards or about how they are to be conceptualized and systematized. But most agree that what gives them their universal
authority is something quite different from their utility in bringing about the
moral agent's wishes. It is usually a corollary of this belief that the status in
being of these standards is not dependent on or affected by whether or not
human beings obey them. Even if they should be universally disobeyed, the
standards stand. The standards prescribe what we should do; they do not
describe what we actually do. As such, they come under the rubric not of utility but of ultimate purpose, if not of human beings then of some larger reality to which human beings belong. The question "Why should we obey the
moral law?" can usually be answered only in words that amount to this: "That's
what we are for." The sheer pervasiveness of this belief is in itself justification for our saying that the rubric of ultimate purpose of human life is indispensable in the analysis of knowledge- or truth-claims.

In part 3 we will find that the discipline of philosophical ethics has furnished
us with a helpful conceptual structure for analyzing theologically the biblical
law, so we shall postpone further discussion of normative ethics until then.

Justice and the Civil Law

From ancient times to the present the status of the civil law has been constantly debated. On the one hand, there are those who argue that civil law
expresses (or evinces) nothing beyond the desires of those who have the
power to enact and enforce it. Therefore, if we should claim about any particular body of civil law that it either agrees with or contradicts some "higher"
principle of justice, we would not be making a truth- or knowledge-claim at
all, since there is no such "higher" principle with any status in reality. On this
position, then, it is inappropriate to ask under which of our two rubrics civil
law is to be understood. Civil law is simply not a body of knowledge. (Not all
who hold this position would advocate breaking civil law, however, since
sometimes it is in our best interests to obey it, even if only for the reason that
those who have the power to enact it often have the power to inflict harm on
those who violate it.)

On the other hand, many argue that truth-claims may indeed be made about
bodies of civil law. From war-crime trials to bumper stickers urging us to
question authority we have evidence of a widely held belief that laws enacted
by political governments, be they totalitarian or democratic, are *in fact* objectively just or unjust, and therefore have no genuine authority unless they are
derived from basic principles of justice that can be known and understood by

all. Yet within this position there seems to be disagreement about how these purported principles of justice are to be understood. Some claim that these principles must provide for something like a final accounting, in which those who have obeyed the just laws are rewarded and those who have violated them are punished. Otherwise justice would not be realized. This view is expressed in the often-repeated quip "You cannot break the law. If you violate it, in the long run the law will break you." Those who make this or similar claims seem to be formulating the knowledge of the civil law implicitly under the rubric of utility; the ultimate sanction for keeping the law is the promise of the desired outcome.

Others who argue for the objective status of principles of justice, however, see no need for such rewards and punishments in the end. For them it is sufficient to answer the question "Why obey the laws of justice?" with the simple words "That's what it means to be truly human." In this case the formulation of the principle of justice is implicitly formulated under the rubric of ultimate purpose of human life. Since these two views of justice figure prominently in the biblical debate about idolatry and Israel's faith, we will postpone further discussion of justice until part 3.

History

If history is an intellectual discipline that produces genuine knowledge-claims, and few would doubt that it is, how is that discipline to be understood and what is the nature of the knowledge? Do historians formulate knowledge under one or the other of our two rubrics? The debate on this question has been carried on for a long time. On the one hand, there are those who argue that proper history must be understood to be a science, the events of history being connected by laws that are verifiable (in the sense that any scientific laws are verifiable), thus making an otherwise inchoate jumble of events understandable. Within this camp are those who think that it is the business of history to produce historical laws (just as it is the business of physics to produce physical laws) by which the events are connected. Others are willing to let other sciences (mainly psychology, sociology, economics, political science, etc.) supply the laws, making it the task of the historian to show the connection between events by the use of these laws. History carefully written in this way would provide the reader—and indeed the world—with useful information about how to avoid the recurrence of the small and great disasters of the past. Such a history would be ethically or morally neutral (in the way that we will see other sciences to be ethically or morally neutral in part 2). Keeping in mind our two rubrics, we can say that history practiced in this manner would be done under the rubric of utility.

On the other hand, there are historians who argue that history belongs not to the sciences but to the humanities, it being an essential part of the historian's task to employ objective ethical or moral standards in the selection, evaluation, and organization of the facts of a particular period. For example, any historian of World War II who failed to pronounce Nazism to be evil would be abnegating one of the historian's fundamental responsibilities. Those who argue this position would implicitly understand history to be formulated under the rubric of ultimate purpose.

Incidentally, the argument is often made that history cannot be a science because the historian cannot possibly include all the facts of a particular period but must, on the basis of some hypothesis, select and interpret a limited number of the myriad facts. But the same limitation is imposed on the physicist; no physicist, in formulating a theory, can possibly become acquainted with all the facts that such a theory would comprehend and explain. If history, on the one hand, and the physical sciences, on the other, are indeed to be distinguished from one another, it will have to be done by choosing some other feature.

These examples of knowledge-claims in areas other than science and theology should be sufficient to add support to the claim that our two rubrics are indeed widely, if sometimes only implicitly, employed in human intellectual pursuits. Let us now turn to the history of philosophy for our final examples.

Third Set of Examples: History of Western Philosophy

The history of philosophy is far too vast and complicated to be comprehended within our simple pair of rubrics. Nevertheless, if we define *philosophy* as the ongoing critical attempt to construct a conceptual framework (world) within which to explain the total range of human experiences, we can see that many great philosophers have continually employed the two rubrics in that attempt. When Plato rejected the atomistic worldview and replaced it with an ultimate reality of ideas or forms, at least one purpose was to make ethical judgments understandable as something more than subjective feelings; something like the rubric of ultimate purpose was at work here. Aristotle's scheme of causes, including a first and a final cause, clearly suggests an attempt to satisfy both rubrics, and that scheme has endured in much of the subsequent history of philosophy. In the early modern period, Descartes and especially Francis Bacon are examples of many thinkers who found the philosophy they had studied to be sorely inadequate to deal with the emerging experiences of their world, especially in the field of science. Bacon's dictum that knowledge is power is a clear call to make the rubric of utility operative in the formulation of anything that is worthy of the name "knowledge." But Immanuel Kant was filled with awe not only by the starry heavens above (science), but also by the moral law within; in his philosophy, therefore, both rubrics had to be operative.

In this century, the logical positivists, in proposing their logical-empirical criterion of meaning, made the rubric of utility the sole operative one in producing truth and therefore had to relegate ethical and religious utterances about ultimate purpose to the emotive realm, where they had neither truth nor falsity. Philosophy often proceeds on the principle that the squeaky wheel gets the grease. When new experiences raise issues that cannot be dealt with in a satisfying way within the conceptual framework of the "received tradition," that tradition is challenged and the demand is made on the intellectual institutions to provide a new conceptual framework adequate to the task.

During the last half of the twentieth century in this country there have been several squeaky wheels, two of which will serve as illustrations. The Vietnam War occasioned the first. The student protests arose in large measure because young people were being asked to give their lives in an effort for which they saw no moral justification. But when students called on the prevailing "received tradition" on American campuses to give answers to moral questions, all that the supporters of that tradition could do was to shrug their shoulders and say that moral questions were outside the limits of knowledge and could not be discussed in a rational manner.

The other squeaky wheel emerges as the result of the rapid increase of knowledge in the field of biology. Because of this new knowledge, we can now do things that we scarcely dreamed of only a few years before, and we must now decide whether or not to do them. We cannot put off these decisions, yet the prevailing ethical traditions seem to give us no guidance. Where in the ancient or modern texts can you find a commandment that says, "Thou shalt not clone human beings"? Whether or not our generation of philosophers will be able to develop a conceptual world in which these and other squeaky wheels can get their needed grease—a conceptual world in which questions of utility and questions of ultimate purpose of human life can be dealt with in a way that is understood to be rational—remains to be seen.

These three sets of examples from our intellectual tradition show the pervasive use of our two rubrics. We will thus end the excursus in the hope that a case has been made for thinking of the rubrics as having an important basic function in the formulation of knowledge and therefore not as gimmicks.

Common Features of Science and Biblical Theology

Even though science, on the one hand, and biblical theology, on the other, are formulated under different rubrics, as rational intellectual activities they have in common three important features. First, they are both intended to be systematic and logically consistent, or holistic. Since in certain circles today both logic and system are scorned as being cold, hard-hearted, and impersonal, it might be wise to defend them in a preliminary way here. In the sciences, the field of pharmacology will serve as a fitting example. When a physician prescribes a drug for me, I expect certain results and not others. I usually take the drug in confidence that the appropriate systematic disciplines of chemistry and biology have guided the development of it. But sometimes, as we all know, a drug can have unexpected, even disastrous side effects. What, then, are we to do to reduce the chances of such outcomes? Certainly not to abandon system and logical consistency and replace them by hodgepodge logical inconsistency, for to do so would only increase the chances of disaster, and *that* would indeed be cold, hard-hearted, and impersonal. If the term *holistic* has any useful meaning in the field of medicine, it is certainly to suggest that we should be *more* systematic and logically consistent, making certain that we have considered all pertinent systematic fields of knowledge in the efforts to cure disease. In the sciences, then, it is the *rubric*—to maximize useful knowledge—that makes systematic and logically consistent thought imperative.

In the field of biblical theology, it is also its rubric—to produce knowledge of what the world must be like if it is our ultimate purpose to love others with faithful loving-kindness—that makes system and logical consistency so important. In theology I must never say anything about the biblical God that would cause someone to conclude that I have God's command or permission to hate or despise anyone, or to ignore anyone's need. It is *lack* of systematic and logically consistent thinking about God that has so often led people to do acts that oppress others in great and small ways. Theology is most warm, kind-hearted, and personal when it embraces *under its rubric* systematic and logically consistent thinking.

The second common feature of science and theology is what I shall call *conceptual conservatism*. In both disciplines, when new experiences occur (as they constantly do), we first try to comprehend them within the conceptual scheme that at that time is the received tradition. We simply do not, at every new experience, reinvent a world. We shall see in parts 2 and 3 examples of this feature in both science and biblical theology.

The third common feature is just the opposite of the second, and I shall call it *conceptual revolution*. In both disciplines, when new experiences cannot be comprehended by the conceptual scheme of the received tradition, in spite of all our efforts to make it do so, that conceptual scheme must be modified—something has to give. Thomas Kuhn has made us abundantly aware of such revolutions in science. Equally obvious are such revolutions in biblical theology, both in the biblical literature itself and in the development of systematic theology since biblical times. Recent episodes of consciousness raising within various liberation movements are examples of conceptual revolutions in theology. It is important to notice that in both science and theology it is *loyalty to the rubric* that necessitates the revolutions.

Meaning, Method, and Truth in Science

The Rubric of Utility and the Putative World of Science

Chapter 3

Introduction to Part 2

Answer to Critics of Science
Who Demand Disinterestedness

Purpose and Structure

The purpose of part 2 is to test the first basic thesis of this book: *that science as a rational human intellectual activity develops creditable knowledge-claims under the rubric of utility and that these knowledge-claims are about the putative world of science.* To accomplish this purpose part 2 has the following four parts:

First, there is a disclaimer to dissociate myself from those who would deny this thesis out of hand by complaining that the scientific method is so deeply flawed in its conception or in its practices, procedures, and techniques that it cannot produce creditable knowledge of the world. My argument against the complainers is in the form of the adage "The proof of the pudding is in the eating." If the knowledge-claims about the world that are produced by the scientific method have all the earmarks of creditable knowledge of the world, then the complaint against the method is apparently unwarranted. But before we dismiss the complaint out of hand, we should suspect that perhaps the words *knowledge* and *world* are being used with different understandings in our thesis, on the one hand, and in the complaint, on the other. We will follow out this suspicion soon. Throughout part 2 we should keep in mind that it is *our thesis* (the pudding) that is being put to the test by the apparently creditable knowledge-claims about the world produced by the widely accepted practices of science (the eating). It is *not* the intention in part 2 to judge, and perhaps attempt to correct, the practice of science and its knowledge-claims by using our thesis as the criterion. (At the end of part 2 there is a discussion of when and why it might be appropriate to do so.)

Second, there is in chapter 4 a discussion of two views of the definitions of *knowledge, meaning, truth,* and *world.* The purpose for introducing these two views is crucial to our argument. One very common pattern of finding flaws in a method that produces knowledge-claims is to begin with a view of what knowledge *must* be, and then, using that view as the criterion, to ask if the questioned method produces knowledge as that view defines it. If the method should fail the test, then that method would be judged to be flawed. In this work I reject that pattern and use this one instead: If any method (either scientific or theological) has been designed to produce knowledge-claims *of a particular type,* then that method is to be judged by whether or not it does what it was designed to do. If some *preconceived* view of what knowledge must be does not coincide with knowledge as that method produces it, then it is the preconceived view, and not the method, that is to be found flawed, at least as a criterion for judging that method, regardless of whether it might be applicable in some other situation.

The first view of knowledge and the world is *metaphysical realism,* a view that I take to have been originally preconceived—that is, in its original form it was held prior to, and therefore independent of, any consideration of the scientific method. This widely held view is often only implicitly held and therefore unexamined. It is therefore important to get this view out into the open, lest we assume it to be "true" without realizing that we are doing so, and therefore use it as a criterion to judge the adequacy of the scientific method.

The second view of knowledge and the world, a view that I shall call *putative realism,* is the one that is implicit in my thesis. I use the term *putative realism* rather than the familiar term *instrumentalism* because the latter term begs a question that I do not wish to beg. I will explain this question when I present putative realism in chapter 4. I believe that this view of putative realism is *not preconceived;* one purpose of this chapter is to determine whether or not it is *well conceived.* In chapter 4 we will discuss it in such a way as to make clear the distinctions between it and metaphysical realism. We will notice that each of these views of knowledge of the world places its own demands on any method that claims to produce its kind of knowledge. Accordingly, if the scientific method produces knowledge different from that which a particular view of knowledge demands, then that particular view is flawed and will have to go. A preliminary criticism of metaphysical realism is given in chapter 4.

Third, to test our thesis, there is a discussion of some of the salient features, practices, aspects, procedures, and techniques of the scientific method as it has come to be understood. Since metaphysical realism is the widely accepted *received tradition* that I am arguing against, two questions will continually be asked: (1) Is metaphysical realism a necessary assumption or presupposition for any of the procedures and techniques of the scientific method? My answer will be no. (2) Do the procedures and techniques of the scientific method produce "knowledge of the world," as that expression is understood in metaphysical realism? My answer here will also be no. In answering these questions we discuss some of the perplexing and vexing problems that arise when the view of metaphysical realism is presumed or accepted, and then ask whether or not those problems are lessened or eliminated if the view of putative realism is adopted.

If the demands of our view, putative realism, but not the demands of metaphysical realism are satisfied by the practices of science, then our thesis that science produces creditable knowledge of the world has been substantiated. Thus, by showing that the adoption of putative realism eliminates many of the vexing problems alleged by the complainers, we will have accomplished the purpose of the chapter. Notice again the direction of the argument. I am arguing *from* the apparent—indeed palpable—success of the scientific method in producing knowledge of the world *to* a view of reality that accommodates that success. I am *not* arguing from a view of reality already accepted as the correct one on some other grounds to the acceptance or rejection of the scientific method as a proper one according to whether or not it produces knowledge that meets the criterion contained in that view.

To repeat, since the scientific method is quite successful in producing a useful knowledge of the world, we will adopt a view of the world (putative realism) that is implicit in and required by that successful method. We will not accept and adopt a preconceived view of the world (metaphysical realism) and then partially or completely reject the scientific method because it does not—or cannot—produce knowledge-claims that satisfy the demands of that preconceived view. I am stressing this because much of the widely read, current discussion of the relationship between science and theology is explicitly or implicitly based on the acceptance of metaphysical realism in one form or another. (In this current discussion Edward O. Wilson is perhaps one of the most widely read scientists and Ian G. Barbour perhaps one of the most widely read theologians who espouse metaphysical realism. Richard Rorty is perhaps the most widely read critic of metaphysical realism.)

If we are successful in this argument, then we will have attained a clearer understanding of *science on its own terms,* and we will have prepared a framework in which we can develop a similar understanding of *biblical theology on its own terms*—and a framework in which we can compare and contrast the two. We will then find it unnecessary to denigrate science in order to "make room" for theology, and vice versa. That is, it will not be necessary to make an either/or choice between the scientific method and the method of theology in the biblical mode.

Finally, if we have been successful in our purpose and shown our view to be well-conceived, then it will be appropriate at times to reverse the procedure

and to use our view as the criterion for judging whether or not certain practices that some people call "science" should go by that name. We will discuss
why this apparent circularity is not vicious but is instead quite justified.

Answer to Critics of Science Who Demand Disinterestedness

It is increasingly common—even stylish—to disparage science in certain
academic or intellectual circles, especially where the cause of the humanities
is championed. Because science is concerned with human wants, its critics
allege, it is presumably biased by those wants, and because it is intimately
associated with technology, it is necessarily tainted by materialistic greed.
When those who are sympathetic to the sciences hear such slurs, they often
stridently respond that the only motive of scientists is the pure love of knowledge for its own sake.

This rash criticism of science is in part understandable, since several centuries of the ascendancy of the sciences have left many people in the humanities feeling unwanted and unloved. The success of the scientific method in
producing useful knowledge has been accompanied by an increase in the prestige and academic budgets of science faculties in many liberal arts institutions
and a corresponding decrease in the prestige and academic budgets of the
humanities faculties. This success has brought with it the implication that the
only knowledge worthy of the name is scientific knowledge and that intellectual activity in the humanities, if it pretends to produce knowledge-claims, is
at best on the fringe of respectability and at worst merely frivolous. (See
Edward O. Wilson's *Consilience* and Richard Dawkins's *River out of Eden* for
recent books that give this impression.) The disparaging of science that concerns me is not the legitimate—and indeed laudable—criticism of such unwarranted claims made about science in the wake of its great success in producing
useful knowledge. It is rather the disparaging that seems to be motivated by a
desire to engender in the audience an emotional bias against science as a legitimate intellectual activity for producing genuine knowledge. It is this carping
on both sides from which I wish to dissociate myself completely.

As I attempt to analyze this faultfinding, it seems to me that two distinct,
unjustified complaints are being made about the adequacy of science. The first
is that in its *very conception* modern science is based on assumptions or questions that are not worthy of being considered by anyone who has honorable,
humane sensitivities and motives. The second complaint is that in its *internal
workings* science relies on techniques and procedures that are unreliable or
unable to produce creditable knowledge and that because of this, science is

not totally acceptable as an intellectual activity unless it can overcome these inadequacies. Sometimes it is even suggested that these inadequacies can be overcome only with an infusion of concepts, techniques, and procedures from the humanities. The first of these complaints—that science is flawed in its basic conception—I will deal with now. The second I will deal with only briefly in this disclaimer, and then in more detail later.

To dissociate myself from these two critical complaints, it is not enough simply to say that I do not agree with them. I must first try to discern the assumptions or presuppositions on which they are based and then to state clearly my own presuppositions that are different. Let me begin anecdotally.

On several occasions when I have suggested to colleagues in the field of science that the scientific method is a response to the human question of how we can control our environment to get what we want and that its rubric is thus one of utility or power, I have been immediately and almost completely misunderstood and have caused offense. On the one hand, the words "control," "get what we want," and "power" immediately raise the image of the mad scientist of fiction, fiendishly at work in the laboratory to discover means to take over and dominate the world. On the other hand, the word "utility" suggests an image of the scientist as a tool of crass commercialism, slavishly devising unneeded gadgets with which to lure and exploit an innocent public. "Where in your suggestion," they ask, "is a place for the dedicated scientist, whose only activity is the disinterested pursuit of knowledge for its own sake?"

Let us focus on this response, for behind it lies an assumption, or preconception, that is common to many scientists and critics of science alike—the assumption that any acceptable method for producing knowledge, whether it be science or theology, must be motivated solely by the disinterested pursuit of knowledge for its own sake.

But when this assumption is applied to science, it raises expectations quite different from the expectations of many whom we commonly think of as the pioneers of modern science. These pioneers were in revolt against what they sometimes referred to as the "Aristotelian" method. (That they were not being entirely fair to Aristotle is not our concern here.) That method, which characterized much of medieval science, went something like this: To arrive at pure knowledge of reality, untainted by any bias of our personal interests or ambitions, we must begin with absolutely unassailable statements, propositions, or principles—that is, we must begin with *universal* statements (for example, statements of the form "All *a* is *b*") whose truth-values (either *true* or *false*) are absolutely beyond doubt. Such statements cannot be based on sense experience, for we all know that sense experience is limited and often unreliable. Therefore these statements must have a truth-value that is self-evident to human reason apart from sense experience. In the history of philosophy such statements have sometimes been called synthetic, a priori propositions. (I was taught in high school that the axioms of geometry were such self-evidently true statements about the real world.) Since such statements would be unquestionably true, it follows that all other statements that can be *deduced* from them by use of the rules of logic would be equally true and that no other statements would be so. (Again, I learned in high school that Euclidean geometry was to be understood as such a system of truth about reality, for in geometry the *proof* is an instance of logical deduction.)

If this so-called Aristotelian method is the correct one for producing pure knowledge of reality, what must we do if knowledge gained from sense experience is incompatible with knowledge gained by the Aristotelian method? We must, of course, deem the knowledge gained from sense experience to be false. (Again, I was taught in high school that if the properties of a geometrical figure that were deduced from the axioms differed from the properties obtained by sense experience aided by the most accurate instruments we possessed, it was always the latter set of properties—those obtained by sense experience—that had to be denied. On the very first day of class we were told to throw away the protractor and ruler that had come with the textbook because they would be of no use whatsoever in arriving at the truths of geometry. Keep this example in mind, for we will return to geometry later.)

It was this deeply entrenched kind of thinking that the pioneers of modern science were up against, and they vehemently opposed it because it did not produce the kind of knowledge that enables us to improve the human lot in the world. They wanted a knowledge that was responsive to human needs and interests. Hence, for example, Bacon insisted that *knowledge is power or utility*. Since that time, as the practices and techniques of the scientific method have been developed, modified, and honed, this principle has been determinative. Much of the material in the rest of this chapter is an attempt to substantiate this idea.

If I were a dyed-in-the-wool advocate of the Aristotelian method, I might well say to these upstart scientists, "You are debasing knowledge by thinking of it as *useful*. True knowledge is to be sought and cherished for its own sake, and not for anything so ignoble as the power it gives us to control facets of our world to meet our wants. Knowledge is to be *contemplated*, it is not to be *exploited*." It is indeed ironic, then, when twentieth-century advocates of the scientific method bridle at the suggestion that it is a method formulated under the rubric of utility so as to produce knowledge that enables us to control, and instead think of it as a method that, unguided or influenced by any human interests, leads us to a truth that is valuable for its own sake. One is tempted to say that with friends like these, science needs no enemies.

Why, then, do the words "disinterested search for truth for its own sake" have such a noble ring, especially when used in partisan debate? It is, I think, because we have confused two quite different sets of motives: (1) motives on the basis of which human beings collectively devised the scientific method in the first place, and (2) the various motives on the basis of which separate individuals become professional scientists or employ scientific knowledge.

I take the first set of motives to be honorable and good. If the human condition of need, privation, oppression, and suffering is a legitimate concern of mine, then the scientific method as a means to produce a knowledge that will help to ameliorate that condition is a distinct improvement over the Aristotelian method and needs no apologies to be made for it. It is therefore not intended as an offense to say that modern science seeks knowledge that is utility or power. Let me stress again that I do not consider the rubric of utility to be the *wrong* rubric, nor do I consider the rubric of ultimate purpose to be the *right* one. They are equally important in my view, and *neither one is disinterested.*

The second set of motives, however, is a different matter, for it is a mixed bag indeed. Some individuals become scientists from the best of motives, such as the desire to develop knowledge that will enable us to cure or prevent genetically transmitted diseases, or to ensure an adequate food supply for an ever-increasing population. Others do so for innocuous reasons, such as the desire to make an adequate income in a prestigious vocation in relatively pleasant surroundings, and perhaps to win a Nobel Prize. Still others do so from base motives, such as the desire to develop knowledge to abet a villainous political tyrant in his efforts to conquer the world and cleanse it of undesirable ethnic minorities. Likewise separate individuals use scientific knowledge from similarly diverse motives. (Such employment of scientific knowledge is what is meant by the term *technology*.) It is when we mistakenly take these mixed motives of the second set as the motives for developing the scientific method itself that we are apt to think of science as morally flawed in its very conception.

Before we move on from this topic there are two points that we ought to notice. One is that the motives in the second set do not in themselves determine whether or not an individual will become a good practitioner of the scientific method. Sometimes those who become scientists from the lowest of motives become good scientists, often to the great distress of most of the world. On the other hand, some who become scientists from the best of motives are unable to make the theoretical breakthroughs that a world in pain and suffering hopes for. The other point is this: *Within* the practice of modern science there *is* a desirable attitude that resembles disinterestedness. Because the rubric of science requires us to try to maximize utility, we ideally seek to produce knowledge that is systematic and complete rather than disorganized and piecemeal. A highly generalized theoretical knowledge is in the long run the most useful, because it can be applied to the widest range of tasks, some of which have not yet been thought of. (Recently I heard this generalized knowledge referred to as the long-sought theory of everything.)

In order to develop such generalized knowledge it is often necessary for theoretical scientists to work in areas that are remote from any practical application. (The big bang theory is an example of scientific, theoretical knowledge-claims that seem to have no utility or immediate relevance to our human wants and needs.) Scientists who work in such areas of theory, therefore, often speak of their attitude or stance as one of disinterestedness. But we should notice that this disinterestedness never prompts them to abandon the modern scientific method and retreat into the Aristotelian method of medieval thought. They are disinterested *within* the rubric of utility, but never disinterested about which rubric to work within. We will have more to say on this point later when we discuss the "original sin" in science.

I trust that I have now adequately dissociated myself from those who disparage science by saying that it is flawed in its very conception because it is intrinsically concerned with and biased by human wants and needs. The other complaint—that in its *internal* workings science relies on procedures and techniques that are incapable of producing genuine knowledge—needs only brief mention here, because we will discuss it in detail when we examine the implications of metaphysical realism. This complaint, it seems to me, also stems from unwarranted expectations about scientific knowledge—in this case expectations that arise from *a deeply embedded metaphysical position.* This complaint calls to mind the familiar story about the bumblebee: According to the laws of physics, it is impossible for the bumblebee to fly; but the bumblebee doesn't know the laws of physics, so it flies anyway. The moral of the story is, of course, that we who claim to know the laws of physics had better reexamine those laws. By analogy, then, we have this story: By following the procedures and techniques of modern science it is impossible for anyone to produce genuine knowledge; but the scientists who follow those procedures and techniques don't know this, so they produce reliable knowledge anyway. The moral of this second story is that we should examine carefully our concepts of "genuine" and "reliable" knowledge, because scientists are certainly producing something that seems genuine and reliable to me. This is what we will attempt to do in chapter 5.

Chapter 4

Two Views of the Nature
of Knowledge of the World

*T*he concept or definition of *knowledge* is neither self-evident nor grasped in a few words. It is, instead, deeply imbedded in one's view of the world and of the relationship between knowledge and the world, and it changes when that view changes. In this chapter we will examine two such views in an attempt to clarify the concepts of "knowledge" and "world" in each. Then in chapters 5 and 6 we will ask which view of knowledge better accords with or "fits" the accepted features of scientific practice. Only then will we be able to deal with the second complaint and answer the question of whether or not the procedures and techniques of science are capable of producing knowledge of the world.

In both of the views discussed here, the method of science is understood to be the same and is not under dispute. The proponents of neither view are necessarily suggesting that the procedures and techniques of modern science are in doubt and that therefore scientists should change the way they go about doing their work and alter the truth-claims that come from it. But in the two views to be discussed, the concepts of *meaning* and *truth* differ from one view to the other. In the view of *metaphysical realism,* because of its understanding of *meaning* and *truth,* there are indeed serious and vexing difficulties concerning the ability of the scientific method to produce true knowledge-claims. In the view of *putative realism,* because of *its* understanding of *meaning* and *truth,* these difficulties largely vanish. Our question, therefore, is this: Which view gives the better account of the meaning and the truth of the knowledge-claims about the world that are produced by the scientific method?

The First View: Metaphysical Realism

An early version of metaphysical realism, usually called *naive realism,* is often implicitly and uncritically held. A popular contemporary version, called

critical realism, has been promulgated because of widely recognized difficulties with the naive form. It seems to me that one version or the other of
metaphysical realism is held by the vast majority of people who participate in
the debate about the relationship between science and religion. Consequently,
this view furnishes their understanding of *meaning* and *truth*, and it is the view
I consider to be preconceived.

Naive Realism

In its barest essentials naive realism can be stated as follows: The real world—
the metaphysically ultimate reality, the world that is the object of all genuine
knowledge—exists in itself quite independently of our experience or knowledge of it. This real world as it exists in itself is the *natural* world or the world
of nature. It contains all that there is. It is the foundation on which all our
knowledge-claims rest, and it is the criterion by which all our knowledge-
claims are to be judged. (It should be noted that the term *metaphysical* does
not mean "nonphysical." It refers to *whatever* the ultimate reality might be,
"physical," " mental," or "spiritual," or some combination.) Genuine knowledge is a verbal representation of this nonverbal metaphysical reality. This
representation is thought of as a point-to-point correspondence between the
nonverbal features of metaphysical reality, on the one hand, and the verbal
features of the statements that constitute our knowledge-claims, on the other.
Hence, the theory of meaning and truth is called the *correspondence* theory.
One understands the *meaning* of any statement that makes a knowledge-claim
if one in some way mentally grasps the structure of the nonverbal reality to
which it claims to correspond. The *truth* of the statement is a function of how
closely the features of the statement do indeed correspond to the features of
the *real world,* as that term is understood within this view.

Since the scientific method is an *empirical* method, one that bases all knowledge on experience, we must include in the view of naive realism the additional
assertion that *sense experience,* which is nonverbal, is a more-or-less accurate
picture of the nonverbal ultimate reality and therefore is the intermediary
between the nonverbal ultimate reality and the verbal scientific knowledge-
claims. First, there is the nonverbal real, metaphysical world. Second, there is
our nonverbal sense experience that corresponds to it and is a more-or-less
accurate representation of it. Third, there are our verbal knowledge-claims that
correspond to our nonverbal sense experience (see Fig. 2).

To verify or confirm the truth of a scientific statement about the world, one
must ascertain that these two correspondences do in fact exist. A common
metaphor intended to aid our understanding of the first correspondence—the

METAPHYSICAL REALISM				
Real Metaphysical World (nonverbal)	Correspondence One	Experience (nonverbal)	Correspondence Two	Knowledge-claims (verbal) (true or false)

Figure 2

one between the real world and our experience of it—is that of an object in the world and a photograph of it. I understand the meaning of the photograph when I mentally grasp that it purports to be in point-to-point correspondence with some object in the world. The "truth" of the photograph—only in the sense that we say, "Pictures don't lie"—is a function of how well the features of the photograph do indeed correspond to the features of the object in the world. This correspondence is taken to be relatively nonproblematic. Just as I can tell when a camera is faulty and produces distorted images, so I can tell when someone's sensory equipment is faulty and thus produces faulty experience. The second correspondence—the one between our nonverbal sense experiences of the real world and our verbal knowledge-claims—is also taken to be relatively nonproblematic. From experience I can gather and record the true facts about the real world, and then with those facts and the rules of logic I can come to true scientific knowledge of the real world.

If we explicitly or implicitly adopt this view of knowledge as the appropriate one for understanding the assertion that the scientific method produces true knowledge-claims about the world, then we thereby make the additional claim that *the scientific method (and perhaps only the scientific method) produces knowledge that corresponds to metaphysical reality.*

Critical Realism

Some who accept the view of metaphysical realism have recently called for a revision in the understanding of both correspondences of this naive version. Let us consider first those issues requiring revision in the understanding of the second correspondence—the one between our nonverbal experiences and our verbal truth-claims that are ultimately formulated as scientific theories—since they are the simplest to deal with. These are the developments that lie behind the often-repeated claim "All facts are theory laden." Since Kuhn's publication of *The Structure of Scientific Revolutions,* it has become a part of the received tradition in the philosophy of science that the path from sense experience to even the simplest knowledge-claims is not a straight one. There are no facts until there is at least a rudimentary theory—a simple hypothesis—in accordance with which we organize experience into facts; and it has long been recognized that we cannot *prove* theories from such facts by logic (or even *disprove* them, Karl Popper notwithstanding). Concerning these developments in science there is little if any disagreement between metaphysical realists and those who reject metaphysical realism. In chapters 5 and 6, when we discuss the procedures and techniques of the scientific method, we will deal with these issues in more detail.

The other issues in science—those that require revision in understanding the other (the first) correspondence, the one between metaphysical reality, on the one hand, and sense experience of it, on the other—are exceedingly more complex. These developments are within scientific theory itself and have culminated in what many consider to be the latest, most creditable, basic systematic scientific theoretical knowledge-claims about the universe. As we discuss these knowledge-claims, it is important for us to keep in mind (1) that these claims are the state-of-the-art product of human intellectual activity in accordance with the scientific method, and (2) that metaphysical realism requires these claims to be in correspondence in some conceivable way with the ultimate metaphysical reality. In other words, the new developments raise this question: Given what we now know about the history of the universe from the beginning up to now, what can it possibly mean to say that our experience *corresponds to reality*? (**Warning! Please proceed no further until you understand that this discussion is not about whether the theory of evolution, or perhaps some other theory, ought to be accepted as scientifically sound. It is about whether any scientific theory whatsoever can, should, or does produce "truth" as that term is defined in metaphysical realism.**)

The theoretical knowledge-claims that constitute the current received tradition and raise questions about the view that experience corresponds to metaphysical reality may be presented in a scenario. I adapt the word from the world of the theater, where a scenario is the synopsis of a story in which the critical movements of the plot are clearly displayed in the parts of the synopsis. In our scenario the story is the entire history of the universe from the beginning to the present, but we will concentrate on the period from the beginning to the arising of human consciousness or experience, since that is the period crucial to the claim that experience corresponds to ultimate reality (the first correspondence). The fundamental laws or theories of science guide the movement of the plot, since it is these laws that are to make every step in the story conceivable and therefore understandable. The parts or episodes to be mentioned are those critical steps along the path from, at first, lifeless matter, through the appearance of life, and then to the much later emergence of *consciousness* or "mind." These are the steps that must be made understandable by the laws, if the demands of metaphysical realism are to be met. Otherwise we shall have to rely on some deus ex machina in place of understanding. Our scenario can be presented as follows:

The Scenario

The universe that we know today is billions of years old, and it existed long before there were any living, much less sentient, beings. Before such beings arose, there were no knowledge-claims and no truth, since only sentient beings can make knowledge-claims, and truth is a characteristic of knowledge-claims. But we now know (because *we* are sentient beings) that from the beginning the material stuff of the universe moved in accordance with the laws of quantum mechanics, in Einsteinian space and time. The laws of chemistry, which are often used in explanations of events in this early period, are themselves derivable from the basic physical laws.

A few billion years ago on our planet a marvelous and critical event happened. Some of that material stuff, in accordance with those laws, was in such a configuration that it caused other bits of matter to become configured in a similar way; thus began the self-replicating of material configurations from which all life that we know arose. At one time the appearance of this self-replicatory phenomenon was thought to be the emergence of a new quality or property (life) that is in principle inexplicable on the basis of what went on before. If this were the case, then the basic laws of science could not have been guiding the plot of our scenario, and we would have to look elsewhere for the guiding principle. But the inexplicability of the emergence of life is now believed *not* to be a *principled* one. Rather it is thought to be occasioned by the sheer magnitude of the number of bits of matter whose individual properties would have to be known in order to construct an explanation of why particles in this configuration result in replications. Many contemporary scientists are attempting to duplicate in the laboratory this phenomenon of producing life from inert matter. If they should succeed, the emergence of life would be in principle explainable by the basic laws of physics that now explain everything up to that point. The confidence of those working in this field is not some wild alchemist's dream; it is founded on the solid knowledge they now have of the molecular structure of what seem to be the most basic forms of life. (Some believe that chaos theory may provide a clue as to how to construct such an explanation.)

We need not wait until such an explanation is provided, however, because we *do* now know quite well the laws in accordance with which living entities, once they are present on the earth, replicate, divide into various species —some surviving and others disappearing—develop eyes and nervous systems and brains, and so on. Many of these laws, usually called collectively the theory of evolution, are now—thanks to the development of instruments once thought to be technically beyond possibility—expressed in terms on the molecular level. These laws, once we understand just how the laws of physics explain the origin of life itself, can in turn be explained by the basic laws of physics.

Explanatory Note on *Reductionism*

This process of explaining the laws of the more complex sciences by the more basic laws is known as *reduction*. Thus the laws of the social sciences are to be proximately derived from (reduced to) the laws of psychology; the laws of psychology reduced to the laws of biology; the laws of biology reduced to the laws of chemistry; the laws of chemistry reduced to the laws of physics. There is debate about whether such reduction, especially for laws of the human sciences, is possible or even desirable. The question of its *possibility* is not a trivial one for the metaphysical realist, because it is a question about the true nature of ultimate reality, and for many it seems to be a question that can be answered only by scientific research. Therefore, some researchers, especially those in the so-called harder sciences where the laws and theories are more nearly exact, believe that the history of scientific progress—and especially the direction of that progress—overwhelmingly supports the hypothesis that all genuine scientific laws are capable of being reduced to the basic laws of physics, and that all scientific research ought to take *reductionism* as a working assumption.

Other researchers, perhaps especially those in the human sciences of psychology, sociology, anthropology, economics, and political science, where conscious decisions are at least part of the subject matter and where the laws are less precise and almost invariably stated as probabilities, believe that the history of science points to the opposite hypothesis. As an example some might cite the inability to explain consciousness itself on the basis of molecular activity (see below) as convincing evidence that the hypothesis of reductionism is false and that progress in their fields is to be achieved by making the assumption that the laws of psychology are different in kind from the laws of the physical sciences and cannot be reduced to them. If the latter group— the antireductionists—should "have it right" about ultimate reality, one of the important implications would be that not just the physical sciences, and not just the sciences, but also other disciplines, such as philosophy and theology, could be significant sources for knowledge of the ultimate metaphysical reality. Many metaphysical realists who want theology as well as science to have something to say about metaphysical reality are, therefore, antireductionists. We should note that if the antireductionists have got it right, so that several irreducibly diverse disciplines contribute to the knowledge of ultimate metaphysical reality, it would be difficult to understand how we could say anything coherent about that reality.

On the other hand, the opponents of metaphysical realism claim that neither of these hypotheses about reductionism is a scientific hypothesis, but that each is a metaphysical hypothesis and that scientific research is irrelevant to a decision about which one corresponds to ultimate metaphysical reality. This does not mean that it makes no difference which way research is carried out. It does mean that research patterns are to be determined by something other than the alleged truth or falsity about some alleged metaphysical reality.

Now even the most complex entity known, the human brain, that traditionally mysterious "black box" into which went stimulus and out from which came response, has been demystified. Every stimulus is in reality some bits of basic matter causing changes in the configurations of matter within the body. Some stimuli come proximately from within the body; some come from the outside. Thus every bit of activity of the human being—every aspect of response—is explainable by laws that are themselves derivable from basic laws of matter. Heredity and environment are not *basically* different kinds of causal factors in human conduct; they are different only in the routes by which the causal chains have traveled before they converged to cause response. Thus the "disposition" to act in a certain way, often attributed to one's heredity, is not some mysterious property that has miraculously emerged. In principle it is no more mysterious than a lightbulb's disposition to give off light when the outside stimulus of appropriate voltage is applied. Every human action, from the very simple, such as the blinking of an eye, to the moderately complex, such as taking a test, and on to the very complex, such as the writing of a theory of evolution or composing the music for a grand opera, is basically explainable in the same way. Some explanations will be more complex than others.

The scenario is not yet complete; two topics, which are quite problematic and are much in dispute, remain to be discussed. They are (1) the status and place of *consciousness* (which I assume that everyone reading this paragraph has) within the theory, and (2) the status and place of *determinism* within the theory. Both of these are of utmost importance, because if the theory is "true" as that word is understood in metaphysical realism, then what the theory says about them is the truth about ultimate metaphysical reality. But before we discuss these topics, let us pause to notice some aspects and implications of the theory thus far. Let us begin by noticing that the observer—the one who has *experience* in the naive version—is no longer a "disinterested outside observer," uninvolved in the "objective world" being observed. The view of John Locke (1623–1704) that the experiencer's mind is a passive blank tablet, a *tabula rasa,* on which experience stamps an impression, now seems hardly appropriate.

In the modern view, "observation" is the interaction of two parts of the universe, an interaction in which the observer alters whatever is being observed just as surely as that which is being observed alters the observer. Furthermore, this interaction is in accordance with well-known laws, which are not different in principle from the laws by which we know and explain the fact that when we use a thermometer to take the temperature of an object, we thereby change the temperature of that object. Furthermore, experience itself is not at all what it appears to be. It is molecular activity in the brain, which is the effect of the convergence of two exceedingly complex chains of causes. If this molecular activity in the brain is *really* what experience is, then the notion of experience as correspondence has lost all its meaning. Although within the theory experience can—and should—be thought of as the necessary *effect* of molecular activity, it is a confusion of language to say that experience, an effect, *corresponds* to its cause. The relationship of effects to their causes is nothing at all like the relationship of the details of a photograph corresponding to the details of a friend's face.

Therefore, the present state-of-the-art theory, as we have discussed it thus far, hardly meets the demands of metaphysical realism. The two types of correspondence—the first between the real world and experience, and the second between experience and verbal knowledge-claims—have disappeared. Experience does not correspond to *anything;* it is an intermediate link in a causal chain that leads without gap from hereditary and environmental stimuli at the input end to vocal chords vibrating in a certain pattern or fingers on a computer keyboard moving in a different pattern at the response end.

In the present theory, this understanding of experience has another implication that is strangely at odds with the demand of metaphysical realism—the demand that a true knowledge-claim be one that by definition corresponds to metaphysical reality. *If this theory is true by virtue of its corresponding to the fundamental structure of absolute reality, then I can never know that it is true.*

And, for that matter, neither can the scientists who have toiled for generations to formulate it. Let us see why:

If I, a layperson seeking to become scientifically literate, hear this theory at a lecture or read it in a textbook and afterward decide that as a knowledge-claim it is true, how does this theory—the one that I have just judged to be true—explain my judgment? Certainly not by saying that I *recognized* it to correspond to metaphysical reality; rather it says that I made the judgment simply because the molecules in my brain at the time of my judging the theory to be "true" were in a condition that caused my vocal chords to vibrate and my lips to move in a coordinated pattern. What I as a scientifically untutored layperson mistakenly believe to be my *weighing the evidence* on both sides and coming to a *rational decision* is known by the scientist to be *in reality* the converging of several causal chains in my brain, the outcome of which (my decision to accept the theory) is explained *not* by anything at all like a correspondence to ultimate reality but by the basic laws of science (which are analogous to the laws of the resolution of forces in basic mechanics).

And what about the scientist who has worked on the theory, using all the appropriate techniques and procedures of the scientific method to come to the conclusion that the theory is true? How is her behavior explained by the theory? The scientist, not being an untutored layperson, knows that her behavior is ultimately to be explained in the same way that she explained mine. And if two scientists disagree about some aspect of the truth-claim, how is their differing to be explained by the theory? Again in the same way that my behavior is explained. And how is their difference adjudicated? Hardly by appealing to metaphysical reality as a criterion and judging that the position of one scientist more closely corresponds to that reality than does the position of the other.

Moreover, if the first scientist should at some point revise her theory, what does she, as an educated science professional and not a scientifically illiterate layperson, say? Should she say, "Earlier I was wrong because the molecular parts of my brain caused me to say what I did, but now I understand I was wrong because I can see that my earlier view did not correspond with ultimate reality"? Of course not, for if she should revise her theory again, she would have to say the same thing; this could lead to an infinite regress, not to a correspondence. If we try to salvage the view of metaphysical realism that says the theory's truth depends on its relation to metaphysical reality by dropping the idea of correspondence and replacing it with the idea of causation, which the theory suggests, then we have gained nothing. We have given up any possibility of *knowing the truth,* because, according to the theory, *every* truth-claim, be it *true* or *false,* would be *caused by* ultimate metaphysical reality. In summary, if any true theory is true by virtue of its correspondence to metaphysical reality, then *according to this theory* no human being can ever have even the slightest idea whether any knowledge-claim is true or false.

Since, as it seems to me, we are unable to make any progress by continuing this tack, let us return to the scenario at the point where we digressed. Perhaps if we take seriously the present *indeterminacy* theory in physics, and then unite it with the emergence of *consciousness*, we can restore some sense to the idea of the scientist as a *disinterested outside observer* who is capable of making statements that correspond to ultimate reality and are not simply caused *by* it.

The Scenario Continues

At some time during the evolutionary development of the nervous system and the human brain—just when is not necessary for our scenario—another marvelous event took place on our planet: Some organisms began to be *conscious*. What *is* necessary for our scenario is that the emergence of this new marvel—consciousness—be explainable in principle in the terms or concepts of the basic laws of the material world, the laws that have been operable from the beginning and by which all events up to now have been explained. At first consideration it seems that this emergence of consciousness is analogous to the emergence of life that came much earlier and it can therefore be explained, at least in principle, by the interaction of an exceedingly large number of molecular entities in the brain. We already know that certain material parts of the brain can be *correlated* with certain aspects of consciousness, so that if those parts are artificially altered by accident or experiment, the associated aspects of consciousness are likewise altered.

Perhaps, then, if we just knew more about the minute workings of the brain we would learn in principle how the molecular activity there comes to be *experienced* as colors, noises, aches, hungers, and so forth, none of which bears any *conceptual* likeness to the properties of molecules. But it is this conceptual *un*likeness that makes the emergence of consciousness in the brain nonanalogous to the earlier emergence of living organisms from inert matter. In that earlier emergence, inert matter, on the one hand, and living entities, on the other, are understood to be basically alike, having the same conceptual characteristics; they can be examined under the same microscopes, measured with the same instruments, subjected to the same physical forces, the same chemical agents, the same radiations.

In other words, living matter is not understood to be a new kind of reality but the same kind of matter (as basic particle physics understands it) in a heretofore-unrealized arrangement. It is this sameness that gives us the foundation for hope that the emergence of life from inert matter can be explained by the basic laws of physics or by laws that can be derived from them. But in the later emergence—that of the conscious mind from the nonconscious material brain—we do not have two entities that are fundamentally of the same kind. It would be ludicrous to say that we can examine the brain and the "mind" under the same microscope to determine the values of their properties, because brain and mind are conceptualized in incommensurable terms. As we will see in chapters 5 and 6, scientific laws explain causal connections of things that have commensurable conceptualized properties that can be assigned values by agreed-on experimental procedures. *Correlations*, such as those between brain activity on the one hand and aspects of consciousness on the other *are not scientific explanations* and ought not to be confused with them.

In spite of these conceptual difficulties, some metaphysical realists remain undaunted and claim that because scientists have solved seemingly impossibly difficult problems in the past, we can expect them to do so in this case; they are confident that at sometime in the future a purely physical explanation of consciousness will be forthcoming from diligent scientific research. Other metaphysical realists less sanguine than these acknowledge the impossibility of deriving anything so patently nonphysical as consciousness from physical matter. In order to avoid the metaphysical dualism implicit in claiming the mind to be an emergent entity that has consciousness, simply say that "mind" is only another name for "brain," that "experience" is only another name for "brain activity," and that "consciousness" is not the name of anything at all. Perhaps the most to be said about consciousness is that it is an epiphenomenon, playing no role whatsoever in anything, especially in the processes that produce knowledge-claims. As intriguing as are these two attempts to deal with consciousness, given the existence of matter and the physical laws, it is difficult to see that either contributes anything to our understanding of what *correspondence* means and therefore to the claim of the metaphysical realist that a true scientific knowledge-claim corresponds to metaphysical reality.

Let us leave the scenario again and summarize. Our attempt to make some sense of the correspondence theory of truth by adding consciousness or "mind" to the entities of ultimate reality has not been successful. Even if, contrary to what we have seen here, it were demonstrated by scientific research that consciousness were really an emergent property that could be explained in its entirety by the molecular activity of the brain and the appropriate laws of the material sciences, would we be any closer to understanding what it would mean to say that the contents of experience correspond to reality as it exists in itself? Not at all, because the theory itself would explain those conscious experiences by saying that they are what they are by virtue of the molecular activity in the brain and the inexorable laws of natural science and not by virtue of correspondence. We are still in the same impasse that we were in before we introduced consciousness into the scenario. Again, the effects of a cause do not *correspond* to that cause. Solving the perennial problem of how mind and matter interact, even if we could do it, would not really salvage the correspondence theory of truth and the view of metaphysical realism. So let us return again to the scenario, discussing *indeterminacy* and asking if it can make correspondence understandable.

The Scenario Concludes

In our scenario thus far we have paid most attention to what the laws say about the activity in the most complex entity known, the human brain. Perhaps we have overlooked something at the opposite end of the spectrum, the least complex of all entities, the simple ones from which all complex ones are formed. According to present theory in quantum mechanics the electron is not what it was once conceived to be. We now know that it is not a simple classic particle with a discrete mass, a discrete location in space, and a discrete velocity. In some experimental situations it seems to have some of those characteristics, but in others it seems to have the characteristics of a wave. Most interesting is that it does not have a simultaneous location and velocity. There is an irreducible indeterminacy, so that being more precise about its location requires us to be less precise about its velocity, and vice versa. This indeterminacy at the very heart of matter at its most simple is of interest to the metaphysical realist who is trying to make sense of the expression "correspondence to reality."

All along in our scenario we have been assuming that the laws that govern all material events are strictly deterministic, not probabilistic. But if the laws of the most basic matter are only probabilistic, so that a given state of matter does not strictly determine its effect but only makes it more or less probable, then between the molecular activity in the brain, on the one hand, and our conscious thoughts, on the other, there will not be strict determinacy but an irreducible minimum "slippage." Could this slippage be precisely what gives us, as observers, the free will to become "outside observers," capable of judging whether or not our experience corresponds to ultimate reality?

Before we attempt to answer this question, we need to examine the idea of indeterminacy more carefully, for there is still controversy about how it should be understood. As we examine three possible interpretations, let us continue the assumption that metaphysical realism is the correct view within which to understand the assertion that scientific truth-claims are true about the world. Therefore, the *big* question is this: Is ultimate reality deterministic or not?

The first interpretation of indeterminacy in the basic laws of quantum mechanics is one we have already touched on. In science, all experimental procedures by which laws are tested and confirmed require empirical measuring, and every act of measuring necessarily alters the value of the property being measured. Whenever we measure, we interfere. When we are measuring large objects, the interference is small enough to be ignored when gathering data for confirming a law. But when the object whose properties are to be measured is an electron, the interference cannot be ignored. It is this insurmountable fact, some say, that accounts for our inability to confirm anything but probabilistic laws about subatomic activity. When we move above that level, the inability disappears. If this interpretation of indeterminacy is accepted, then indeterminacy is not necessarily a characteristic of ultimate reality; it is a characteristic only of laws and is explained by our inability to make measurements accurate enough to eliminate it. And if this interpretation is accepted, then our scenario is not significantly altered; we are still not able to make any sense out of correspondence. But this interpretation is far from being universally accepted.

The second and third interpretations of indeterminacy both acknowledge that the act of observation does indeed alter the state of that which is being observed, but both deny that that is the explanation for our present inability to develop deterministic laws about basic matter. The second interpretation makes two points: (1) We cannot make deterministic laws about matter because a degree of indeterminacy *is* a characteristic of ultimate reality, as the present laws declare, and (2) the present laws have been so consistently confirmed that it is virtually impossible to doubt them. If one accepts this second interpretation, and many do, then metaphysical reality is indeed to a degree indeterminate, and the implications of this for the correspondence theory of truth will have to be explicated.

The third interpretation stresses (1) that all scientific laws (or theories), no matter how well confirmed, are subject to revision; and (2) that the indeterminacy in the present theory suggests that it should not be accepted as the "final" truth about matter, but that a new, deterministic theory should be hoped for. Einstein's remark that he could not believe that God would play dice with the universe seems to be an endorsement of this interpretation. To accept this third interpretation is to commit oneself at least in hope, if not in confidence, to the ultimate determinacy of whatever is real. Therefore, for those who do accept it, and many do, it is still premature to make the claim that indeterminacy is an objective characteristic of ultimate reality, and would therefore make possible an understanding of what correspondence to reality might mean. Therefore, it is only the second interpretation that might have serious implications for salvaging the correspondence theory of truth.

Before we inquire about those implications, there is one other interpretation of the determinacy-indeterminacy debate that we should introduce here, even though it is not directly linked to the view of metaphysical realism. It could, perhaps, make the discussion of the three previous interpretations quite beside the point. Ever since the Scottish empiricist David Hume (1711–1776) criticized our ordinary definition of "cause" as a necessary connection between events, many Western philosophers have been reticent to talk about our knowledge of causation. Hume's criticism is roughly this: In our ordinary life we may experience that all events of a particular type are always followed by events of another particular type. This invariant sequence leads us to say that the first event (the cause) *causes* the second event (the effect), and to think of this causal relationship as a *necessary connection*. Thus we think these causes that link events to one another to be just as much part of the real world as are the objects that make up the events.

But if we are empiricists, we must specify the experience by which we observe this alleged necessary connection. We cannot see, hear, touch, taste, or smell this causal connection, however, in the way that we can experience the events that are presumably connected by it. Because we can have no empirical (or scientific) knowledge of causes themselves, they are not a part of objective reality. They are totally subjective and are supplied by the observer. The only things that we can (and do) empirically experience are the thus-far-invariable sequences of events, and by force of habit we "supply" the necessity to the sequence. Many today accept the force of Hume's criticism without accepting his suggestion that it is *habit* that motivates us to supply the subjective necessary connection. But it does seem clear that if we follow Hume's criticism, then the question we referred to earlier, "Is ultimate reality deterministic or not?" is the wrong question and should be replaced with the question "Why do we want to explain the events of the world with deterministic, or 'necessary' laws?" (In explicating putative reality, in contrast to metaphysical reality, this is the question we will ask.)

In our scenario as things now stand, it seems to me that lack of agreement about how the theories of indeterminacy are to be understood and interpreted makes it unprofitable to attempt to include further scenes. The plot has become too uncertain to guess what the future turns in it will be. So let us close the scenario now, and ask the question that we deferred when we discussed the second interpretation of indeterminacy: If a measure of indeterminacy is a feature of ultimate reality, does this fact enable us to *know* that knowledge-claims do indeed correspond to reality?

As we have already noted, one difficulty with the view of metaphysical realism, with its correspondence theory of truth, is its inability to make sense of the concept of "being in error" or of "getting it wrong"—not in the ordinary ethical sense of those terms but in the sense we have in mind when we say, "In your answer to question 3 on the exam, you really *got it wrong.*" If all of our acts, including the writing of an answer on an exam, are the inexorable results of molecular activity in the brain, what can it mean to say that those acts, which are by hypothesis unquestionably *real* acts in the *real* world are nonetheless *wrong*, and are somehow worthy of condemnation?

For example, when I read Edward O. Wilson or Richard Dawkins, I cannot escape their deep feeling of righteous indignation over those who have *got it wrong* about evolution, their profound approbation of those who have *got it right,* and their conviction that those who have got it wrong *should* get on the ball and get it right! I do not question their indignation, which on some issues I share. What I do question is whether the view of metaphysical realism in any way at all justifies either their or my indignation. To be indignant over those who inevitably have it wrong because of the molecular activity in their brains (which are but parts of the ultimate metaphysical reality), it seems to me, would be itself a display of extreme irrationality. And to say that those who have it wrong should have it right would be tantamount to saying that ultimate reality should be different from what it actually is. And approving those who have got it right would be as pointless as congratulating ultimate reality for being what it is. Thank you very much, but metaphysical reality can get along very well indeed without our approval *or* disapproval!

Let us try to clarify this point with an illustration. Professor Roe has just returned a set of graded quiz papers to her biology class. After class sophomore Doe complains about the F on his paper. She explains, "The right answers to the multiple-choice questions are a, c, b, b, d, e, a, a, c, b. You got six of them wrong. Therefore you have flunked the quiz." With a smile somewhere between wry and sheepish, Mr. Doe responds, "But you shouldn't blame me for the wrong answers. Blame my heredity and environment. As you explained last week in lecture, I really didn't have a thing to do with either. Gotcha!" Professor Roe, who has been down this road a time or two herself, retorts with a smile more weary than wry, "Mr. Doe, you shouldn't blame me for flunking you. You should blame my heredity and environment. After all, I didn't have a thing to do with either one. Gotcha!" Clearly, this game could continue until one of the participants dies. What we seem to long for, and indignantly demand that there be, is a genuinely *responsible* observer who can look at the real world, on the one hand, and Mr. Doe's answers (knowledge-claims), on the other, and say definitively that they do or do not correspond. Our demand is somewhat like the demand of the freshman (not a sophomore, of course) who at the beginning of a course said to me, "Don't tell us what *you* think the Bible means; tell us what it *really* means."

So we are now back to the question "Does a measure of indeterminacy in the ultimate metaphysical reality, and therefore in *us*, enable us to be responsible observers of this alleged correspondence?" Those who take comfort in the measure of indeterminacy in quantum theory and answer the question affirmatively argue along this line: It is self-evident that in a totally causal world—a world completely governed by deterministic laws—there can be no *responsible* beings, only *reacting* objects. And (despite David Hume's philosophy), either (a) complete determinacy or (b) some indeterminacy is an objective, metaphysically real feature of reality. Only with at least some indeterminacy, some *freedom* from causal necessity, can we be free to be responsible. Confident in their definition of *causality*, they are equally confident in their definition of *responsibility*: it is free will, the absence of determinism. And now, science has shown that there is real, objective, metaphysical indeterminacy in us.

But how, we should ask, does adding a small measure of freedom from determinism by our heredity and environment enable us to be responsible in any sense at all, much less in making objective judgments about the correspondence of truth-claims to ultimate metaphysical reality? It seems to me that it could only make us *less* responsible, if that were possible. Now Professor Roe would have to respond to Mr. Doe, "You shouldn't blame me for flunking you. You should blame heredity, environment, *and a small measure of absolute arbitrariness,* none of which I had anything to do with. Double gotcha!" This is not a response that is likely to motivate Mr. Doe to study harder before the next quiz.

Fundamental Criticism of Metaphysical Realism

It seems to me that if we, accept the view of metaphysical realism, then we can make no sense of the claim that the scientific method produces true knowledge-claims about the real world. The difficulties that we have seen in the previous discussion can be dealt with under three headings. The first is "Correspondence." If I am to conclude that two things, A and B, correspond to one another, I must first be *independently* acquainted with each, and then by comparing them decide that they do in fact correspond. The view of metaphysical reality that defines truth as correspondence demands that ultimate reality, on the one hand, and scientific truth-claims, on the other, must correspond if the latter are to be true. By employing the scientific method, which has an indispensable empirical content (experience), I can and do have an independent acquaintance with the knowledge-claim (see Fig. 2, p. 45). The link between *experience* and *knowledge-claim* is the second correspondence in Figure 2. But I have absolutely no independent acquaintance whatsoever with ultimate metaphysical reality that would enable me to compare *metaphysical reality* with *experience* to see if they correspond. Thus there is no possibility of establishing the first correspondence in the figure.

Note carefully that empirical experience is *not* acquaintance with ultimate reality. If it were, then all the objects I dream of would be metaphysical reals. Empirical experience is only one aspect of my making a scientific knowledge-claim. I can compare your face to a photograph of your face to see if they correspond, because I can be independently acquainted with each. I can compare one scientific theory to another scientific theory and judge whether or not they correspond, because I can be independently acquainted with each. But it is nonsense to talk about my comparing a scientific theory to ultimate reality because, according to the hypothesis of metaphysical realism, the way I know metaphysical reality is through the very theory by which it is known. Thus the analogy suggested earlier—that the photograph of a face is to the face itself as experience is to metaphysical reality itself—is totally inapt.

The second heading is "Determinacy." The concept of determinacy is important in our understanding the scientific method and its knowledge-claims. The view of metaphysical realism requires that determinacy (or indeterminacy), because it is a feature of a theory, be understood as an objective feature of ultimate reality. Thus it is an *object* of our scientific search. The thesis of this book is that this understanding fails to recognize *why* we want knowledge in the first place, why knowledge is important to us as something other than an object of disinterested contemplation, why it is the *scientific* method and not some other method that yields the desired knowledge, and why we want *responsible* scientists who do not falsify their data. Our view of putative realism will suggest an understanding of *determinacy* that regards it not as a fact of ultimate reality that is either true or false, but as a *rule* for stipulating how the scientific method must be carried out if it is to produce what we want it to produce. An analogy that is often used to make this point is that of a game. If we think of science as a game, then determinacy is a rule about how the game is to be played and, like all rules, is neither true nor false. It is an *imperative,* and responsible players must follow the rules. Otherwise, no matter what else they might be doing, they definitely are not playing the science game.

The third heading is "Responsibility." It is impossible for me to imagine that the scientific method could produce reliable knowledge-claims about the world without responsible scientists. However, as we have seen, if we conclude from current scientific theory that the metaphysical reality is either (a) totally determinate or (b) partially indeterminate, then it is impossible, on either conclusion, to explain how a practicing scientist, who is a part of this totally determinate or partially indeterminate reality, could be a *responsible* scientist. Defining *responsibility* as (partial?) freedom from determinacy got us only deeper into *nonresponsibility*. The thesis of this book suggests that we should treat the concept of responsibility in much the same way as we treated the concept of determinacy— not as a factual matter to be discovered by the scientific method itself, but as a stipulated rule that we *bring to* the method so that it will do the important thing that we want it to do. It is inconceivable to me that a responsible scientist, after years of research on the molecular structure of the human brain, should conclude from such research that the expression "responsible scientist" is just meaningless noise. The claim of this book is that contrary to the claim of metaphysical realists, responsible scientists are making knowledge-claims *not* about metaphysical reality but about a putative world under the rubric of utility, a world therefore in which there are no responsible scientists—in fact no responsible people at all. Responsible people belong in another putative world.

In conclusion, then, I see no necessity for adopting the view of metaphysical realism as a presupposition for understanding what the scientific method is accomplishing. Indeed, I take it to be an unnecessary obstacle to such an understanding. However, it is easy to understand why someone who *does* adopt metaphysical realism as the proper view of knowledge, would then say about science, "By its internal practices and techniques it is unable to produce knowledge of the world."

I do not take this route of despair. The practices and techniques of the scientific method *do indeed* produce something that seems to me to be knowledge of the world. *Bumblebees do in fact fly.* Therefore, I take the alternative to such despair. I suggest for adoption the view that I have called *putative realism,* and we will put it to the test to see if it succeeds by having its demands, which are different from the demands of metaphysical realism, met by what the scientific method does indeed produce.

The Second View: Putative Realism

This view begins with that part of the thesis of this book that can be stated as follows: *Knowledge-claims generated under the rubric of utility are about a putative world.* As we elaborate this view, we need again to keep our attention focused on the concepts of *meaning* and *truth,* asking how in this view these concepts are related to the concept of *knowledge of the world.* Only if we do so can we deal with the question of whether or not the procedures and techniques of the scientific method are adequate for producing knowledge. Also, and especially, we should keep in mind what was said in chapter 2 about the *primacy of experience.* This second view can be summarized as follows:

In our ordinary lives we experience wants or desires. Some of them are satisfied in the ordinary course of events without our doing anything and others, after we have taken deliberate action. But some are never satisfied, regardless of what we do. We would like to improve this situation so that in an ever-larger number of circumstances the actions that we take will be followed by the outcomes that we want. How can we achieve this desired improvement? In our everyday experience of the world we have noticed many apparent cycles, rhythms, and patterns in the natural events. We have also noticed that in our trial-and-error attempts to satisfy our wants and desires we have been able to succeed in doing so by taking advantage of these cycles, patterns, and rhythms. For example, we have taken advantage of our observation of the periodic changes of the seasons of the year by planting crops when certain experiences that signal the beginning of the growing season occur, but not at other times. If we do not squander the resulting surplus, we will have enough to eat in the other seasons to avoid the unpleasantness of hunger that would otherwise follow. Therefore, we conceptualize, postulate, or posit the world as one consisting of "stuff" that is more or less orderly. The greater the number of orderly cycles, rhythms, and patterns that we are aware of, the greater will be the number of opportunities for us to take advantage of and thus to fulfill our wants. If the "stuff" is completely orderly, then our being aware of its order will enable us to maximize such opportunities.

This world that we, under the rubric of utility, have conceptualized as orderly "stuff" is now our *putative world,* and *it* becomes the "object" of our scientific search for knowledge. Since the objective of our search is this putative world, we will call it the *objective, natural world;* we will call the "stuff" that things in it are made of the *real* stuff; the events that we say truly or really happened are the events in this putative world; statements about this putative world will be the statements that we say have *truth* or *falsity.* As this search becomes more and more sophisticated and develops into a critical rational human intellectual activity, it exhibits the three characteristics that were mentioned at the close of chapter 2. First, it aims to produce *systematic* knowledge, since complete orderliness is the very essence of a system; and, as we have seen, a world consisting of completely orderly "stuff" maximizes our ability to control the outcome of our acts. Second, at certain times our search for knowledge of this putative world will be *conservative,* in that it will more or less tacitly take for granted the prevailing (a) concepts of what the "stuff" is and (b) statements of the regularities exhibited by that "stuff." And third, at times our search will exhibit *revolutionary* characteristics. These revolutionary characteristics will show themselves when, in spite of all our best efforts to do so, we are not able to expand the orderliness of our putative world if we continue to accept the prevailing concepts of the "stuff," or the statements of the regularities, or both. In order to increase the orderliness of our world and thus to increase utility, we will have to change our conception of what the "stuff" of the world is, our formulations of its orderliness, and therefore our judgments about what events have happened in the world. *And we will keep changing these until we get a combination that works.* When we make truth-claims about what events have occurred in the world, about what objects are real, and about what laws of nature are true, these claims are being made about this putative world. These three characteristics of our search are dictated by the rubric under which we are operating—the rubric of utility.

In this view of putative realism, what, then, is *knowledge?* It certainly cannot easily be thought of as a set of statements that in any way correspond point to point with a nonverbal entity called metaphysical reality. Indeed, it seems that we have asked the wrong question about knowledge. It might even be thought of as a loaded question—one that tempts us to accept implicitly the very assumptions that we ought not to accept. We should ask not, "What *is* knowledge" but "What does knowledge claim to *do* if it has been generated under the rubric of utility?" This latter question is one that can be answered with some clarity: *Knowledge of the world* is a systematic set of statements (theory) that in conjunction with other statements (statements about our possible acts) enables us to produce further statements that predict the experiences that will follow our possible acts (statements of the results), thereby maximizing utility. Knowledge, therefore, functions as a prediction device. The *meaning* of knowledge, therefore, *is* this function. If this, then, is what a knowledge-claim is, what is the *truth* of a knowledge claim? To judge that a knowledge-claim is true is to judge that it performs its function optimally.

Explanatory Excursus

Putative realism has antecedents in the pragmaticism of Charles Sanders Peirce (1839–1914) and later in logical positivism. Whether this view says anything about knowledge different from what these earlier views say, I am not sure. What it *does* do is this: By focusing *initially* on the motive and rubric out of which this knowledge arises, and only *later* on the problem of how this knowledge is to be verified or confirmed, it explains (1) why the scientific method rather than some other one (such as the Aristotelian method) has been chosen (or devised) as the appropriate one to produce useful knowledge, and (2) why this view of knowledge (putative realism) rather than metaphysical realism or some other view is the appropriate one for understanding scientific knowledge-claims. This circularity is apparent and appropriate because in this view knowledge may be thought of as a *tool,* and *not a copy of metaphysical reality.* We design a tool to do a job well, and then we judge the tool by how well it does the job.

I stated earlier that I preferred the term *putative realism* to the term *instrumentalism* because the latter term begs a question that I wished not to beg. Let me now explain. The term *instrumentalism,* when used by metaphysical realists, subtly conveys their claim that "real" knowledge must be what metaphysical realism defines it to be, and so pejoratively suggests that instrumentalists have abandoned reality and truth and have replaced them with fictions or convenient lies. The view that I advocate does not abandon reality and truth. Instead it challenges the definitions of those terms as they are given in metaphysical realism and redefines them to bring them into accord with the procedures that all scientists constantly employ to determine them. Scientists who are instrumentalists distinguish fact from fiction—truth from falsehood—with precisely the same procedures that scientists who are metaphysical realists use to do so. This insinuation that the metaphysical realist stands on some higher ground than does the instrumentalist is found in two recent books by two eminent metaphysical realists who represent quite different positions on the relationship of science and religion. Let us briefly consider these.

In *Religion in an Age of Science* (1990), the theologian Ian Barbour defends his position of critical realism this way: The word *truth* means "correspondence with reality." Reality, however, is "inaccessible to us," so we must employ four "criteria of truth" in assessing a theory: (1) "agreement with data," (2) "coherence," (3) "scope," and (4) "fertility." Barbour contrasts himself with instrumentalists, who "adopt a pragmatic view of scientific language," the pragmatic view being the one that says "a proposition is true if it works in practice." He finds pragmatism unsatisfactory because he thinks it is concerned only with the fourth criterion of truth, fertility. He ends his argument with this statement: "Even to ask the question 'could a false idea have useful consequences?' shows that we distinguish between the meanings of truth and usefulness." Thus Barbour has not very subtly accused instrumentalists of being those who are willing to tell a lie if it gets them what they want.

But what Barbour has done, in my opinion, is to miss what the difference between metaphysical realism and instrumentalism is about.

In the first place, instrumentalists are just as concerned about all four of the listed criteria as are the metaphysical realists, and for a very important reason: By employing all four criteria in judging a theory to be true, the instrumentalist believes scientists are *maximizing* utility. These *pragmatists-instrumentalists,* who are definitely anti–metaphysical realists, are definitely concerned with *this* question: When is a scientific theory sufficiently confirmed for us to accept it as a reliable guide to accomplishing the broadest range of tasks in life with as few unexpected side effects as possible? They are not trying to find ways to cheat and get by with it. And they are definitely *not* concerned with the question "When and on what grounds can we say that a scientific truth-claim corresponds to metaphysical reality?" What Barbour has not explained is how or why, by following the four criteria, scientists produce truth-claims that *do* correspond with metaphysical reality. The four criteria pertain to what we have called the second correspondence, and, as we shall see, they are acknowledged by virtually all scientists; but they have nothing whatsoever to do with that crucial first correspondence, the one between metaphysical reality and sense experience. So in the following sentence Barbour simply asserts in the second half what he has categorically denied in the first half: "But because reality is inaccessible to us, the *criteria* of truth must include all four of the criteria mentioned above." Furthermore, when he says that by asking, "Could a false idea have useful consequences?" we are showing "that we distinguish between the meanings of truth and usefulness," he has put his finger on the issue but has failed to recognize it. The pragmatist could well respond, "Indeed we are, and I am suggesting that we *redefine* the word 'truth' so that we can still distinguish truth from falsehood without implying that 'truth' means 'correspondence to reality.' Throughout the history of intellectual life much progress is made when we recognize the wisdom of redefining terms." (34, 35)

In a similar vein, Edward O. Wilson, the eminent biologist, makes no effort in *Consilience, the Unity of Knowledge* to hide his disdain for all thinkers who do not hold his version of metaphysical realism, dismissing them as "mad men and a scattering of constructivist philosophers." Wilson, quite rightly in my opinion, praises the almost incredible accomplishments of scientists who, by following the widely held criteria for distinguishing science from pseudoscience, have done much to produce scientific knowledge-claims of ever-expanding generality. Among these scientists are the special ones who have their names indelibly inscribed in the scientific textbooks because they have discovered something. But Wilson seems to fear that if metaphysical realism is not vigorously defended, then these past accomplishments will be debased, the justification for science will vanish, and the joy and thrill of scientific work will be lost. In other words, Wilson is not content to let science be concerned only with what we have called the second correspondence; he seems to require that science have as its *proper* task the establishment of the first correspondence. Scientific knowledge-claims must be grounded in and legitimized by an ultimate metaphysical reality (which is for him, of course, a *physical* reality). Let us cite his position:

> Here is the argument. Outside our heads there is freestanding reality. Only madmen and a scattering of constructivist philosophers doubt its existence. Inside our heads is a reconstitution of reality based upon sensory input and the self-assembly of concepts. Input and self-assembly, rather than an independent entity in the brain—the "ghost in the machine," in the philosopher Gilbert Ryle's famous derogation—constitute the mind. The alignment of outer existence with its inner representation has been distorted by the idiosyncrasies of human evolution, as I noted earlier. That is, natural selection built the brain to survive in the world and only incidentally to understand it at a depth greater than is needed to survive. *The proper task of scientists is to diagnose and correct this misalignment.* The effort to do so has only begun. No one should suppose that objective truth is impossible to obtain, even when the most committed philosophers urge us to acknowledge that incapacity. In particular it is too early for scientists, the foot soldiers of epistemology, to yield ground so vital to their mission. (60–61)

Since Wilson's position is essentially the view of metaphysical realism that we have already discussed, I will make only a few comments.

First, Wilson's position, with such terms as "inside the head," "outside the head," "concepts," and "objective truth," is far from self-evident, presuppositionless truth. His position is itself "theory laden." I believe there *is* a context in which that language is perfectly acceptable—the *putative* world of science that is formulated under the rubric of utility. It is precisely by conceiving the putative world within these concepts and then organizing experience under the rubric of utility that scientists have been able to formulate marvelously reliable truth-claims. I do not believe that the language in any way supports the view of metaphysical reality.

Second, in the first part of the paragraph quoted above, Wilson, properly in my view, exorcises the ghosts in the machine. But suddenly in the last part of the paragraph they reappear as scientists, who have all sorts of ghostly characteristics. They have a *proper task*. They must not yield to the urgings of the most committed philosophers who *tempt* them to abandon their *proper* task of realigning the misfit between the outer real world and its inner representation. They *diagnose* and *correct* that misfit, but without any hint of how they can even know that there *is* a misfit, much less diagnose and correct it, if they cannot know that outer real world independently of the experience, which allegedly now does not align properly with it. But most surprising of all, human evolution, once explained by *idiosyncratic* natural selection, now seems to be *teleologically* driven: to reach the telos of objective truth is the proper task of the scientists.

With two small but significant emendations, both of which require us to shift from metaphysical realism to putative realism, Wilson's view in this paragraph would be in my opinion not only acceptable but also very important. First let us relocate the "mind" (the machine-like brain that is free from ghosts) from the metaphysical reality to the putative reality formulated under the rubric of utility—the rubric that requires us to strive for knowledge-claims that are totally deterministic and of the widest generality, since such knowledge-claims will maximize utility. It was when scientists abandoned studying the brain as a ghost-inhabited machine and began to study it under the rubric of utility, with its deterministic *imperative,* that useful knowledge began to emerge. To study human beings in this manner neither requires nor implies a commitment to some metaphysical view about what human beings "really" are. What it does require from the scientist is a responsible commitment to the rubric.

The second emendation is to shift the proper task or mission of the scientist—to diagnose and correct the misalignment—away from the first correspondence to the second correspondence. As I have already claimed, and will continue to claim as we examine the procedures of the scientific method, it is to improve the fit between experience (the given) and scientific knowledge-claims (the goal) that the various procedures of science are employed—and it is precisely these procedures that distinguish science from pseudoscience. I see no reason to perpetuate the illusion that it is the task of the scientist to discover objective metaphysical truth.

Finally, I find it difficult to believe that scientists who are able to carry out their work without the presupposition of a metaphysical god are nevertheless unable or unwilling to carry it out without the presupposition of a metaphysical reality to which their knowledge-claims must be aligned. This unwillingness to give up metaphysical realism seems to be based on a fear that if serious scholarly pursuits are not grounded in metaphysical ultimate reality, then they will be deprived of their rigor, their power, and their ability to give joy. In his chapter 9 on the social sciences, Wilson argues—appropriately in my view—that if the social sciences are to become proper theoretical sciences, they must not be content to construct only "lateral" sociological or cultural laws but must relate these by "vertical" causal connections to the theories of psychology, the brain, biology, and ultimately the basic theories of physics.

In other words, social scientists must make reductionism an essential guideline in their agenda. Why have the social scientists not yet attained the rigor in their field that characterizes the genuinely theoretical sciences? It is, for Wilson, apparently because the postmodernist scholars have tempted them to abandon *epistemology* and to substitute in its place *hermeneutics.*

Hermeneutics, in Wilson's opinion, "waves aside the synthetic scientific method, demonstrably the most powerful instrument hitherto created by the human mind. Lazily, it devaluates intellect" (190). Wilson twits "the distinguished philosopher Richard Rorty" for making "playful" distinctions between epistemology and hermeneutics that are appropriate only at cocktail time, and not in serious scholarly discussion. Wilson's argument seems to be this: Science produces true knowledge-claims about *metaphysical reality* by rigorously following the scientific method. Therefore, if that method is not itself well founded by the discipline of epistemology, its results (scientific knowledge-claims about metaphysical reality) are not reliable. Nonrigorous hermeneutics, if it replaces rigorous epistemology, deprives science of its scholarly rigor. If this is indeed Wilson's argument, then it fails to recognize the point of the debate about epistemology and hermeneutics. That debate has nothing to do with rigor versus nonrigor but has everything to do with *metaphysical realism* versus *anti–metaphysical realism* as the appropriate view for understanding why science should be—and *is* so commendably—rigorous.

Let us look at the debate more closely, dropping the pejorative term "postmodernist" and using the more accurate, though more cumbersome, term "anti–metaphysical realist." Perhaps as deeply imbedded in our Western intellectual tradition as the view of metaphysical realism is the view that one of the tasks of philosophy is to develop a properly grounded theory of epistemology on which a method for acquiring knowledge of ultimate reality can be based. Thus, before work can begin in any field of inquiry that hopes to produce truth-claims, it must "get its method straight" and be able to recognize that it is "straight" not by what it later produces but on strictly a priori philosophical arguments. The view of the anti–metaphysical realists is that no such epistemological theory is possible, and it is a mistake to think that to produce one is the proper business of the discipline of epistemology. Method, like a theoretical knowledge-claim produced by it, is constantly on trial, and, in science as long as sense experience continues to occur, the scientific method is subject to revision.

Hermeneutics is the term widely used to suggest that when a knowledge-claim or a method for producing such a claim is revised, the revision is not required by some reference to metaphysical reality. It is made instead by reference to the purpose for which we devised the method and by how well it serves that purpose. Hermeneutics, therefore, is not an invitation to abandon rigor. It is instead a call to *concentrate our rigor where it counts*. In science the imperative is to produce knowledge that will maximize utility. What leads us to revise or not is our human judgment about whether the methods, or the knowledge-claims produced by them, are accomplishing their intended purpose. Thus, when scientists began to drop the presupposition of a metaphysical god as a necessary premise of the scientific method, it was, as we today can see, a *hermeneutical* decision that such a premise did not enhance the ability of the method to produce knowledge-claims that would maximize utility. It was not because they suddenly recognized that an epistemologically sound method, grounded in metaphysical reality, required the premise to be dropped.

In summary, both rigor and joy are better served by anti–metaphysical realism than by metaphysical realism. It seems to me that the task of producing useful knowledge for the purpose of ameliorating the human condition is much more likely to motivate one to maximum rigor in one's work than is the task of realigning truth-claims with metaphysical reality—and much more likely to be a joyful task. The claim that one is seeking absolute metaphysical truth, and moreover that one has the epistemologically well-grounded way to find it, smacks too much of the "Aristotelianism" that modern science opposed with such vigor. The hermeneutic approach does not oppose or avoid the demand for *vigor*. It does oppose the demand for *conformity* that arises from any group claiming to have the way to absolute metaphysical truth. Science has proved itself to be the least oppressive when it turns away from Aristotelianism and embraces the Baconian dictum that knowledge is power for the betterment of the human condition. Wilson's obvious sectarian-like zeal and vigor, in my opinion, would be altogether appropriate if they were employed in the service of a science conceived in accordance with the Baconian dictum, and not in the service of a science that claims to have the inside track to objective metaphysical truth.

Conclusion

Let us now briefly summarize these two views, metaphysical realism and putative realism, stressing the differences between them that we must focus on as we ask which view better "fits" the scientific method.

The view of metaphysical realism has been developed without any consideration of a motive from which we desire knowledge, and therefore without consideration of a *rubric* to guide and shape the development of a method to attain knowledge. Here, presumably, is a "generic" understanding of *knowl-*

edge, meaning, truth, and *world.* Truth is a correspondence between the non-verbal metaphysically real world, on the one hand, and our verbal utterance, on the other. Therefore, any method whatsoever that purports to produce truth about the world must verify, or at least confirm, that this correspondence does indeed exist. Thus this view of metaphysical realism puts a demand on *any* method that makes truth-claims—scientific, theological, Aristotelian, or whatever—to produce confirmation of this correspondence. Any method that fails to do so forfeits its right to be called a method of generating knowledge.

The view of putative realism, on the other hand, has been developed with our motive for wanting knowledge, and therefore with the rubric for developing that knowledge, very much in mind. Since, according to our thesis, the rubric for the scientific method is one of utility, the view of putative realism puts this demand on the scientific method: Produce knowledge of a world that explains why any event in that world of a specifiable type is followed by another event in that same world of a specifiable type. In other words, produce knowledge of a completely causal world, *and do not consider your work completed until you have done so*! Therefore, determinacy is not a characteristic of the world that science somewhat incidentally discovers; it is instead a requirement that responsible human beings have in mind as they devise the scientific method in the first place. This imperative would be totally inappropriate if the motive for our wanting some kind of knowledge in the first place were either different from our motive for wanting scientific knowledge, or were ignored altogether. This is a demand that knowledge *do* what it is supposed to *do.* Ideally, knowledge *as it is defined in this putative view of reality* will do what knowledge under our rubric is supposed to do, maximize utility, because it explains to us why an event of one specifiable type—an act we perform, for example—is followed by another event of a specifiable type—the result of that act. In other words, it reduces to a minimum the chances that in acting to get what we want we will have unexpected and unwanted side effects.

We are now ready to move to the next chapter of part 2, in which we will test our thesis by checking to see if the procedures and techniques of the scientific method do in fact produce knowledge as it is defined by this view of putative realism, but not as it is defined by the view of metaphysical realism. In testing our thesis, we will repeat many of the criticisms of metaphysical realism that we have made here.

Chapter 5

Testing Our Thesis by the Procedures and Techniques of Science

The Tasks

It is not our purpose here or elsewhere in this book to attempt an exposition and analysis of all the procedures and techniques that make up the scientific method today. But we must attempt to specify at least the *tasks* that any procedures or techniques that are a part of the scientific method are expected to perform, for it is these more-or-less permanent tasks that generate the always-changing procedures and techniques. I have tried to be consistent in using the term *scientific method* in the singular, and the terms *procedures* and *techniques* in the plural, to draw attention to my claim that all the activity of modern science is done under the *one* rubric of utility, although *many* procedures and techniques may be involved in that activity. Some others use the term *scientific methods* to indicate that the activity includes many techniques and procedures. But one thing I wish to avoid suggesting is that the scientific method is an algorithm—a specifiable set of steps that if followed will lead inexorably to the desired end of true knowledge-claims.

Where shall we begin? We cannot just arbitrarily stipulate these tasks. That would be a bit too "Aristotelian." On the other hand, we cannot after careful study conclude that we have once and for all discovered what these tasks are. We have already noted that in just about any intellectual pursuit we begin with the received tradition. This is the conservative aspect of intellectual activity. So we shall begin with the received tradition about what scientists do. It may be that as we proceed we will find it advisable to alter the received tradition in one or several ways, but this should not surprise us, since there is always the revolutionary aspect of intellectual activity to keep in mind.

Let us begin, then, with a perfectly ordinary question and its equally ordinary answer. Q: "What is it that scientists are doing?" A: "They are discovering the laws of nature." Although the question is perfectly ordinary, it is not a perfectly unloaded one, since it calls for an answer stated in a specific way. Suppose we had asked instead, "What is science?" Eventually we might have come up with somewhat the same answer, but probably our first inclination would have been to try to formulate the answer according to the demands of metaphysical realism: science must be some kind of a thing, so let's try to state what kind of thing it is. After floundering and eventually resorting to a dictionary, we might then say, "It would be a lot easier if we told you what scientists are *doing*." Such an answer would indicate that we find it easier to think of science as a guided activity than to conceive of it as some obscure, difficult-to-grasp *reality*.

Already we would have been indicating that the putative view of reality eliminates some vexing problems created by adopting the metaphysical view of reality. We would have been acting on what we might call the dictum of putative realism: "Ask not what it *is;* ask what it *does*." I am not suggesting that we be overfastidious with such words as *is, thing,* and *entity* but that we be aware that they change their significance when we move from metaphysical realism to putative realism. (In the same vein, we might notice that in academic circles it is common nowadays to hear professors say, "I *do* biology"; "I *do* history"; "I *do* theology"; or "I *do* literary criticism." This manner of speaking, I believe, is not totally a matter of fashion.)

Now that we have finished this brief digression, let us return to the answer given to our original, loaded, question: "Scientists are discovering the laws of nature." This answer, I believe, is a fairly reasonable formulation of the received tradition, and few people, whether they "do" sciences or not, would seriously quibble with it as a starter. Most would agree that scientists perform many different tasks in the course of their work but that all of these are ancillary to the main task of discovering the laws of nature. Immediately in this answer the words *laws, nature,* and *discovering* suggest three distinct tasks on which the various techniques and procedures of science must focus. Let us consider each of these words briefly, and then in some detail.

Laws

Since the laws of nature (or theories) are the final product of the scientific method (technology, in our way of speaking here, is not a product of the scientific method but the application of knowledge produced by that method), and since laws are verbal entities formulated as *statements*, the procedure for formulating words into law-like statements will require some care. All laws of nature are statements, but surely not all statements are laws of nature. So we must ask, What is the difference between law-like statements and non-law-like statements? Since one of the functions of *formal logic* is to supply "templates" for all types of statements, this procedure of science will require at least a passing acquaintance with logic. Shortly we will try to make such an acquaintance. But knowing just the *form* of law-like and other statements does not tell us how to "fill in" the forms. So other procedures will be needed to instruct us concerning what to put in the blanks. Furthermore, we have to specify how a hypothesis, which is a law-like statement, differs from a law of nature.

Nature

Since the laws are *of nature,* we will need some procedures and techniques to enable us to bestow on that virtually empty word *nature* some content. The received tradition says, roughly, that the natural world is made up of objects existing either at rest or in motion in space and time. Thus far we have used the generic term *stuff* to stand for these objects. What are the procedures and techniques by which we give this generic stuff more specificity? The necessity of having such procedures and techniques is seen when we realize that the received tradition was not always what it is today. At one time in Western thought the stuff was thought of as a plenum rather than as specific objects. At another time the received tradition said that the stuff was a mixture of earth, air, fire, and water. A few centuries ago the stuff was conceived as a collection of very small—indivisible—billiard balls. How has the conception of the stuff changed through the history of thought to become what it is today in quantum mechanics? The procedures and techniques that cluster around the word *nature* can be thought of as those having to do with the task of conceptualization. In ordinary language, How do we decide what the world is made of? Sense experience is a factor in answering this question, but it is hardly the only one.

Discovering

If scientists are discovering the laws of nature, how is it decided that a law-like statement, formulated according to the rules of logic, with its blanks filled in with concepts of the stuff, has at last been "discovered" to be a law? When, if ever, does a statement cease to be a hypothesis and become a law? These and similar questions are about the task of *confirmation,* or *verification* as it once was called. Here procedures and techniques of many kinds are employed. First, there is a role played by experience, since the received tradition insists that science is an empirical discipline. If *observation* is different from just *having sense experience,* what is the difference? What role do instruments play? If the laws are about the objects moving or resting in space and time, how do we measure space and time? And perhaps most important, since logic is also about the structure of valid proofs, does the practice of science discover the laws of nature by *proving* them to be true with the rules of logic? One question we might think about is why some scientists now refer to their work as the *inventing* of laws or theories. If it is appropriate for them to do so, what would *confirming,* or *verifying,* or *proving* an invention to be *true* mean, if anything? Does this usage suggest a shift away from metaphysical realism and toward putative realism?

This brief discussion of three principal tasks that the scientific method should accomplish gives a notion of the array of the techniques and procedures involved in producing scientific knowledge. It should also suggest that the naive view of the scientific method cited below is far from adequate for understanding how the procedures and techniques do produce laws and theories of nature. As we now turn to examine some of these in more detail, keep in mind the structure of the argument of this chapter: These techniques and procedures *do indeed* produce *knowledge.* The question is, Is that knowledge what is defined and demanded by metaphysical realism, or is it what is defined and demanded by putative realism? A similar but slightly different question is, Is metaphysical realism a necessary presupposition of even one of these techniques or procedures?

It would be convenient—indeed terrific—if the techniques and procedures of science could accomplish the tasks required by "law," "nature," and "discovering" separately, one by one, in a specified order. Then knowledge would be what naive metaphysical realism demands it to be; and the naive view of the scientific method might then be summarized as follows:

Critiquing the Naive View of the Scientific Method

Sense experience puts us unambiguously in touch with the *real world* with reasonable accuracy. We may need instruments in certain situations to aid our senses, and when we do, we know how to devise appropriate ones. Thus we have telescopes, microscopes, yardsticks, protractors, clocks, scales, thermometers, gauges, and so on. With instruments, as with everything else, there is always room for improvement, and when the need arises we will try to make more accurate instruments. But these tasks of observing the world are straightforward in that they can be accomplished independently of and prior to the other kinds of tasks—and indeed they must be, because they supply the data for the subsequent tasks. Thus by sense experience, aided by instruments, we can observe what the components of the "stuff" are, what their locations in space and time are, how much they weigh, what their velocity is, what their temperature is, and what the value of any other relevant property is. In short, we determine the facts of metaphysical reality by experience, and these facts can be recorded in a lab book.

Once we have gathered the facts—the data—but only then, can we begin the tasks of formulating law-like statements or hypotheses, because laws are statements of regularities found in the facts of the real world. With statements of the gathered facts before us as premises in a logical argument, we, by the rules of logic, infer a hypothesis, a law-like statement. Then we confirm the hypothesis by experiments. When we have conducted replicating experiments a number of times sufficient to banish doubt, we declare the hypothesis to be a law of nature—the scientifically proved truth about ultimate reality.

The previous short summary, or something much like it, is, as we have noted earlier, a rough expression of naive realism. I have heard it taught to undergraduates who are not science majors as all they need to know about the scientific method. It is taken by many people to be an account of what scientists *must* do and *actually* do in order to produce genuine knowledge of ultimate reality. Two criticisms should be made about this naive view of the scientific method.

The first criticism is of the claim that experience puts us in touch with ultimate, metaphysical reality and thus establishes the first correspondence in Figure 2 (p. 45). In our discussion of metaphysical realism in chapter 4 we have already found this claim to be without foundation: conceptually it is meaningless to say that experience corresponds to something else unless we have independent knowledge of that "something else." But there is no procedure or technique in the practice of science that claims to establish such independent knowledge of ultimate metaphysical reality.

It should be stressed here that this fundamental *conceptual* impossibility of establishing the first correspondence has nothing to do with the practical problems that allegedly arise from the imperfections of our sensory organs, or from the imperfections or inaccuracies of our scientific instruments that aid our observations, or from the fact that since all scientists are human beings, our "picture" of the world is based on experience that is unique to our species.

Had evolution taken a slightly different turn, it is suggested, our experiences and therefore our knowledge-claims about the world would be quite different from what they are now. If we, like metaphysical realists, believe that knowledge of reality depends on the first correspondence, then these problems are superfluous trifles, since it has already been shown that no experience whatever can be said to correspond to reality. If vision itself cannot put us in touch with metaphysical reality, then the *fact* that I have astigmatism is not a *problem.*

However, if we are putative realists and think of "knowledge of the world" as that expression is defined in the putative view of reality—in which knowledge is developed on the basis of experience *as it occurs* and under the rubric of utility—then the conceptual impediment of the metaphysical view is eliminated and these alleged problems will have to be dealt with, and indeed are. It is sufficient now simply to mention that scientists, in spite of such alleged problems, do indeed produce knowledge that has utility; but they also *by the very laws and theories thus produced* (1) are able to assert that members of other species do have experiences that are different from ours, and (2) are able to explain the imperfections and inaccuracies in ourselves and in our instruments and at times recommend procedures to correct them so as to increase utility. Notice carefully that these recommended corrections will not enable us to experience *metaphysical reality* more clearly than we did before or more accurately than the nonhuman animals do. What they *will* do is give us additional *experiences* that will enable us to construct a *putative* world of greater utility.

It is only *within* this putative world, and not within a metaphysically real world, that we can speak about our sensory organs being imperfect, or our measuring instruments being inaccurate, or our eyesight being different from that of the animals. I cannot imagine that without science as it is now practiced we could possibly know that different species have different kinds of experiences, or could understand color-blindness, or could perform cataract surgery successfully, or could design electron microscopes, or do the countless other things we do to improve our ability to *observe*. The view of putative realism does not require us to begin with a perfect, omnispecies set of sensory equipment before we can produce knowledge that has utility. But it does require us to base knowledge on the rubric of utility and on experience as it does indeed occur.

Are we, therefore, to conclude that the scientific method is internally flawed in its procedures and techniques and is therefore unreliable as a producer of knowledge? Not at all! In the first place, I am unable to identify any procedure or technique in science that even *pretends* to verify or confirm the first kind of correspondence that is required by metaphysical realism. In the second place, and related to it, there is the clarity with which it can be seen that all the procedures and techniques of the scientific method have been designed to establish the *second* kind of correspondence mentioned above— the correspondence of our nonverbal experience, on the one hand, to the verbal knowledge-claims of science, on the other. It is to that correspondence that we must now turn. As we do so, keep in mind the main claims of this chapter: (1) that the procedures of the scientific method do indeed produce knowledge of a *putative* world (not knowledge of the metaphysically real world of the other view), (2) that this knowledge has its base in experience, and (3) that this method is guided by the rubric of utility. Furthermore, we have now made the additional claim that the procedures of this method (to produce this correspondence of sense experience to the putative world) are not simply linear but are better described as circular or spiral. Our second criticism of the naive view previously stated is not that the scientific method cannot produce true knowledge-claims but that the techniques and procedures for producing the second correspondence are far more complex than the naive view suggests them to be and are best understood within the putative view of reality.

Since this second kind of correspondence is between two "things" that we are more or less familiar with, we must consider each one in some detail. Let's begin with the verbal things, the knowledge-claims. (We will get to sense experience a bit later.) Since knowledge-claims are statements, and *logic* is about statements, if nothing else, this might be the best place to become acquainted with it or to review some relevant points about that discipline, which unfortunately is regarded by many as arcane, heartless, and cold, if not downright brutal. As in most of our other discussions, so also in this one, we begin not at the beginning but with the received traditions that most of us are somewhat familiar with.

Logic, Warm and Humane

Most people, even those who disdain logic, recognize that there are certain pairs of statements that cannot both be true. If one of them is true, the other has to be false. Formal or deductive logic is about the features of such statements that make them have this kind of relationship. It asks the question, What is there about a statement that makes its *truth-value* (its truth or falsity) entail the truth-value of some other statement? It is in the attempt to answer this question that the rules of logic have emerged. Let us begin our discussion with an example, admittedly contrived, of a student's use of what is called a *valid logical argument.* Once we have grasped the cogency of the argument, we will be better able to understand what logic is about and how several of the key terms of logic are used.

A student, Tom Jones, enrolls in a logic course not because he desires to learn what logic is about but because the course fulfills the graduation requirement in philosophy, which he has to get out of the way, and Logic I is offered at a time that is convenient for him. The course syllabus distributed on the first day of class contains this statement: "If you pass the final examination with a grade of C or better, then you will pass the course." He stores this bit of information in the back of his head, thinking that it might come in handy later, and indeed it does, because his grade average going into the final is considerably below the passing mark—not because he is inept but because he has not done his homework. Knowing, however, that all he has to do to pass the course is to make at least a C on the final, he bones up for it with just this goal in mind.

After the examination Mr. Jones feels confident that he has made the grade, and two days later when the graded finals are distributed he is delighted to see that his has an unmistakable C as the grade. A week later, however, when he receives his course grades from the registrar's office, he is infuriated to discover that he has been given an unmistakable F in Logic I. Armed with his copy of the syllabus, his final examination paper with the grade of C on it, and the registrar's report with grade of F in Logic I on it, he storms over to the instructor's office, only to learn that the instructor has departed for a year's sabbatical leave in Europe. He then proceeds to the dean's office to lodge an official complaint against the instructor. His argument is this: The final examination grade is C and the course grade is F. But the syllabus clearly states that if the final exam grade is C then the course grade will be passing. Therefore the syllabus lied. The dean, who in her teaching days had taught a few courses in logic, immediately recognizes the force of his argument, for it has the *valid* form: If C on the final exam is the case, and if non-P for the course is the case, then it cannot be the case that C guarantees P.

But the dean knows that logically valid arguments do not prove the truth-values of their conclusions; they only prove that the conclusion follows necessarily from the statements that are called the premises. Therefore, if the premises are not all the case, then the valid conclusion is not necessarily true. Therefore, she can save the instructor from a serious charge of lying if she can establish that at least one of the premises is false—in this case that "Tom's final exam grade is C or above" or that "his course grade is F." Because the instructor has a reputation for being scrupulously fair with his students, she formulates her own valid argument: *If* the syllabus is correct, *then either* the final examination grade is incorrect *or* the registrar's report is incorrect (or perhaps both). Since Tom has his examination paper with him, she asks if she may read it. He hands it to her, and as she reads it she is quite satisfied that the paper deserves the grade of C that the instructor had written on it. Convinced, then, that the first disjunct is true, she wonders if the second disjunct could be false because of a clerical error. Her experience has taught her that such errors do occasionally happen. She calls the registrar's office and asks if someone could check the computer entry for Tom Jones's Logic I grade against the instructor's written grade sheet. The check is made, and sure enough, an error had been made. There was also a Toni Jones in the class, and it was her grade that was F. Tom Jones's grade was a passing one. Case closed—or is it? One does not have to be a logic nerd to understand every step of this episode thus far. Keep it in mind, for we will refer to it again.

This story, which is about how the truth-values of some statements may determine the truth-values of other statements, illustrates what logic is about, and it seems to me to be anything but arcane, heartless, cold, and brutal. Indeed, the dean's knowledge of the rules of logic enabled her to act warmly humane toward all parties. Using this illustration, let us try to be more precise about some of the words that we have used.

A logical *proof* is called an *argument,* but the word does not suggest that a dispute is actually taking place. An argument is a set of *statements,* or *propositions* as logicians usually call them, some of which are called *premises* (but some arguments may have only one premise), and another statement (usually one) called the *conclusion.* In the logic that we are discussing, every statement has one and only one of two possible truth-values, *true* or *false,* even though we may not know which it is. The argument does not require that the premises be true, but it proceeds on the assumption that they *are* true. There is a very common expression in our language: "Let us *for the purposes of argument* assume such-and-such to be true, and see what would follow if it were." The "such-and-such" in this expression is a premise or a collection of premises. In some arguments we strongly believe the premises to be true; in other arguments we strongly believe the premises to be false; in still other arguments we have no opinion about the truth-value of the premises.

But in all arguments, *for the sake of argument,* we assume the premises to be true, because we are interested to find out what other statements will be necessarily true *if* the premises are true. In any argument that is called *valid,* the conclusion follows *necessarily* from the premises, and therefore if the premises are true, then the conclusion *must* be true. Therefore a valid argument always has a hypothetical form and can be cast as an *if-then* compound statement: "*If* the premises are true, *then* the conclusion must be true." In a valid argument it is said that the conclusion can be *deduced* or *inferred* from the premises; the rules of logic are called the rules of valid deduction or the rules of inference. Ordinarily, then, it is the function of logic *not* to prove that the conclusion of an argument is *true*, but to prove that the conclusion follows from the premises. It is important to keep this in mind, because it is often wrongly claimed that the laws or theories of nature are conclusions to logically valid arguments and therefore are proved to be true by the scientific method, which is an inherently logical method. Generally, if there is uncertainty about the truth of the premises of a valid argument, there is a similar uncertainty about the *truth* of the conclusion, even though it is a *valid* conclusion. Note carefully that a valid conclusion is not necessarily a true statement. We might also note here that often in the practice of science a law or theory is taken as one of the premises of an argument in which the conclusion is a statement with the form of a fact, not of a law. In its internal techniques and procedures, science does more than just begin with factual premises and conclude from them laws and theories.

It is helpful when studying the rules of logic to distinguish clearly between the *meaning* of a statement on the one hand and its *truth-value* on the other. Generally, we can know the meaning of a statement about the (putative) world quite independently of its truth-value, and, as we noted in part 1, the alleged truth-value of such a statement is always subject to change on the basis of future experience. If we did not know the meaning of a statement, we would have no idea of how to go about determining its truth-value. Until we know its meaning, a "statement" is only a collection of words—or worse, a collection of noises or wiggly lines. Ordinarily this distinction between meaning and truth-value is easily grasped and causes no confusion. For example, in ordinary discourse everybody knows what the statement "All apples are red" means, and everybody knows that it is false. However, when in logic we *symbolize* the *forms* of statements we can sometimes become confused when a statement contains within it a negating word or particle, such as *no, not, non-,* or *un-*. It is a common mistake to assume that a statement containing such a negating word or particle thereby has the truth-value of false. Let us take an example. The statement "The lightbulb is not on" has in everyday life a clear meaning that no one in our culture would be the least bit confused about. And equally clear is the fact that the statement can be true or false. But when we start to symbolize the two possible truth-values of this statement, we can easily lose track of what we are doing. When logicians are speaking, they indicate that the statement is true, or has truth-value "truth," in several ways:

It is the case that "The lightbulb is not on" is true.
It is the case that "the lightbulb is not on."
It is true that "the lightbulb is not on."

In each example the statement, whose meaning we clearly understand, is within the quotation marks, and the words outside the quotation marks assert that the truth-value of that statement is "true." However, if logicians wish to assert that that same statement is false, or has the truth-value "false," they use similar words with appropriate changes:

It is the case that "The lightbulb is not on" is false.
It is not the case that "the lightbulb is not on."
It is false that "the lightbulb is not on."

It is easy to lose track of just what is being asserted, or just what truth-claim is being made. But the situation is further complicated by the fact that each one of the entire lines above is itself a statement, and that therefore it has a truth-value of its own.

The difficulty illustrated here is not one that is created by introducing logic into an otherwise clear situation. It is a difficulty inherent in ordinary language itself. Often in college faculty meetings, after a complicated motion or resolution has been debated and the vote has been called for, someone with a Ph.D. who has the motion or resolution in writing before him, will ask, "If I vote aye, am I voting for or against the proposed change?" Others then laugh, but the truth is that they are just as confused as the questioner is. And as often as not, the dean's answer, which is always correct because she has taught logic and has studied the motion carefully beforehand, is that if you vote aye, you are voting against the proposal. In the state of Oregon where there are often several propositions on the ballot to be decided by the voters, the same question is raised by the wording of a large number of them, with the same answer: If you vote yes, you are voting against the change that is being proposed!

Logical symbolism has been invented, not to complicate the matter, but to simplify it by eliminating ambiguities that are built into certain words and phrases in everyday language and to reduce every statement to its precise form. When this has been done, then the form can be dealt with in arguments by the application of a few simple rules, without having to worry about the content, including the number of negatives. It is possible to do this because the logical relations between premises and conclusions that make arguments valid or invalid are relations of the forms of the statements, not their content.

So let us now turn our attention to forms, using as the content the contrived story of Tom Jones and his Logic I grade. As we do so, let us keep in mind that these statement forms can be thought of as templates, with blanks to be filled in by the specific content later.

Logical Forms or Templates

Several different ways of symbolizing statements have been invented, but we will use the one in which the smallest unit to be symbolized is a simple statement, and such a statement will be symbolized with a single lowercase letter, usually chosen to suggest what the content of the statement is. But once we have symbolized it, we can forget about the content. In our story, the arguments of the student and of the dean contain two simple statements: "Final exam grade is at least C," which we will symbolize as c, and "Course grade is passing," which we will symbolize as p. Simply to put the symbol on paper as a premise is to assume for the sake of argument that its truth-value is "true," although later we could change our minds about its truth-value. Technically, then, c and p are not statements, but statement forms, and therefore have no truth-values. They become statements when the blanks, represented here by the letters, are filled in with statements; only then do they have truth-values. In an argument form, every instance of a particular letter must be filled with the same statement, or must be thought of as representing the same statement. When we say, "Let us assume that p is true," we mean, "Let us assume that a statement represented by p is true."

Logical Operators

Simple statements can be transformed into compound statements by the use of logical *operators,* which have carefully specified meanings. We will use four such operators, although we could get by with fewer. In our case, frugality will usually be sacrificed to increase convenience. (If you ever took a course in Euclidean geometry, you will remember that all theorems could be proved directly from the axioms; but once a theorem had been proved, it was much simpler to use that theorem in proving subsequent theorems. Our decision to use four operators is somewhat like allowing proved theorems to be used instead of going back to the axioms each time.)

The first operator is the *conjunction* operator, whose meaning is virtually the same as the word *and.* Its symbol is the ampersand, which is placed between two statements to make a conjunction. Thus the compound statement $c \& p$ is read, "c and p are both true," or "c is true and p is true," or simply "c and p." If some ambiguity would result without them, parentheses are used to enclose the statement. (Incidentally, the word *but* in everyday language usually has the same logical meaning as *and* and therefore is symbolized with the same operator. The two compound statements "Tom passed Logic I, *but* Harry flunked Logic I" and "Tom passed Logic I, *and* Harry flunked Logic I" function in the same way in almost any logical argument. Any number and combination of statements, simple or compound, can be joined by the conjunction operator into a compound statement. All statements formed by this operator are called conjunctions. Because a conjunction itself is a statement, it has its own truth-value. And again, simply to write the conjunction on paper as a premise is to assume for the sake of argument that its own truth-value is "true." Thus, in the conjunction (c & p) there are three distinct statements, each with a truth-value. This conjunction could be read, "It is true that both c and p are true," or simply "c and p."

The second operator is symbolized by the *negation* sign, ~. When the negation operator is placed before a statement, it creates a new statement that has the opposite truth-value from that of the original statement. Thus ~p is a compound statement of the original p and negation sign. The original p and the new ~p must have opposite truth-values. Such compounds are often called negations, but that term must not lead us to believe that all statements called negations are necessarily false. At the risk of being repetitive, let us take another obvious example:

Judge: Do you swear to tell the truth?

Witness: I do.

Judge: The previous witness says that the light was red. But you have just sworn on your oath that it is false that the light was red. Were you telling the truth?

Witness: Yes, your honor. I swear that my statement, "It is false that the light was red," is the truth, and the whole truth.

The witness could be telling the truth, in which case his statement, which has the form of a negation, is true. On the other hand, the witness could be committing perjury, in which case his statement, which is still in the form of a negation, is false. So a compound statement that has the form of a negation can be either true or false. The only requirement is that it have the opposite truth-value of the original statement that it negates.

The negation operator can be put in front of a compound statement that has been formed by any operator. For example, we might have the statement, ~(c & ~p), which is a negation of a conjunction in which one of the component statements (a *conjunct*) is itself a negation. This statement would probably be read in this way: "It is not the case that *c* is true and *p* is false."

The third logical operator is symbolized by a bold capital **V**, called the *disjunction sign*. When it is placed between two statements, it forms a new statement that is called a *disjunction,* and the two component statements are called *disjuncts.* Thus *c* **V** *p* is a disjunction. It is usually read, "Either *c* is true or *p* is true, or perhaps both are true." Notice that the disjunction has a precise meaning, whereas in everyday discourse the "either-or" combination is ambiguous. When a parent says to a child at afternoon snack time, "You may have either a candy bar or a glass of chocolate milk," the possibility of having both is definitely being prohibited by the "either-or" combination. In a different context if an instructor says to an advisee, "Either Economics 101 or Sociology 101 fulfills your general graduation requirement in the social sciences," no one understands this statement to mean that you are prohibited from taking both. This latter usage is called the weaker sense of "either-or," and the former is called the stronger. Sometimes in everyday life serious misunderstandings arise from the hearer's misunderstanding of the speaker's usage. In logic the disjunction is always understood in the weaker sense. In some formulations of logic an additional operator is introduced to cover what is included in the stronger sense, but the stronger sense can be expressed with the operators that we will use, so in this case we will practice frugality. The disjunction is itself a statement, and therefore it has its own truth-value. What is prohibited is that the disjunction be true when both of the disjuncts are false.

The *implication* operator is the last one for us to discuss. It is symbolized by $\supset$. When this operator is placed between two statements, a compound statement called an *implication* is formed. Thus $c \supset p$ is an implication; it is usually read, "*c* implies *p*," or "If *c* is true, then *p* is true." The statement to the left of the symbol is called the *antecedent* and the statement to the right is called the *consequent.* Either the antecedent or the consequent may be either a simple or a compound statement. Thus $(c \ \& \ \sim p) \supset \sim(c \supset p)$ is an implication, with its own truth-value. It may be read this way: "If *c* is true and *p* is false, then it is false that *c* implies *p*." This is the form of the accusation that Tom Jones makes against his Logic I instructor. What a true implication prohibits is a true antecedent and a false consequent.

The *implication* is important for our discussion for two reasons. First, it is one of the most common formulations for a law-like statement and will therefore serve to explicate what laws and theories are and do. Second, all logical arguments (in the formulation of logic that we are discussing) have the form of an implication, with the antecedent made up of the premise(s) of the argument, and the consequent being the conclusion of the argument. This being the case, we can think of the scientific method as our collective efforts to invent or discover law-like statements (called implications) whose truth-values will never be made false by the truth-values of the component statements in those implications. In other words, we have as our goal laws that are not made false by the facts of the putative world. We will explicate this after we look at argument forms.

We need to discuss one further attribute of the implication. A true implication does not entail that either the antecedent or the consequent is true. In our story the instructor's statement in the syllabus, "If you pass the final examination with a grade of C or better, you will pass the course," does not guarantee that anyone in the class will pass the final with a grade of C or better, or that anyone in the class will pass the course. The statement is still true, even if the entire class is made up of total failures. Therefore, if we infer from the truth of an implication that the existence of anything is being asserted, we can be sorely disappointed. Therefore a complete system of logic will require some way of indicating when a statement has existential import and when it does not. However, for our purposes we do not need to go into how that is done.

The Rules of Inference

Let us now assume (for the sake of the argument of this chapter) that we have a complete set of templates, into which any statement whatsoever can be fitted. Since the validity of any *argument* depends on the *forms* of the *statements* that make it up, and not on their specific content, we now need to turn our attention to the *rules of inference* that stipulate forms of valid arguments. These rules are few and fairly obvious, but here again more rules than are strictly necessary may be given in any logic text to add convenience, so frugality may be sacrificed.

In the rules of valid inference that follow, I will first give the rule in ordinary language. Then below that on the left I will give its form as an argument with the premises above the solid line and the conclusion beneath it. On the right I will give its form as an implication, with the premises as the antecedent and the conclusion as the consequent. If there are several premises, they will be represented as a conjunction of the several statements. Thus, a valid argument form can be represented as a statement form, which will have its own truth-value, and *the truth-value of any statement with a valid argument form is always true*.

Rule 1. If a statement is true, then its negation is false:
(If c is true, then $\sim c$ is false.)

c $c \supset \sim(\sim c)$
___
$\sim(\sim c)$

Rule 2. If two or more statements are true, then their conjunction is true.
(If c is true and p is true, then the statement c and p is true.)

c $[(c)\ \&\ (p)] \supset (c\ \&\ p)$

p
___
$c\ \&\ p$

Rule 3. If an implication is true and its antecedent is true, then its consequent is true.
(If c implies p is true, and c is true, then p is true.)

$c \supset p$ $[(c \supset p)\ \&\ (c)] \supset p$

c
___
p

Rule 4. If an implication is true and its consequent is false, then its
antecedent is false.
(If c implies p is true, and p is false, then c is false.)

$c \supset p$ $[(c \supset p)\ \&\ (\sim p)] \supset \sim c$

$\sim p$
___
$\sim c$

Rule 5. If a disjunction is true and one disjunct is false, then the other disjunct is true.
(If $c\ \mathbf{V}\ p$ is true and c is false, then p is true.)

$c\ \mathbf{V}\ p$ $[(c\ \mathbf{V}\ p)\ \&\ (\sim c)] \supset p$

$\sim c$
___
p

Rule 6. If the antecedent of an implication is true and the consequent false,
then the implication is false.
(If c is true and p is false, then $(c \supset p)$ is false.)

c $(c\ \&\ \sim p) \supset \sim(c \supset p)$

$\sim p$
___
$\sim(c \supset p)$

There are other rules for forming valid arguments, but for the purposes of our discussion we will let these six rules represent all the valid argument forms. (Also, in almost every logic textbook there is a discussion of invalid argument forms, which are innumerable. There are several of these that at first glance— and sometimes at second glance—appear to be valid, and these are listed as *fallacies.* It is not necessary for our purposes to list these.) But we must say some further things about the *valid* argument forms that are important for understanding the role of logic in science. First, notice that because every valid argument form can be represented as an implication (as it is in the right column on the facing page), every *valid* argument form therefore has a truth-value, and *that value is always "true,"* regardless of the truth-values of the component statements in it, which are represented by the letters, *provided that in the argument the same statement is always substituted for the same letter.* Thus in Rule 3, there are two component statements, c and p, each of which appears twice. If we substitute any statement whatsoever for c both times it appears, and substitute any statement whatsoever for p both times it appears, then the resulting compound statement will be necessarily true. The rules, then, have the form of *tautologies,* statements that are always true, regardless of the truth-values of the component statements. Notice very carefully in Rule 3 that in the formulation on the right there are two separate implications: first, the statement $(c \supset p)$, which is one of the premises, and second, the entire statement. In this example it is only the second statement, the entire argument, that is a tautology and necessarily true. The first implication is either true or false, and its truth-value *is* determined by the truth-values of the components c and p.

The argument form in Rule 3 is the crucial one for our purposes here, for it is the basic form for both (1) a scientific *explanation* of an event, and (2) the *prediction* of an event that will follow an act, both of which are crucial to knowledge under the rubric of utility. In this argument form, the first implication, $(c \supset p)$, represents in the simplest way a natural law, while c and p represent facts in the world. If the law of nature is true, then if a fact c happens, a fact p will also happen. In this case, we would say that fact c and the law $(c \supset p)$ together *explain* fact p. Likewise, the possible fact c and the law together *predict* that if we do act to accomplish c, then p will follow.

We are now at the point where we should be able to see why the scientific method does not *prove* the laws of nature to be true by the use of logic. In the naive linear view of the scientific method, which we examined above, it is assumed that sense experience gives us the facts (represented here by c and p). Then with these facts in hand as premises and with the rules of valid inference at our command, we should be able to deduce valid consequences (the law of nature) that would be true if the facts (the premises) are true. And, as we have seen from the beginning of our discussion, logic at its very heart is about how the truth-values of some statements determine the truth-values of other statements. So let us look through our rules to see what valid argument forms have statements of facts as premises and statements of law (implications) as conclusions.

Only Rule 6 appears at first glance to have that pattern, but notice carefully that in Rule 6 the conclusion is not a law (an implication), but the *negation* or falsity of one. So by the use of logic we can argue *from* the presumed truth of the antecedent and the presumed falsity of the consequence *to* the *falsity* of the law. From no other combinations of the truth-values of the antecedent and the consequent can we argue to a valid conclusion about the law. This argument form is the one that Tom in our story employed to make his claim that the statement on the syllabus was a lie (was false), and this form of argument is used often in the practice of science.

Another way to understand why proving a law of nature to be true is impossible is to consider what is usually called *inductive* logic, in contrast to *deductive* logic, which we have been discussing thus far. In the example we will use here, the premises are alleged facts of the natural world given in sense experience, and the conclusion is a law of nature; but in an inductive argument, no claim is made that the conclusion follows *necessarily* from the premises. Suppose that many times in the natural world we have observed c followed by p, and we have never observed c not followed by p, no matter how hard we have looked, nor how many times we have contrived instances of c to see if in these there was at least one in which p did not follow. With each of these many instances as a premise, we might then conclude the implication $(c \supset p)$. If just one instance of c without p following happened, then the conclusion would indeed appear to be false. But as long as no such negative instance has happened, the law stands. In some contexts such conclusions will be considered to be quite reliable, and, indeed many procedures in the practice of science employ such *inductive* inference.

It should be clear, however, that as long as experience continues to occur, we can never be sure that $(c \supset p)$ is always true. Furthermore, it should be equally clear that many of the law-like statements in modern scientific theory did not arise by first observing many particular facts and then generalizing by induction to the universal statement. It is difficult to think of the modern theories of the atomic structure of the elements as having been arrived at by simple induction. Our point here is not to disparage induction, for perhaps a kind of induction is at the very heart of the basic scientific procedures. The point, rather, is to emphasize that neither deductive nor inductive logic is capable of *proving* the laws of science to be true. That they are incapable of doing so might be a serious matter indeed if the scientific method had to meet the demands placed on it by the view of truth in metaphysical realism. However, without this ability to prove the laws of nature to be true, scientists continue to produce knowledge of ever-widening utility, as required by the rubric of the putative view of reality. Scientists are not in the habit, when they find it helpful to abandon a long-held law of nature, of throwing up their hands in despair and saying, "Since by neither deductive nor inductive logic can we *prove* laws of science to be true, we should abandon our work." Ask not what truth is; ask what it does.

Does what we have said about logic mean, then, that although we cannot prove laws to be true, we can indeed prove some of them to be false? As we have noticed, in a valid argument the truth-value of the conclusion (in this case "false") has the same uncertainty as the truth-value of the premises. So before we can say that we have proved a law to be false we must be absolutely sure about the truth of the alleged facts stated in the premises, and of course we can never be absolutely sure. It is at this point that we encounter some of the most significant procedures and techniques of the scientific method. We have yet to discuss the way in which sense experience gives us *the facts,* and we will do that soon. So for now we can only say this much: By several techniques and procedures we may be able to save a law from this deadly fate—of being proved false by the facts—by changing the way we gather the facts. We can suspect that our equipment was dirty; we can assume that our clocks and meter sticks were inaccurate; we can change the way we conceptualize the world. Especially if the law is part of a long-standing received tradition and has served well as guide to our conduct as we seek to fulfill our desires, we will be most reluctant to declare it to be false. In our story, the dean was reluctant to give up the received tradition that the instructor was an honest man. We will look at her argument soon.

Before we end our logic discussion, we should deal with one further question: "How do we know that the rules of logic really do state valid argument forms; how do we know that in an alleged valid argument the conclusion must follow from the premises?" One answer sometimes given is that because we are rational creatures, we by our very nature have an insight into the logical structure of reality, and that the rules of logic simply reflect that reality. This answer sounds a bit "Aristotelian," and I think that there is a simpler explanation. It is that every thing asserted by a valid conclusion has already been asserted by the premises, but not always in an obvious way. The rules of logic are to help us avoid saying in the conclusion more than has been said in the premises. If this sounds too simple and trivial, keep in mind that when we enter into important contracts, we pay lawyers considerable amounts of money just to give this kind of help. Language is often confusing, and it is sometimes difficult to know what we have asserted to be true (and contracted or promised to do) by our words. Sometimes our words say more than we thought we had said or had wanted to say. Sometimes they say less. Either mistake can have disastrous results in business, science, or theology.

Chapter 6

Making Laws Fit the Facts;
Making Facts Fit the Laws

*L*et us return to the contrived story of Tom Jones and his bout with logic. We will not treat the story as an *example* of logic in science, for the law-like statement, the implication printed in the syllabus, is hardly a law of nature. We will instead treat it as an analogy, but we need to remind ourselves that all analogies are imperfect and should not be pressed beyond their usefulness. As an analogy, this story will illustrate several of the points we have made thus far.

When Tom enters the classroom, one of the first things he notices is this statement in the syllabus: "If you pass the final examination with a grade of C or better, then you will pass the course." This interests him greatly, because his desire is to pass the course, and any information about what will help him fulfill that desire is not to be overlooked. This "law," which has, for him, great utility, can be symbolized $c \supset p$. As an implication, it is a law-like statement. (I suggested in chapter 5 that this statement does not fit our usual understanding of a natural law, for we think of laws of nature as having a force that is derived from the "objective" causal structure of reality, but this implication on the syllabus has only the force of the instructor's integrity. It is a promise, not a law. However, we should not be too quick to reject any likeness other than the logical form. Since the time of David Hume we have learned not to speak too confidently about just what *causation* is. It seems not to be observable by sense experience in the way that stars, trees, and even protons are.

(Many scientists of the early modern period were not reluctant to suggest that in their search for the laws of nature they were inquiring about the mind of God. Since no necessity could be discerned in the laws themselves, the very choice of the laws of the universe, and the constancy of those laws, were attributed to the integrity of God. Much earlier, the writer of Gen. 8:22 had attributed the orderliness in nature—"seedtime and harvest, cold and heat, summer and winter, day and night"—to God's faithfulness to a covenant, that is, to a promise. Einstein's often-quoted remark "I shall never believe that God plays dice with the universe" seems to be in the same vein. Such remarks are not scientific justification for the existence of God, but more like theological justification for the existence of science. I am not suggesting that we adopt them as such. I am merely suggesting that the scientific method does not rest on some direct insight into the nature of causation or on some unproved "faith" that the universe is causal in its very nature, but rather on the rubric of utility that requires us to seek to make causal or deterministic laws in order to maximize utility.) Since Tom has no reason to doubt the instructor's integrity, he assigns the implication the truth-value "true." Knowing more logic than he yet has words with which to talk about it, he deduces from the implication what he can do to pass the course. He uses the law as a prediction device.

Since Tom is young and has no great investment in the received tradition that instructors are to be trusted, when the prediction based on the integrity of the instructor's word fails to come about, he has no difficulty in taking the revolutionary step of calling the instructor a liar. The dean, on the other hand, is older and does have a vested interest in the received tradition, so she takes the conservative approach. Her argument makes the *law,* the statement in the syllabus, $c \supset p$, the *premise,* and makes the negation of a conjunction, $\sim(c \,\&\, \sim p)$, the conclusion. Notice that in this case the law is not something to be tested or *confirmed.* Its truth is taken for granted, and it becomes the basis for a research project (a minor one, to be sure, so she doesn't apply for a research grant). And by her research she has extended the applicability of the law to an area where it had not been tested before.

It would be easy to conclude at this point that the case is closed. But experience never ceases to occur in the dean's office. As soon as Tom Jones has left satisfied, the dean begins to think about Toni Jones, the student who received the course grade of F in Logic I. She then remembers that Toni is a freshman whose tests and records from high school were so outstanding that she received a prestigious scholarship and advanced placement. What happened to her that made her fail the course? While she is wondering, there is a knock on the door, and Toni is shown in. She has copies of all her test papers in the course, including the final, all of which have the grade A on them. She also has her copy of the registrar's report, with F in Logic I for the course. And she also has a letter from the financial aid office, informing her that her scholarship has been revoked because she has failed a course. Toni did not bring a copy of the syllabus, because the "law" had not interested her when the course began. Her interest had not been in how merely to pass the course; it had been in how to get an A instead of a B.

The received tradition is under attack again, but this time the situation is not so easily resolved. All of Toni's work indicates that she has earned a course grade of A. The instructor's grade sheet in the registrar's office clearly shows an F. A new research project is called for, this time with an ethical difficulty. (Notice that scientific research is sometimes prohibited by ethical considerations.) The dean would like to look at the instructor's grade book, but it is apparently locked in his desk, and the departmental secretary does not have a key. The only key this side of Europe is in the custodian's office. Should she get it and search the desk for the grade book? Though doing so would greatly simplify the research project, do the rules of academic ethics allow it? Finally the dean, in consultation with the chair of the faculty ethics committee, decides that the interests of the student outweigh the rights of privacy of the instructor, and she takes the appropriate action. When the grade book is located, she examines it, and breathes a sigh of relief. Apparently while the instructor was working on the grade book, he was also drinking a cup of coffee. A bit of it had spilled on the page with Toni's grades, and the course grade A had been hit by a drop that caused it to run, making it look to tired eyes very much like an F. A slow letter to the instructor in Europe eventually reaches him, and an equally slow reply arrives, confirming the diagnosis and stating his relief that no permanent injustice had been done. The received tradition is saved again. Case closed. Or is it? With a little bit of ingenuity you can think up further experiences occurring in the dean's office, some of which may force her finally to give up the received tradition concerning the instructor's integrity. But if this revolutionary step is called for, the "new" received tradition must not only satisfactorily explain just the new experience; it should explain all the old experience as well and give a reasonable account of why the instructor had earned such a good reputation earlier.

We have for the time being said enough about logic as a discipline that provides us with forms or templates for statements and valid arguments, and we have seen why logic cannot *prove* the laws and theories of science to be true. Before we consider the very important function of logic in system building, we must first turn our attention to how we fill in the blanks in the logical templates with the facts of the world.

Experience and Observation

We have already suggested that there is a difference between *having experience*, on the one hand, and *observing the facts,* on the other. Experience simply occurs, but to observe the facts of the world we must have some clue as to what to notice and what to ignore in the raw experience. Generally, we do not have to search for a clue; it is given in the received tradition (Kuhn's paradigm), which in some circumstances can be quite rudimentary and in other circumstances quite sophisticated indeed. In those sciences that have developed beyond the very simplest stages, the received tradition consists of the accepted laws and theories of the discipline and the accepted ways of making observations of the facts. Hence, the facts are always "theory laden." Anyone who is not tutored in the theory of a fairly advanced science has almost no idea of how the experts in that field justify saying that they have observed certain facts. The untutored can presumably have the same sense experiences as the experts, and yet have observed nothing of note.

To appreciate this distinction, let us look again at Figure 1 (see p. 11). But this time we will use it for quite a different purpose. In chapter 1 we used it as an analogy for understanding the difference between the two rubrics, one of utility and the other of ultimate purpose. Here we will use it as an analogy for understanding how within science under the rubric of utility different scientific theories can give rise to different sets of facts. Keep in mind that this is only an analogy, not an example of two different theories. If we let the assertion that Figure 1 is a picture of an older woman stand for theory A, and the assertion that Figure 1 is a picture of a younger woman stand for theory B, it can be seen that even though our sense experience is presumably the same in each case, a different set of facts emerges for each theory. An observer who is "locked in" by theory A almost automatically—by second nature, we say—sees an older woman, and may initially be unable to see a younger woman or to understand why anyone else can. In each case, it is the theory that tells us what kind of "stuff" the natural world consists of and how to interpret experience.

With this analogy in mind, we can appreciate how strong a hold the received tradition in science can have. The Newtonian theory in physics, after it became widely accepted, ceased to be thought of as a hypothesis still needing confirmation and became the received tradition. In effect, the Newtonian principles became the truths of the world. They dominated generations of scientists, determining the facts they observed and guiding their research as they extended the scope of physics to cover new areas of inquiry. According to this theory, the stuff of the natural world is made up of Newtonian particles, and facts of the world are about these particles moving in accordance with Newtonian laws.

In short, then, without a theory to guide us, our experience yields no materials with which to fill the blanks in logical templates and thus form statements of facts and statements of laws and theories. Ordinarily it is the received tradition that supplies us with theories. Yet the received traditions themselves must have been at one time new hypotheses that challenged and eventually superseded inadequate or outmoded traditions. The circularity here is apparent: without facts from experience, we can have no laws or theories; but without laws or theories to guide our experience, we can have no facts. But the circularity is probably better thought of as spiral-like, because each time around, the old received tradition of the theory may be replaced by a new and sometimes improved model. Before we ask what determines when the received tradition is no longer adequate and how new hypotheses are devised, we will consider an additional factor that makes the determining of the facts of the natural world even more complicated.

Earlier, in the discussion of the rubric of utility, it was suggested that the rubric requires us to maximize utility, and that to do so we must have as our ideal a putative world that is unified by a system of deterministic laws, or by a unifying theory. Few things are more obvious than that this ideal has not yet been attained and that the possibility of attaining it is beyond our reach as long as experience continues to occur. Because the rubric arises in response to our unfulfilled human wants and desires, it creates in the practice of science an ever-present tension. On the one hand, we demand from science knowledge that will make possible fairly quick, if not instantaneous, gratification for some of our specific wants. On the other hand, we demand knowledge of broad generality to increase the chances that the means by which we satisfy some of our wants will not have unexpected side effects that will frustrate the satisfaction of other wants.

Since the rubric of utility arises from our wants, and since human wants seem to have no limits, the various branches of science, along with their specializations, have proliferated in order to address the areas into which human wants divide themselves. Within many branches of science the tension mentioned above has led to the rise of specialists; some focus their work on solutions to pressing problems, and others focus on what are sometimes called the broader or more theoretical issues. Thus the academic world of science has not just one received tradition, but many; not just one prevailing theory, but many; not just one "stuff" of the natural world, but many; and consequently not just one circular or spiral movement of thought, but many. The "real things of the natural world" that some physicists talk about have little similarity to those that some biologists, psychologists, economists, or political scientists talk about. In short, we do not yet have that one "theory of everything" that has long been sought.

In some fields of science that focus on certain areas of human wants, scientists have been able to make knowledge-claims that approach the ideal of deterministic theories. In other fields, scientists have not been able to do so and are at present content to live with probabilistic laws or theories, although the ideal continues to beckon. Under the rubric of science, which requires the maximization of utility, probabilistic laws are better than no laws at all. Earlier it was said that some scientists think of their task as inventing laws or theories rather than discovering them. If this is apt, then it is appropriate to compare theories with any other human invention. Few of us who find automobiles or computers to be of utility in our daily lives would think of postponing buying one until they have been perfected. Likewise few of us would think of not acting on the latest theories in science because they have not yet been perfected. The putative world of science is constantly being improved or upgraded, and as long as the process goes on, the laws and theories—as well as the *facts* of the putative world that are imbedded in them—are subject to revision.

For the purposes of this chapter, the point of the present discussion is this: *Experience,* contrary to the claim of metaphysical realism, does not put us in touch with a metaphysical reality that exists independently of it, and to which it corresponds. Consequently, the scientific method does not begin with "the facts" and proceed from them to the goal of theoretical knowledge-claims. If we judge the scientific method by whether or not it does what the view of metaphysical realism demands of it, we must find it fatally flawed. On the other hand, if we judge the scientific method by the view of putative realism, we find that when it is obedient to its rubric of utility, it indeed produces knowledge of ever-widening reliability.

The complaint that scientific knowledge is not perfect and that tragedies have happened because human beings trusted too heavily on some aspects of it is hardly a fundamental criticism. Many of us can remember that at our own freshman orientation in college the dean warned us that within a few years of our graduation a high percentage of what we learned within the ivy-covered walls would be outdated or just plain wrong. A liberal education therefore did not consist in memorizing "truths" that had been "proved" by the academic disciplines, but in understanding how truth-claims are arrived at and in preparing oneself to participate in the ongoing critical revision of them. Let us, therefore, return to the discussion of the importance of a received tradition in producing knowledge and how the critical operations of the scientific method might deal with it.

Discovering the Laws of Nature

If, as we have asserted, (1) experience is primary, simply occurs, and as to its occurrence is nonproblematic; and if (2) the object of scientific knowledge is not a metaphysical reality but rather the postulated (and problematic) world of putative reality; and if (3) that postulated world and our scientific knowledge of it are formulated together in a somewhat circular or spiral-like manner under the rubric of utility; then we are constantly, if tacitly, asking the question "What must the world be like for us to have the experiences that we do have?" Answering this question is the process of *discovering or inventing the laws of nature,* and in answering it we are not free to postulate a world in just any way that we might, but are governed by two very demanding restraints: First, there is the rubric of utility, which requires us *ideally* to postulate that world as one characterized by deterministic laws and theories of widest scope in order to maximize that utility. Second, we are restrained by experiences as they actually occur, for if we should ignore experience or declare that certain kinds of experiences are out of bounds, our very reason for devising the scientific method in the first place would be abandoned. These two restraints, unlike the purported restraint of the metaphysically real world, *do* something. They are ever present and operative, providing us with criteria to judge the success or failure of any effort to formulate the putative world and knowledge-claims about it. In other words, there is no freewheeling relativism here. It is in this context that received traditions, laws, and theories play a vital role and are to be understood.

From our very earliest days, I presume, we all learned from our parents or from others who raised us to understand our experiences within a received tradition, much of which is implicit in our language. Thus, with the learning of words we became able to distinguish the various objects of our world. By a process much too complicated to analyze precisely, or even to call a method, we began to correlate our experiences with the "stuff" of the world in such a way as to satisfy our wants. As our experiences increased, we understood them within the categories of the received tradition. But as we matured we found it difficult at times to understand some experiences within that tradition, at least as we had learned it, and we had to make modifications. I can remember when I had to modify my received tradition to include the stuff *zebra,* because I had experiences that I could not comprehend with *horse.* The point is that we learn to correlate our experiences, on the one hand, with the various things of the world, on the other, in an informal way that defies easy codification. I would be hard-pressed to specify exactly what sense experiences I would have to have before I could say that I was seeing a zebra, but I have sufficient confidence to know one when I see one (but are there any albino zebras that would shake my confidence?). Similarly, I would be hard-pressed to specify exactly what sense experiences I would need to have to distinguish a younger woman from an older one.

When we move from this early stage of expanding our knowledge to the rational-critical method of modern science, the prevailing theory in a given area of inquiry plays the role of a received tradition, providing us with two essential features, in no particular order: One feature is a conceptualization of the "stuff" of the putative world that makes explicit the defining features or state variables of that stuff, along with the laws or theories (these may be deterministic or probabilistic, depending on the circumstances), written in terms of those defining features and in accordance with which the changes in the putative world take place. In addition are the ways by which we correlate our experience with the features and events of the putative world so that experience in its sheer givenness is transformed into observation of the world. These ways of correlation are seldom codified or made explicit, and are usually learned by a science student in the way that a small child learns to say, after certain experiences, "I see a zebra." Although these ways of correlation are not often discussed in detail, they are essential to the doing of modern science, for without them scientific knowledge-claims would be totally "Aristotelian," completely unrelated to the realm of human wants, needs, suffering, and satisfactions of desires. The second correspondence we mentioned earlier, the correspondence between nonverbal experiences, on the one hand, and verbal scientific knowledge-claims, on the other, could not be made.

Figure 3 may help to make clear the distinctions between (1) theories and (2) ways of correlation between experience and the putative world. In Figure 3 the area above the horizontal line is the realm of experience. As was claimed in part 1, experience is in one sense all that we ever have; it simply occurs; it is in its occurrence unproblematic; and though it is the basis for all our knowledge, knowledge is not the mere recording of experience. Experience is neither true nor false; it simply occurs and makes no knowledge-claims. Below the line is the realm of the putative world, with its theoretical entities and events and the laws and theories that connect them, making possible the explanation and prediction of events. This is the realm of scientific knowledge-claims, which are either true or false. In the realm below the line, logical consistency or validity of arguments is important. It is here that the laws or theories can be construed as statements of implication with which we explain and predict events. But this is the very realm that must correlate with experience above the line as it actually occurs. As we have already seen, scientific laws and theories do not *explain* an experience (which is above the line) as an event caused by an event in the putative world (which is below the line); scientific explanations do not cross the horizontal line; they stay below it. It is, rather, the *ways of correlation* that cross the line, giving scientific knowledge-claims their basis in experience. One event in the putative world, along with scientific theory or law, predicts a second event in the putative world, and only by ellipsis can it be said that the laws have predicted sense experience.

Figure 3 also illustrates one of the great advantages of putative realism over metaphysical realism, one that we have already mentioned. If a reality called

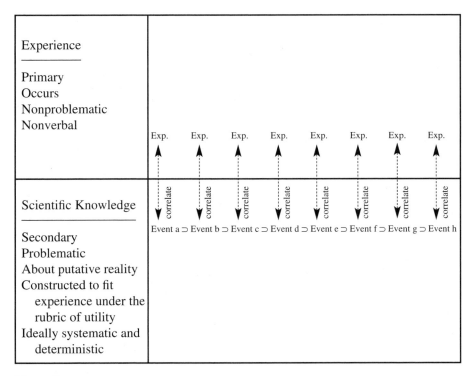

Figure 3

mind has as its defining feature *experience,* and if the stuff of the real world is *matter*, having as its defining features those that are *not experience* but others such as those of Newtonian or Einsteinian physics, then there is the vexing problem of how mind and matter can interact in the process of observation. As Figure 3 shows, the view of putative realism does not solve the problem but eliminates it. In this view there are not two separate kinds of ultimate reality to interact; the putative reality is invented or construed or postulated to *fit* experience as it occurs. If it sounds too glib to say that we have postulated the putative world to fit experience, we need to remind ourselves again that the putative world of science is not a fiction, or worse, a lie, made out of whole cloth. Experience and the rubric of utility are tough, exacting taskmasters indeed. The marvel of science is not that scientists have been able to discover a preexisting causal metaphysical reality. It is rather that there have been in the field of science the great geniuses who have been able to postulate new hypotheses that create a putative world to fit experience under the rubric of utility. When it is said, then, that scientists are discovering or inventing the laws of nature, what is meant is that they are constantly seeking to improve the fit or correlation between the realm of experience, on the one hand, and the putative world, on the other. Since experience, once it has occurred, cannot be altered (although I can reinterpret it, or forget it, or lie to you about it), the fit can be improved only by altering the postulated putative world or the ways of correlating experience and the putative world.

In keeping with the plan of this chapter, we now must look at a few of the procedures or techniques of the scientific method *that do indeed improve this fit*, asking our usual question: Are these given techniques better understood under the view of metaphysical realism or the view of putative realism? The ones we look at will illustrate the three features of a rational intellectual activity: *systematic logical consistency, conceptual conservation,* and *conceptual revolution*.

Systematic Logical Consistency

Since the rubric of science requires us to maximize utility, there will always be the procedure or technique of unifying laws and theories into a systematic logical whole. Thus far we have used the terms *law* and *theory* without distinguishing them. We will now make a rough distinction between them in order to explicate this procedure. As a rule, laws can be thought of as low-level implications, with scope or application limited to commonly recognized and accepted features of the everyday world—features that are part of widespread and relatively unchanging received tradition. Because they are based on such features, we seldom think of them as theory laden, just as we do not ordinarily think of seeing a picture as one of a younger woman to be theory laden, but laws are. At a relatively early stage of a particular science, these laws are thought of as inductive generalities based on many observations of events in the everyday world. At this stage the various laws are not seen as necessarily related to each other, and therefore the evidence for one law is not seen as evidence for any of the others.

As the science develops, however, there is the desire to understand the several laws as themselves dependent on some deeper or higher law-like statement(s) that will give them systematic unity, thus making it the case that the direct evidence for one of the laws is indirect evidence for all the others. Such higher or deeper laws are commonly called *theories*. These theories often are not themselves the result of induction from events of the everyday world, but are instead ingenious inventions devised precisely to perform this unifying, systematizing task. In such a case, systematic logic as we have discussed it is not so much a tool in the thinking up of the theory in the first place as it is a tool used to test it to see if it does the job it was devised to do. In this aspect of theory making, the theory itself provides the *premises* for logically valid arguments from which the low-level laws are deduced as the *conclusions*.

Euclidean geometry is often used as an analogy to make the procedure or technique of theory construction more understandable. In plain geometry we can easily imagine (even if it is not precisely the case) that each individual *theorem* (which is analogous to a low-level law) could have been independently "discovered," in which case the direct evidence for each would have had no bearing on the discovery or acceptance of any of the others. But after a time, as the number of such independent theorems increased, the systematizing demand began to be felt. How can these separate laws (the theorems) be understood as instances of a deeper law, or theory? To answer this question, the genius, Euclid, invented the axioms that provide this unity, thereby making the direct evidence for each of the theorems serve as indirect evidence for all the others. And, behold, this set of unifying axioms provided a most important additional benefit. Now that this new system of geometry had become a reasonable hypothesis about the structure of space, the axioms and theorems could be used as premises in valid arguments to deduce, and therefore to "discover," new theorems that had never been thought of before. Thus the unifying theory (the axioms) became the means not only of unifying existing knowledge but also of expanding the scope of geometric knowledge. Here we can see that a theory, though ultimately tied to empirical evidence, did not itself in the first place arise as an inductive generalization from particulars. Rather, it was invented to do the job of unifying and extending the scope of knowledge. Thus deductive logic played a vital role in the process by which the hypotheses became a theory, and indeed became the received tradition that remained well into the twentieth century.

Conceptual Conservation

In the attempts to systematize and extend the scope of a particular received tradition, the process is at first conservative. We attempt to comprehend all new experience within the concepts and laws and theories of that tradition (Kuhn's "paradigm"). Especially if that tradition has served us well for a long period, we will, as we have noted, think of it as embodying the sure and certain results of science. Much of the work in any given area of science, therefore, is characterized by techniques to extend the scope of the theory to areas that have not yet been subsumed within it (Kuhn's "normal science"). As this process progresses, often new laws are developed to explain the events in these areas and heretofore unknown entities are discovered.

Occasionally, however, events are recalcitrant and anomalies happen—events that do not accord with the received laws and theories of nature. But when they do happen, scientists in our tradition are not prone to exclaim, "An event that breaks the natural law has just happened; it is a miracle; we have proof for the existence of God!" Because the rubric of utility says, "Thou shalt strive to maximize utility by developing deterministic laws and theories," there are techniques to meet anomalies head-on. The first conservative approach is to deny that the event was a genuine anomaly by showing that the events in the situation were not as we assumed them to be.

In my high school chemistry class, when the result of my experiment was not in accord with the laws of chemistry, it certainly did not occur to me to say that a miracle had happened before my very eyes, and my teacher would have tolerated no such explanation of my anomalous results. The laws of chemistry were not on trial; my techniques and accuracy were! If the anomaly happened in an experiment that can be repeated, and if the purported anomaly does not repeat itself, we suspect that we used the wrong reagents or had faulty instruments or had dirty test tubes. Even if an anomaly cannot be satisfactorily explained, however, we prefer to live with the anomaly rather than to give up a highly reliable law or theory. (In part 4, after we have discussed theology in the biblical mode in part 3, we will be in a position to deal more adequately with the whole issue of science, anomalies, and miracles.)

Sometimes anomalies happen with such regularity that this expedient is not open to us, and more drastic measures must be taken to preserve the received tradition. Let us consider one. In some scientific theories the defining characteristics of the entities—such as size, mass, location in space, and velocity—are numerically quantified. Accurate instruments are needed to assign such values if we wish the laws to predict precise results. One instrument needed in physics is the clock. Of all the various clocks, natural or contrived, that are available, how do we choose the most accurate one? It should not surprise us now that sometimes the law itself serves as a criterion for determining that one type of clock is better than another. If, for example, a given law is part of a well-established and confirmed theoretical system, and if the clock traditionally considered to be the state-of-the-art chronometer does not yield results in some exacting situations that are within acceptable limits predicted by that law, we need not change the law but can search for a new periodic device, natural or contrived, that will eliminate the anomalies by giving us the desired results.

Here, then, we preserve the received theory by changing the manner in which we determine the events that happen. In this case, the events are theory laden, and the instruments are chosen to make the events *fit* the theory.

This circularity at first glance seems to be a pure example of fudging, and it would be so if we understood scientific truth-claims to be in correspondence with the metaphysical world. But it is not an example of fudging if we understand scientific truth-claims in accordance with the view of putative realism. In this view, time is not some mysterious reality in the metaphysical world to which a good clock must correspond; time is whatever the clock measures. The clock creates the putative "real" time, and we choose the clock that will give us the time that best enables us to construct laws and theories of maximum utility. But we would choose a new clock only if we can explain *within the laws that the new clock confirms* the reasons why the old clock was not adequate. In this technique of achieving a fit between experience and theory, it is the rubric of utility that prevents circularity from being arbitrary.

Conceptual Revolution

With various conservative techniques and procedures, a received tradition may be saved while the scope of its applicability is expanded and hence its utility increased. Yet there come times when these techniques will not do the desired job. Sometimes new experiences cannot be adequately explained within the conceptual framework of the tradition. Sometimes logical inconsistencies are discovered in the basic theory of the tradition. For whatever reasons, then, a more radical way is needed to meet the imperative of maximizing utility. It is time for a revolution (Kuhn's paradigm shift) in which a greater or lesser part of the received tradition is replaced. Such a shift is not always easily accomplished. Perhaps the most celebrated revolution in modern science is the shift from the Newtonian to the Einsteinian paradigm in physics. It is not difficult to appreciate the fact that not just anybody could have recognized the need for the shift, much less could have envisioned a new paradigm that would successfully address that need. You do not have to be a genius to see that a genius is needed. Let us consider just one process that was a part of that shift.

An essential part of a modern physical theory is its concept of space. For centuries Euclidean geometry furnished that concept. It was the received tradition, and so venerable were its axioms and theorems that it was considered to be a self-evident truth about the real world, and as such it provided one of the best arguments in support of metaphysical realism. Sometimes it was suggested that even God could not create a world that was non-Euclidean, since the very notion of non-Euclidean space is self-contradictory. Few if any scientific revolutionaries were so radical as to suggest that physicists should dare to do what God could not do. Newton's space was Euclidean.

The possibility of doing what God could not do, of using a non-Euclidean space in a theory of physics, arose in the nineteenth century when mathematicians attempted to perfect the systematization of geometry. They discovered that if they denied the truth of the parallel axiom and then used a form of that denial in conjunction with the other axioms to deduce the theorems, they developed a whole system of theorems that were different from the Euclidean ones instead of arriving at the logical contradiction one would expect. But these new theorems were considered to be mere curiosities, with no application in empirical science. Later, when Einstein faced the problem of measuring triangles in astronomical space, where yardsticks will not serve as measuring instruments and where instead one has to depend on light rays traveling at high but finite speeds, he recognized that our *experience* would be different from that predicted by Euclidean theorems. So in Einstein's theory of general relativity space is non-Euclidean. A dyed-in-the-wool medieval Aristotelian might be outraged at the audacity of Einstein, and indeed some early twentieth-century scientists who had become comfortable in the Newtonian received tradition and who, therefore, exhibited a bit of Aristotelianism themselves, were unconvinced by his theory. But it prevailed and has become for many aspects of physics the received tradition.

Two additional observations might be made about a revolution or a major paradigm shift. The first is that the revolution is not so thoroughgoing as to throw out the received tradition completely. A totally new putative world is not postulated. The giants in science usually acknowledge that they are standing on the shoulders of giants. The second observation is that since Einstein, most scientists have recognized that although we have a new received tradition, it too may in turn have to be superseded by a newer one. As long as experience continues to occur, there is always the possibility that the rubric of utility will call for a giant to lead a new revolution.

Let us now ask our regular question about such revolutions. Under which view of reality are the procedures and techniques involved in performing them best understood? It seems to me to be impossible to understand them as confirming a point-to-point correspondence between a reality that exists apart from our experience, on the one hand, and the verbal truth-claims of a theory, on the other. Even the dubious claim that there are some aspects of metaphysical reality, such as the geometry of space, that we know innately, apart from sense experience, is no longer available. But every procedure and technique of the revolution seems to have been designed to do what the putative view of reality demands. They improve the fit between experience, on the one hand, and the theoretical putative world, on the other, so that the utility of knowledge-claims is increased.

Conclusion

It has been our purpose in this chapter to test our thesis that science is a rational human intellectual activity designed to develop creditable knowledge under the rubric of utility and that this knowledge is of a putative world. We have tested this claim by examining a representative selection of scientific techniques and procedures, and we have discovered that they do what this thesis demands that they do but *not* what the view of metaphysical realism, with its correspondence theory of truth, demands that they do. If the arguments here have been cogent, we can now consider the thesis well established, although not *proved* by logically valid arguments. *For the purposes of argument,* therefore, in the remainder of this book I will treat the thesis no longer as a position to be tested but as a criterion by which practices that are claimed to be scientific can be judged and by which certain types of knowledge that are claimed to belong to the body of scientific knowledge can be evaluated. In a sense, then, I will now use this thesis as a received tradition. The circularity here is analogous to the circularity by which new hypotheses in science, originally designed to challenge old received traditions, may eventually themselves become the new received traditions and, as such, cease to be thought of as positions to be confirmed and become themselves the criterion by which other positions are confirmed or disconfirmed.

We will put this thesis to such use in part 4. In the meanwhile, in part 3, we must test our thesis concerning biblical theology as a rational human intellectual activity to develop knowledge-claims under the rubric of the ultimate purpose of human life. Only after that is done will we be able, in part 4, to examine the principal areas of knowledge about which science and theology seem to be in such irreconcilable disagreement. In that part we will discuss the function of creation accounts in science and biblical theology, the comparison of anomalies in science to miracles in theology, and the place of canonical texts in each.

PART 3   Meaning, Method, and Truth
in Biblical Theology

*The Rubric of Ultimate Purpose
and the Putative World of Theology*

Chapter 7

Introduction to Part 3

Explication of the Thesis

*T*he aim of part 3 is to test the second basic thesis or claim of this book: (1) that biblical theology as a rational human intellectual activity develops creditable knowledge-claims under the rubric of the ultimate purpose of human life and (2) that these knowledge-claims are about the putative world of theology, all of the features of which point to the ultimate human purpose of imaging the biblical God, whose character is understood to be faithful loving-kindness. To accomplish this aim the structure of part 3 is as follows:

First, there is an explication of this thesis (or hypothesis), because to test it we must understand its implications and the demands that it puts on any actual human intellectual activity of which it purports to give an account. Just as in part 2 it was our thesis that was on trial, so it is here also. We will be testing the thesis by the theological content found mainly in the biblical material itself, but also in the doctrine of the Trinity in postbiblical times. It is not our intent to pass judgment on such theological content but to ask if our thesis, or perhaps some other thesis, gives a credible account of what is actually there. In other words, we are not trying to decide if the Bible is true; rather we are trying to decide what *kind* of truth-claim the Bible makes—and under what rubric it makes its truth-claims. We will conduct this explication by discussing how knowledge-claims made under the rubric of utility, on the one hand, and the rubric of ultimate purpose of human life, on the other, are alike and different and how their differences require that the methods of theology and science also be different.

After explicating what our thesis entails, we will test it by asking, "Does the material in the biblical texts and in doctrine substantiate it? Does that material do what this thesis requires or entails that it do?" To accomplish this test, I will have to suggest an alternative thesis that I believe many people both inside the community of the biblical faith and outside it uncritically assume to be the appropriate one by which to understand the biblical texts. Since this alternative thesis is commonly expressed as a synopsis of the biblical material, I will present it as such. Then I will present my own synopsis of the biblical material as that synopsis is developed from my thesis. As we examine the biblical texts, we will ask which one of these theses best fits that material, and which one solves the vexing problems so often raised by that material. The pattern of testing here is similar to that in part 2, but of course the thesis and the alternative are different here.

Let me state again why I have chosen this pattern. The conflict between science and religion is very much a part of the current intellectual scene in the United States, if not in the entire world. At the heart of that conflict in this country are the apparently incompatible truth-claims produced by the scientific method, on the one hand, and method of biblical theology, on the other. In part 1, I stated my view that the conflict is occasioned by unconsciously but implicitly held assumptions concerning what these knowledge-claims are all about. If these assumptions are not made explicit, then they will continue to operate as a kind of received tradition and make it virtually impossible to understand the argument of this book. To use the analogy in Figure 1 again, if I see the picture as one of an older woman, but you do not know that and are looking at it as a picture of a younger woman, the chances of your understanding anything that I say about the picture are slim indeed. Consequently, the arguments in this book depend on persons in both science and theology being explicitly aware not only of how those in the other discipline are "looking at the world" but also how they themselves are. Only then is there a chance that the conflict will be addressed and understood.

If in part 3 our thesis rather than the alternative one is sustained, then we will have come to an understanding of biblical theology on its own terms, and thus we will be prepared for the discussion in part 3.

Similarities between Science and Theology

The rubric of human purpose, as it is understood here, assumes the primacy of experience and requires the construction of a putative world. Theological knowledge-claims are as solidly based on experience as scientific knowledge-claims are. Just as human beings have experiences of wants or desires and have constructed putative worlds under the rubric of utility to maximize the fulfillment of those wants and desires, they also have experiences of moral or ethical obligation and have constructed putative worlds under the rubric of ultimate purpose to clarify and understand those obligations. In each case, the rubric is in response to a specific kind of experience but the putative world is intended to comprehend *all* experiences, not just the ones that prompted its rubric.

In science, as we have seen, the experiencing of wants and desires prompts the rubric of utility, which in turn prompts the question, "What must the world be like for us to have all the experiences we do have?" Therefore, the *scientific method* must comprehend in its putative world *under the rubric of utility* not just the usual sense experiences but also the experiencing of moral or ethical obligations if and when they occur. Indeed, much of the work in what are sometimes called the *human sciences* is an entirely legitimate effort to construct explanations for all human moral or ethical experiences and phenomena, as well as experiences of wants and desires. (For example, a social scientist might give a very interesting—or dull—explanation of why I am writing this book and saying the things that I am saying, and such an explanation would be within the putative world of science.) When constructing a putative world with any method that takes experience as basic, no experience can be placed out of bounds as either irrelevant or too privileged to be considered.

Similarly, in biblical theology the experiencing of moral or ethical obligation prompts the rubric of purpose, which in turn prompts the question "What must the world be like for us to have *all* the experiences we have?" Therefore, the *theological method* must comprehend in its putative world *under the rubric of purpose* the experiencing of wants and desires. In the attempt to construct a putative world of theology, in which experience is also primary and basic, experiences of wants and desires as well as experiences of moral and ethical obligation are all relevant. In other words, each discipline attempts to construct *a complete world* under its own rubric. It is important that we do not think of each discipline as using only a fraction of total experience to construct only a part of a world that will later be added to the part constructed by the other discipline. Think again of Figure 1. One half of it is not a picture of an older woman and the other half a picture of a younger woman.

Because theological knowledge-claims, like scientific knowledge-claims, are based on experience (although developed under different rubrics, of course), the view of metaphysical realism with its correspondence theory of truth is just as inappropriate for understanding knowledge-claims in theology as we have seen it to be for those in science. In theology it is conceptually impossible to understand what a point-to-point correspondence of a theological entity, on the one hand, to a doctrinal statement, on the other hand, would be, much less how it could be confirmed. For theology as well as for science it is the putative view of reality that supplies us with an operable understanding of *meaning, truth,* and *reality*. Therefore, when we confront a statement produced under the rubric of ultimate purpose, we must also ask, "What is it intended to *do*?"

We will find in examining theology—as we did in examining science—that there is no freewheeling relativism here, for experience and the rubric of ultimate purpose are its exacting taskmasters. The consequences of ignoring either or both can be, and often have been, most unfortunate, and even shamefully disastrous.

Because theology is a rational human intellectual activity, the method by which its truth-claims are produced will display the three characteristics of any such activity, which we discussed at the end of part 2: systematic logical consistency, conceptual conservation, and conceptual revolution. Theologians explicitly or implicitly strive to produce knowledge-claims that can be systematically unified into one body. Logic, which as we have seen is about how the truth-value of one statement entails the truth-value of another statement, is just as important in theology as it is in science. In science we stressed that one important reason for seeking a unified body of knowledge in which all laws are related by a general theory is to reduce the probability of an act's having unwanted side effects. Similarly, in theology systematic unity of knowledge is desired to prevent us from saying anything about God that would give us permission—or worse, command us—to do anything contrary to our ultimate purpose of caring for all without regard to their merit.

In the effort to produce a systematic, unified putative world under the rubric of ultimate purpose, theology will also exhibit conceptual conservation, in that as new experiences occur it will seek to comprehend them within the framework of the received tradition. And just as in science, so also in theology, at times well-established received traditions can take on the aura of eternal, immutable truths. When it becomes evident to some members of the theological community that the received tradition cannot adequately comprehend the experience of a new situation if the rubric of ultimate purpose is to be obeyed, it is time for a revolution or reformation, in which some aspect of the received tradition will have to be altered. For example, when a received theological truth-claim by valid logical deduction either commands me or allows me to hate you or to oppress you, that truth-claim must be modified. The biblical writings and the history of doctrine supply examples of these three characteristics, just as the history of science supplies them for its field.

Finally, the tension between immediate and broad systematic concerns will have its effect in theology, as it has in science. In science there are major divisions and specialties within divisions, the result of which is the phenomenon of scientists who, because they have different specialties, can hardly talk with one another about their work except in the most vague of generalities. About all they have in common is the rubric of utility. Similar divisions and specializations characterize theology, the effect of which is about the same. It is an implication of the thesis of this chapter that the rubric of purpose is one indispensable factor that gives theology its unity.

Differences between Science and Theology

We need to note carefully two main differences between science and theology. The first is about how the various events within one putative world are related to other events in that same world. The second difference is in the aim of activities within each discipline.

Events within Each Putative World

Within both science and theology, the *rubric* dictates how the events of its putative world are to be linked together. Since in neither science nor theology is knowledge a simple list of experiences that have occurred, but in both, ideally a unified system of events, the rubric in each is operative in determining not only how experiences are formulated into events but also how the events are related to one another. As we saw in part 2, because in science we want knowledge that is useful for satisfying our wants, the events of the putative world of science are connected or linked by causal laws. Although we are not always capable of making the laws completely deterministic and comprehensive, to do so is the ideal commanded by the rubric of utility because such laws will maximize utility. In other words, the putative world of science is *ideally* one in which the basic "stuff" is *nonconscious* and moves in accordance with inexorable mechanistic laws, not in accordance with conscious purposes. To understand *why* an event happens requires no resort to some purpose that a responsible conscious being has in mind to accomplish; the explanation of any event is completely exhausted in the set of nonpurposive events that preceded it and in the laws of nature. Much of the work throughout the history of modern science has been *for the purpose* of ridding theories of any dependence on *purposes* to account for and explain events, not because of perversity, as some critics of science seem to think, but because the method of utility cannot confirm or disconfirm them.

In the putative world of ultimate purpose, on the other hand, the significant events will be understood as those brought about by responsible beings to accomplish some purpose in mind. To ask *why* a responsible human did a certain act is not to inquire about the laws of nature and the previous state of the "stuff" in that person's brain and the relevant vicinity; it is to inquire about that person's motives and intentions. It is to ask for a *teleological* not a *mechanistic* explanation. Because these two types of explanation—two ways of answering the question *why?*—are used constantly in everyday life and are a part of the received tradition that can be traced back to antiquity, we should look at them more closely.

Science's great success in using causal or deterministic, mechanistic explanations to construct useful knowledge perhaps justifies the assumption that if there is any self-evident truth about the world, it is that the world is governed by mechanistic causal laws. Even if we do not know what kind of "stuff" the world is made of or what the laws that govern it are, many claim that we at least know that there is some such stuff and that there are such laws. Indeed, it is a popular view that the very possibility of science is based on this assurance and that the scientific method is the way to discover just what they are. As we have seen, this is a part of the view that we have called metaphysical realism, with its correspondence theory of truth. But if the scientific method is one based on experience alone, we must ask how we experience *causal connections*.

As we have already noted, David Hume, the eighteenth-century Scottish empiricist, sharply criticized the notion that we have either innate or empirical knowledge of causation as a necessary and universal feature of reality. Our position in part 2 was that such *knowledge*, either innate or empirical, of causation was not a necessary *factual* presupposition of science. It is the *rubric of utility,* which is not itself a factual matter but more like a rule or an imperative that commands us to construct a putative world in which events are ordered causally. Science, therefore, accepts causation not as an assumed fact of metaphysical reality but as a marching order to be obeyed if it is to produce and maximize useful knowledge. Accordingly, science does not "prove" that ultimate reality is causally ordered by mechanistic laws. Rather, the success of science shows the importance of using the rubric of utility, with its requirement to construct deterministic laws, if we are to produce knowledge that will be useful to humanity.

If to think of the world as governed by mechanistic laws comes "naturally" to us, it is just as natural to think of the world as one in which many events come about and are explained by conscious decisions of responsible beings with purposes or intentions in mind. It seems to me that this latter mode of thinking underlies virtually all of our everyday discourse about human affairs. It is what history books are made of. Most literature could not be thought of without it. As I participate in casual or serious conversation every day, I am constantly using teleological explanations of my own and others' conduct. When I listen to the conversations of others, many of whom are scientists, I discover that I am not unique in such usage. Furthermore, I experience the link between my conscious intentions and the events that follow with a clarity that is absent in my experience of the mechanistic causal connection between events in the inanimate, nonconscious, world.

For example, when I experience iron filings on a glass plate arranging them-selves in certain patterns when a magnet is brought close to them under the glass, I have no experiential insight into why or how they do it. The *connection* between the events is not itself *experienced*. It is *explained* by (logically deduced from) the relevant natural law of the present prevailing theory, and a statement of the initial location of the iron filings before the magnet was brought near. On the other hand, when I consciously intend to move my right hand up to the computer keyboard and that intention is followed by my hand's so mov-ing, the connection or link between the intention and the event is of a different kind from that provided by a law of nature. Indeed, the *connection* seems to require no explanation at all. To explain the movement of my hand it is suffi-cient to say that I *intended* to use the computer to write this page. (If I intend to move my hand, but it does not move, or if I intend not to move my hand but it does move, *then* I might want scientific laws to aid my understanding.)

Inasmuch as the *doing* of science is itself a purposive human activity, it is entirely appropriate to use teleological explanations to answer why a scientist is performing an act. For example, if a scientist is applying for a research grant, it is not considered odd for the review board, composed of eminent sci-entists, to ask for a *justification* for the proposed (*intended*) research grant. It certainly would not be considered an appropriate justification but would instead be considered sheer impertinence if the applicant justified the appli-cation by stating that, at the time of the writing of it, the relevant factors of heredity and environment (all of which could be analyzed into the states of basic particles of physics) were such that the applicant's hands, in accordance with laws of physics, moved in such a way as to produce the written proposal.

The request for a justification does, however, call for a teleological expla-nation, stating what the applicant intends to accomplish. Not that the mecha-nistic causal explanation is inappropriate *within* a scientific theoretical context, where it cannot be ruled out on principle—though the technical difficulties in formulating it may be overwhelming. The mechanistic causal explanations *are*, however, inappropriate when we move away from the putative world of sci-ence and into the realm where we are asked to justify conscious responsible human decisions, choices, and actions. I am not suggesting that teleological explanations of conscious responsible human decisions, choices, and actions are, at best, stopgap measures to be benignly tolerated until technical difficul-ties can be overcome and mechanistic, causal explanations can be made. I am suggesting rather that mechanistic causal explanations should not be thought of as the "privileged," "real," or "true" explanations, while teleological expla-nations are dismissed as imaginary, fanciful, or false. Each type of explanation should be recognized and defended as appropriate in its own putative world.

It is my present opinion that causal and teleological explanations are incommensurable. Centuries of debating the question of free will versus determinism have not led to a verdict—a fairly good indication that there is no verdict to be reached because the question is ill conceived. In abandoning the notion of metaphysical realism, which *would* require a verdict, and adopting instead the view of putative realism, it is possible to understand each type of explanation as *doing what we want it to do*. It is helpful here, again, to think of knowledge-claims under the two different rubrics as two different tools designed to *do* two different jobs. In a recent survey of home repair experts, the crosscut handsaw and a roll of duct tape were top favorite tools. To the best of my knowledge, no one has even dreamed of inventing a dual-purpose tool to do the jobs of both. The incommensurability of the saw and duct tape is not a problem for those who prize good tools designed to do specific tasks.

For our final illustration on this point, let us contrive another chapter in the life of our imaginary logic student Toni Jones. She indeed fulfills the promise she had shown. She graduates with highest honors and enters graduate school to study the molecular structure of the brain. During the next thirty years many scientific revolutions, major and minor, happen, making much that she had learned in her undergraduate days passé. Remembering her education in the liberal arts, she is undaunted by these revolutions and embraces them gladly, recognizing that in them is the possibility of increasing the utility of scientific knowledge. In recent years she has become a Nobel laureate in recognition of her work in her chosen field—work that has led to a significant revolution. Thanks to her work it is now possible to explain many aspects of human behavior by reference to physical states in the brain and the laws of physics— explanations that could only be dreamed about in her undergraduate days. For the first time in centuries, biologists and physicists are not just talking to one another in polite but guarded terms; they are actively seeking out one another to discuss how the new theoretical breakthroughs bring their disciplines into a systematic unity.

Whereas many hail Dr. Jones's work as a significant advance in scientific knowledge of the human being, others see it as a significant threat to human freedom and morality. The latter ask how human beings can be held morally accountable for their acts if all their behavior is determined inexorably by physical conditions and scientific laws—a question that has been asked for millennia but is now being asked with marked urgency because now it seems that science is at last going to pull off what it has always been threatening to do. When Dr. Jones is asked by the International Society of Science and Ethics to give its prestigious annual lecture, she announces that her topic will be "Moral Responsibility and Scientific Knowledge." Many await her address with bated breath, some hoping that she will finally and definitively lay to rest the ancient superstition that human beings have anything that could be called moral responsibility. Others fear this possibility but also hold out a slim hope that she might find some loophole in prevailing scientific theory that will allow morally responsible human activity to be a legitimate concept within science.

Dr. Jones does neither, and instead of discussing whether or not her latest theory has a place within it for human purposive action, speaks about the moral responsibility of those who choose to be scientists. Human beings qua scientists are to be understood as conscious, experiencing beings who do their work by making deliberate choices to accomplish purposes in mind. Because the very purpose of doing science as it has been understood since the time of Bacon is to produce knowledge that will improve the lot of humankind, scientists are morally responsible to follow the rubric of utility scrupulously, even if their area of work is the human brain. If they should fudge or cheat or lie in an effort to produce knowledge that would satisfy some other rubric than that of utility, they forfeit the right to be called scientists, for they increase the risk that the knowledge-claims they produce will be unreliable.

Dr. Jones even uses her own variation of the "bumblebees cannot fly" story: "Everyone knows that according to the laws of science human beings are automatons and cannot act from conscious motives or purposes. But practicing scientists, who are human beings, have not recognized this, and so they consciously choose to produce laws of science anyway." The moral of her story is, of course, that we must not forget that science is a human rational intellectual activity, invented and engaged in for a consciously conceived purpose. Therefore, the knowledge produced by the scientific method must always be understood *within* the context of its purpose—to produce useful knowledge. When scientists are about their work, *they themselves* are to be understood as beings within a putative world of conscious purposes and intentions. But the *products* of their work, laws and theories of science, are to be understood as truth-claims about the putative world of the rubric of utility. She ends her speech by reminding her hearers that because the knowledge-claims produced by the scientific method may be used for weal or woe, scientists qua human beings have the responsibility to influence the ways in which scientific knowledge is used.

In the putative world of biblical theology, therefore, the most significant "stuff" will consist of conscious, responsible beings acting purposively to bring about intended ends. To explain why a significant event happened is to state that a responsible being intended it to happen and that the necessary means to bring it about were at hand. The language used for such explanations is the familiar, teleological one of ordinary discourse about daily affairs.

It will abound with the terms we have developed over the centuries to speak about our experience of *responsibility:* obligation, ought, good, bad, right, wrong, righteous, unrighteous, sin, blame, guilt, forgiveness, moral character—terms which would most likely have no meaning to anyone who has never had an experience of obligation or responsibility—and terms that have no use, except perhaps in a Pickwickian sense, in the language of scientific theory. Because in biblical theology the ultimate purpose of human life is derived from the character of the biblical God, it is that character of faithful loving-kindness that provides the systematic unity for all the terms in the language of responsibility.

Because explanations of events in theology are teleological rather than mechanistic, the most characteristic genre in which theology is cast is that of a story or narrative *with a plot.* Although the biblical material itself comprises several types of literature, taken as a whole that literature tells a story about what the biblical God is doing in history from the beginning to the end. God's purposive action supplies the main plot of the story, and every act of God in the narrative has its meaning because of its place in the plot. Reading parts of the biblical material without reference to the plot to which they contribute and in which they have their meaning is as inappropriate as reading individual sentences of a murder mystery at random, without any regard to its plot. In other words, the meaning is in the plot. If the biblical material is read under some rubric other than the one of ultimate purpose—the rubric of utility, for example—not only is its significance apt to be entirely overlooked, but also its material is apt to appear to be contradictory. The thesis of this chapter, as a hypothesis, requires that the material that the Bible (which it purports to explain) be a story with a plot that is governed by the purpose that God has in mind. We will test our thesis by the biblical material. Keeping in mind Figure 1 as an analogy, our thesis requires us to read the Bible—in its physical givenness only an inchoate jumble of ink marks—under the rubric of ultimate purpose and to see whether or not the plot "jumps out" at us.

The Aim of Activities within Each Discipline

In our discussion of science as a rational human intellectual activity, we asked the question, "What are scientists doing?" and answered, "They are discovering the laws of nature." In this chapter, if we ask, "What are theologians in the biblical mode doing?" it might seem that the answer should be "They are discovering what the ultimate purpose of human life is." But this is not the case. Even though the question of ultimate purpose supplies the rubric for theology, theological thought in the biblical mode *begins* with a conviction about that purpose and then is compelled to ask, "What is the world like if the ultimate purpose of life is to love one another with a love that is not based on the other's worth or merit?" What is the justification for *beginning* with such a conviction? If it is not a self-evident truth, known apart from experience, from what source does it come? The answer is that biblical faith, and therefore all theological thought that arises from it, begins with the *experience* of being freely and unconditionally loved—loved without regard to any merit that one might possess to earn or deserve that love. In the biblical narrative the Israelites experienced that love in the events of the exodus, and their conviction about that love was that they certainly did not deserve it, nor were they righteous whereas the Egyptians were not.

Subsequent Israelites experienced this love through the testimony of the community, and virtually all theological thought of the community is a reflection on what such love must mean about themselves and the world. Later, a small group of Israelites who became known as Christians experienced that same love in the person of Jesus of Nazareth, and especially in the events of his life that led to his death. Christian theology, always founded upon Israel's theological writings as its received tradition, continues as a reflection on the meaning of such love. This love, traditionally known as *grace*, certainly nullifies any notion that the purpose of human religion is to get God to fulfill our wishes (although the constant temptation of people of biblical faith is to relapse into this belief). The overwhelming conviction is that God's character is faithful loving-kindness, which does not answer the question of how we can get what we want but of the ultimate purpose of our lives. It is our ultimate purpose to *image* that love in all that we do.

All features of the biblical faith follow from this conviction, and we will discuss some of them in the next section of part 3 as we test our thesis. However, we should mention several of them now to get a clearer understanding of the thesis itself.

The first feature is that in the biblical faith the fundamental *revelation* is not a linguistic proposition or a set of such propositions, but the experience of overwhelming unmerited love. It is this experience and the rubric of ultimate purpose that are together the strict taskmasters of theological thought as it constructs its putative world. Theological doctrine that is true to this experience and this rubric will never say anything about God that will permit—much less require—human beings to hate anyone else; instead it will require them to regard all with unmerited compassion.

The second feature of biblical faith that follows from its origin in the experience of unmerited love is this: In the biblical story God is the main character, the one whose responsible, purposive choice gives the story its plot, which leads to the telos, or the fulfillment of the purpose. Consequently, the biblical narrative does not purport to be about *human beings'* search for God; it is about *God's* search for human beings and *God's* restoration of them to the ultimate purpose for which they were originally created but from which they rebelled. All responsible, purposive faithful conduct of human beings is a response to knowing God's acts—a response to having been found by God.

The third feature of the biblical faith to be noted here is that it understands its knowledge-claims fundamentally as a *witness* when they are addressed to the world. It is not the task of theology to *prove,* or *verify,* or *confirm* the truth of its knowledge-claims to a skeptical audience, for to do so is impossible. It is the task of theology to make intelligible to its audience the claim concerning the ultimate purpose of human life imbedded in the plot of the biblical narrative. Just as anyone can understand the plot of any other story without knowing whether or not it is true, so one can understand the claim made in the plot of the biblical narrative without accepting or acknowledging that claim. If, in response to such witness, anyone acknowledges and accepts that claim, theology attributes that response to God's fulfilling in that person the ultimate divine purpose.

With this explication of our thesis, or hypothesis, concerning theology in the biblical mode, we are now ready to put it to the test.

Two Conflicting Views of the Plot of the Bible

My own thesis concerning theology in the biblical mode is significantly different from one that is commonly, but implicitly, held by the general public. It is therefore important to make explicit that commonly held one in order to prevent its functioning as an unconscious, and thus unexamined, hidden assumption. I have referred to it as the *alternative thesis,* and I now present it to make it clear that *it is a position I reject.* It is often formulated simply as a synopsis of the biblical material.

Synopsis for the Alternative Thesis

God is a power who created the world and decreed a set of rules or laws by which all human creatures are to live. In this world I am related to God fundamentally by my *merit* or *righteousness.* If I obey those rules and am thereby righteous, God, who is just, will reward me with good things that I want. If I disobey those rules, God will punish me by giving me bad things that I do not want. God has in one way or another given all human beings some knowledge of these rules, so that everyone has an equal chance to obey and win rewards. God has also created heaven and hell as the ultimate reward and punishment. Hence, rewards on earth and final reward in heaven, and punishments on earth and final punishment in hell, are the sanctions for obeying God's rules. It should be noted that heaven is understood as a place where I get what I most dearly want, and hell is understood as a place where I get what I most fearfully do not want. The practice of religion consists of all those things I must do to make sure that I know God's laws and obey them so that I will enjoy God's blessings here and hereafter. My relationship to others is not an integral part of *my* salvation, although some of God's rules require me to treat others in considerate ways in order to merit my salvation.

Yet I do not always obey God's laws, and I know that I am a sinner. I am tempted in many ways to sin or break the laws, and because I frequently break them, I am doomed unless God, who is just, is also somewhat merciful. The biblical message is that God is indeed merciful. God has provided a way for human sins to be forgiven—for the slate to be wiped clean—so that everyone can have a second chance to be blessed in this life and to get the final reward, heaven. The provision for sins to be forgiven is the sacrificial system, in which I give to God something that I value in order to please God and to get back something that I value even more—good things here and hereafter. Yet even in the sacrificial system I am disobedient. Therefore the merciful God has provided the only truly effective sacrifice, the only begotten Son. Now all that I have to do for my sins to be forgiven is to believe—to have sufficient faith to accept the sacrifice that God has made in my behalf. If I do have sufficient *faith*, God will, in spite of my sins, reward me with the good things I desire here and hereafter. The ultimate religious question for each person, therefore, is this: "Have I done everything necessary, including having sufficient faith, so that when I die I will go to heaven?"

It is my opinion that if we take this synopsis, or one similar to it, as a hypothesis about what the biblical faith is and test it by the biblical material itself, this hypothesis will fail, because it ignores what is central in the biblical plot. Therefore, I shall now present a synopsis of the biblical material that is developed with the thesis of this chapter in mind:

Synopsis for Our Thesis

God, whose eternal and unchanging character is faithful loving-kindness, created the world for a purpose: to reflect or to *image* the character of its creator. Human beings in particular are for the purpose of *knowing* this God and *reflecting* God's faithful loving-kindness to one another in the human community in the world. It is this *character* of faithful loving-kindness, and *not our merit,* that has always been and always will be the basis of God's dealings with human beings. To know God is to know what we are for. But human beings have chosen to reject this God, and therefore to reject this ultimate purpose; we have instead chosen to create our own purposes and to worship gods of our own devising whose business is to reward us, if we obey their rules, with the things we want for our self-made purposes. Thus, *sin* is not fundamentally breaking rules. It is *rejecting the ultimate purpose for which we were created:* to be a community that reflects in our lives together God's character of faithful loving-kindness. This sin—rebellion against the Creator and our ultimate purpose—results in *idolatry,* a religion that thinks of its god as a power that will help us to fulfill our own wishes if we are obedient.

In spite of the fact that humanity has rejected God, God, who is true to the divine character of faithful loving-kindness, does not reject humanity. Instead, God promises to *save* the creation—that is, to restore it to the original purpose for which it was created. Once again human beings will know this God, and in so doing will reject idolatry and become a community of faithful loving-kindness. To accomplish this purpose God makes promises to Abraham and Sarah that through their descendants all nations shall be saved. Biblical history, particularly Israel's history as it is told in the Hebrew Scriptures, is an account of what God does to keep these promises: God provides Abraham and Sarah with a nation of descendants; God gives that nation the Ten Commandments so that it will understand the difference between God and the idols, and thus the purpose of human life; and God gives the nation a land in which it can live as the people—the community—whose purpose is given by God and not by the human pharaoh.

But Israel frequently succumbs to the temptation to make its God into an idol, thus forgetting its purpose and misunderstanding the law. Israel's prophets repeatedly condemn Israel for deserting its God and turning to idolatry; but they proclaim that God, who is faithful to the promises, will bring judgment upon Israel for the very purpose of reminding it again of God's purpose for choosing it. One of the many ways by which the prophets proclaim the ultimate triumph of God's promise to Abraham is to speak of a new David. Just as David, the second anointed king of Israel, united the twelve tribes of Israel into a community under the law of God (the *purpose* of God), so a new King David (a new anointed one, a new *Messiah,* a new *Christ*) shall unite *all nations* by making known to them the true character of God as faithful loving-kindness.

In the Greek Scriptures of the Christian community, the *gospel* or good news is that God is keeping the ultimate promise to Abraham and Sarah in the person of Jesus of Nazareth, the expected Messiah or Christ. By his life, his teachings, and especially his death on a cross Jesus reveals the total character of God and so the ultimate purpose of human life. The resurrection appearances of Jesus to those who experience them are the experiences of overwhelming unmerited love that change them from cowering disciples to fearless apostles. Their hope is that at the culmination of all things God's ultimate purpose for the creation, as that purpose is seen in Jesus' life, will be accomplished. That hope is not based on any human merit; it is based solely on God's character of faithful loving-kindness.

The community of the biblical faith understands itself first of all as made up of those who are to live out this purpose, and second as only servants, the instruments of God by whose witness *God* will accomplish the ultimate telos. This telos—salvation, the kingdom of God—is not our finally getting what *we* want; it is the reign of God's purpose for the whole creation. The ultimate question for the person of the biblical faith, therefore, is not "Have I done everything necessary to go to heaven (defined by my wishes) when I die?" It is "Do I truly understand and live the ultimate purpose for which I have been created and redeemed?"

In testing our thesis, it is *not* our purpose in the first place to attempt to prove the biblical truth-claims to be true. Rather, we will attempt to establish that our synopsis is more accurate than the alternative one in describing the claims that the biblical material does in fact make. We will do the testing by pointing out the salient differences between the two synopses, noting the requirements that each one places on the material it purports to describe, and showing how prominent parts of the biblical material meet or do not meet those different requirements. If, and only if, after the test our thesis (hypothesis) appears to be the more satisfactory one, can it then function no longer as a hypothesis but as a guide to understanding further reading of the biblical material.

The most important thing to notice about the alternative thesis is that it implicitly if not explicitly understands the biblical material under the rubric of utility. If the question "Why should I be religious?" is addressed to that material, the answer according to the alternative thesis is that by being so you will get what you want and avoid what you do not want. A very important implication follows: *Under the alternative thesis the truth-claims of the biblical material are potentially in conflict with the truth-claims of science, since both are formulated under the rubric of utility.* Both sets of truth-claims would be about the same putative world. Therefore, if there should appear to be an actual conflict, it would be at least one responsibility of theology to defend the correctness of the biblical truth-claims against those of science. The method by which that could be done would *not* be the method of science, as we have understood it in part 2, since that method produced the claims under question in the first place. Therefore, *some nonscientific method,* external to both science and theology, would have to be employed.

Those who hold the alternative thesis about the *meaning* of the biblical narrative and who also hold that that meaning is *true,* often claim to establish or prove on grounds external to the meaning of the biblical text that the Bible is the authoritative word of truth. The difficulty, if not impossibility, of proving that biblical truth-claims are indeed true and that therefore conflicting scientific truth-claims are false, does not, of course, have any bearing on whether or not the alternative *thesis* is correct. It could be the case that the biblical writers are indeed making their truth-claims about God under the rubric of utility, in which case the claims of the Bible and those of science could not both be true. Then one would be forced to deny one or the other or both. It seems to me that the hidden assumption of this alternative thesis underlies much of the discussion of science and religion in the public arena today: If the Bible tells us how we can get what we want, the Bible and science cannot both be true.

My thesis, with its accompanying synopsis, rejects the alternative thesis not because of difficulties establishing that the Bible is true over against any conflicting claim of science but because, in my opinion, the alternative thesis ignores what is one of the most insistent and persistent claims of the biblical literature: namely, that the God of Israel is not an idol and is not to be thought of or worshiped in the way that idols are. The difference between Israel's God and an idol is not merely that they are called by different names; nor is it that Israel believes its God to be the only one who can really give them what they want. The basic and essential difference is that whereas the idol is understood to be the personification of powers that we can control for satisfying our wants, Israel's God is understood as the one whose own character gives all creation, including human life, its original, continuing, and ultimate purpose. The major implication of this difference in *rubric* is that when the biblical material is read under our thesis, the question to be asked of the passage is "What does this passage *in the context of the biblical plot* say about what we are *for?*" In keeping with our view of putative reality (in contrast to metaphysical reality), the *meaning* of a knowledge-claim is not about a point-to-point correspondence of a statement to some unknowable metaphysical entity; it is in what it *does.*

Because the biblical material is far too large to be examined here even in a superficial survey, I think the best way to test our thesis will be as follows: Keeping in mind Figure 1, with the picture that can be seen as either a younger woman or an older woman, we will "look at" several important biblical themes that perennially have raised vexing problems. As we do so, we will ask if these vexations are occasioned because we are looking at the material under the rubric of utility and if they are reduced or eliminated by looking at them under the rubric of ultimate purpose. We will also have to keep in mind the three common features of any intellectual activity, be it science or theology: a quest for systematic consistency, conceptual conservatism, and conceptual revolution.

We are not now concerned with the question of whether science or the Bible is correct about such matters as evolution and miracles but only with the question of which *rubric* the biblical writers were guided by. We will thus postpone a discussion of the contemporary debate about creation accounts and miracles until part 4 when we will be better prepared to tackle it, and we will concentrate here on the *theological* issue of how creation stories, miracles, and other vexing topics are to be understood if our thesis concerning the biblical faith is taken. Some of these topics are as follows: community versus individualism, original sin, God's special treatment of Israel, the Ten Commandments, the attitude toward and treatment of enemies, the apparent incompatibility of absolute justice and absolute mercy, suffering, sacrifice, worship, the use of masculine titles for God, faith versus works as the means to salvation, law versus gospel, and monotheism and the Trinity.

As we might suspect, if the biblical faith arises from an experience that shifts the rubric from utility to ultimate purpose, these topics will have revolutionary new meanings. Granted, biblical thought, like scientific thought, is conservative and thus begins with received traditions about most religious concepts. The passing of time, however, brings new situations, and with the constant demand to unify those topics into a consistent view of God and human beings, the various biblical writers will be forced by the rubric of ultimate purpose to modify and revise what has been said about them earlier. What will remain constant is the conviction that the ultimate purpose of human life is to image faithful loving-kindness toward others without regard to their merit.

Since we often find models, illustrations, and metaphors useful in clarifying to ourselves and to others the relationships among words or concepts within an intellectual system, I shall now introduce two metaphors as aids in grasping the difference between the two suggested synopses of the biblical faith. These are not perfect models in every detail, of course, so we will not expect more from them than they are able to deliver.

Archery under the Rubric of Utility

In the recreational activity of archery I have but one target, the bull's-eye. Since I know the rules, I know what I must do in order to get the prize or reward that I want. "Righteousness" is hitting the bull's-eye, and "salvation" is the prize. "Sin" is missing the bull's-eye or missing the mark, and the consequence of sin is missing out on salvation. "God" is a just judge or scorekeeper, who must give me what I deserve. Since I am not morally perfect, I do not always hit the mark and therefore do not deserve salvation. Fortunately, the scorekeeper is not fanatically just but tempers justice with mercy, providing me with a "sacrificial" system that makes it possible for me to cover my misses. Perhaps to preserve a semblance of justice, the scorekeeper will introduce a substitution rule to allow his son's perfect score to count for my own and will place upon the son the punishment I deserved. Thus the amount of sin is balanced with the proper amount of punishment. The good news is that since someone else has achieved the required score for salvation for me, all I have to do to receive it myself is simply to accept it.

Several implications of this metaphor should be noted. God, who plays the role of the scorekeeper and referee, has no purpose for my life. The rules of the activity are ground rules (means), not statements of my ultimate purpose (ends). Justice and mercy are opposites: justice means that I get what I deserve, and mercy means that I don't get what I deserve. And there is no reason for my making any effort to hit the bull's-eye if I can accept the son's score as my own. Why not sin the more that grace may abound the more? A further implication is that in this game I am not a team player. I am concerned only to get my own salvation, and my relation to others is of concern only if the ground rules require me to treat them in certain ways in order to get my reward.

Basketball under the Rubric of Ultimate Purpose

In basketball there are two goals, one of which is most definitely *not* properly the goal of our team, and the other of which *is* properly ours—the one for which I was recruited when the coach found me hanging out on the sandlot and promised to do everything possible to make me a good member of his team. From the moment I joined up, the coach has kept his promise, and I am now in a game doing everything that I have learned from him. I am a slave to our basket, using every talent and skill I possess to advance the fortunes of our team. In a moment of excitement the ball gets loose, and we all go for it, tapping it madly in the air as we go around and around in circles.

Finally I gain control of the ball, but in the confusion I head toward the wrong goal. I, of course, do not know this, and as the noise of the crowd gets louder, I think that I must be doing quite well. I use all my skill in a heroic effort to make a basket. But just as I am about to lay one in, out of all the noise I hear the voice of my coach, and he is using theological language: "God damn you, Chalker, turn around!" When those words get to me, I undergo an overwhelming change in *rubric*. I fall to my knees and use theological language myself: "I'll be damned! Woe is me." But I do not stay on my knees. I get up, and (forgetting double dribbling) I turn around and head for the right goal, the one for which I was originally recruited. I have been saved by grace—by the coach's *faithfulness to the promise* he made to me. It was not my effort that turned me back to my purpose—to true righteousness. When I was a slave to sin, headed for the wrong goal, I was convinced of my righteousness and was making quite a show of it. And when I am saved by the coach's grace, I do not keep going in the wrong direction, saying, "Why not sin the more that grace may abound the more?" No, with renewed effort I strive for my true purpose. I now again become a slave to righteousness.

Furthermore, in condemning me the coach was *totally just* and *totally merciful*. If when I was headed for the wrong goal the coach had thought, "I love Chalker so much that I will not condemn him," and had called out, "Chalker, baby, I love you," I would not have turned around but would have continued straight to "hell." When I have abandoned my true purpose, the only way the coach can save me—be gracious and merciful to me—is to condemn me. In this situation justice and mercy are not opposites or contradictories but are the same thing. When I abandon my purpose, I stand under the coach's total judgment, but in judging me the coach is exercising total faithfulness to his promise to do everything possible to fulfill in me the purpose for which I was recruited.

The implications of this metaphor for theology should be obvious. God is not so much a referee as a coach. The concept of ultimate purpose is the central one and redefines most other theological concepts. Laws are not ground rules that specify techniques to control God; they are about our ultimate purpose. God's judgment is not the withholding of mercy or love; it is the necessary expression of it when "we have turned to our own way." The *good news* and the *good life*—God's grace and our obedience—cannot be separated, for the gospel is God's keeping the promises to Abraham and Sarah to restore us to the community of compassion that reflects God's character.

We will now turn to the biblical narrative, asking if its plot substantiates our thesis and not the alternative thesis.

Chapter 8

Testing Our Thesis

From Creation to the Ten Commandments

The Creation

Creation accounts, by necessity, are reflections under the appropriate rubric on our knowledge of the present (since we were not present in the beginning to experience it). The creation accounts in the early chapters of Genesis fit this pattern, bearing marks of a received tradition about the past that was current during Israel's early history, with that tradition here being interpreted under the rubric of ultimate purpose as Israel experienced that purpose in the exodus. The Creator God is none other than the God whom Israel comes to know in the exodus, the one whose character is faithful loving-kindness. This God creates a world that is very good, providing all creatures with what they need to fulfill their purpose (1:31). Human beings are created to *image* God's very character of faithful loving-kindness as they live together on this good earth (1:26–27). The command to subdue the earth is not a command to rape nature but a command that in all dealings with the earth we are to remember that it is God's creation, to be used by us solely in accordance with our ultimate purpose.

In the second chapter begins another somewhat parallel account of the first times. Here the Creator is specifically identified as the God of Israel by the use of the term commonly translated "LORD God," with all letters of LORD in upper case. The Hebrew word being translated by LORD is YHWH, the name of the God of Israel. Many scholars today pronounce the name Yahweh, but many Jews consider it too sacred to be uttered. The important thing for us to notice is that in many if not most appearances of this term "LORD God" in the Hebrew Scripture, the usage is polemic and is to be read "The God YHWH, and *not* the god Baal." Baal was a principal idol of the Canaanites, and Israel generally understood idols to be construed by their worshipers as powers that could be controlled by religious observance. Therefore, if we today read the term "LORD God" as a sort of generic term for the deity, we will miss the biblical insistence that God is to be understood under the rubric of ultimate purpose and not utility. We should notice that in the story of the garden of Eden, the creation as YHWH intended it is not complete as long as Adam is alone with the animals. Not until there is a nascent *community* of creatures who can *know* the Creator, and so know what they are for, can the creation image the character of the Creator. What is important here is not the difference between the man and the woman but the likeness: both can know the character of the Creator, and both can live their lives not from just instinct but from the knowledge of what their purpose is. Both are ethically responsible beings.

The Fall and Original Sin

In Genesis 3 the plot continues with an account of the original or fundamental, basic sin. The man had been commanded earlier not to eat of the tree of the knowledge of good and evil. Now the serpent tempts the woman to eat of it, saying that if they do so, they "will be like God, knowing good and evil" (3:5). Since here, also, it is the reflection on the ultimate meaning of life as it is revealed in the exodus that gives this somewhat enigmatic temptation its meaning, let us look ahead for a moment to the period after the exodus, when the biblical understanding of sin takes shape.

Israel's great prophets understand in the light of the exodus that just as Yahweh is qualitatively different from the idols, so sin is qualitatively different from merely breaking rules and thereby diminishing our chances of getting what we want. It is a total rejection of Yahweh's purpose for human life and substituting for it some purpose that we choose for ourselves; it is each human being's playing in his or her own life the role of God, being the determiner of purpose. This rejection of God's purpose results in our no longer reflecting the image of the Creator. Now rather than caring for one another, we find ourselves estranged from one another.

If I choose the purpose for my life, and you choose the purpose for your life, these two purposes may seriously conflict with each other. In that case I must not only be the "god" of my own life; I must also attempt to be the determiner of the purpose of your life, and you must attempt to do likewise concerning me. In other words, we each try to turn the other into an object—a thing to satisfy our own purposes. The typical biblical term for this attempt to determine the purpose of another's life is "oppression." In our relationships with one another we will constantly jockey for position, each guarding against letting the other know just what we are up to, lest in doing so we lose our advantage over the other. However, this rebellion against the Creator is far from the abandonment of religion. In practice, this original sin almost always manifests itself as religion—a religion in which the god is conceived under the rubric of utility rather than ultimate purpose. Original sin, therefore, is not, as in archery, missing the mark we are aiming at; it is turning to the wrong basket.

If our thesis is the correct one for understanding the biblical text, then this is the meaning of the temptation and the sin in the garden. The man and the woman are tempted to be like God—to take the place of God in deciding the ultimate purpose of their lives. The result of yielding to that temptation is that they are no longer to each other what they were created to be. In choosing to be estranged from God, they become estranged from each other, this latter estrangement being evidenced by the fig leaves. This twofold estrangement is the universal human condition; but it is not one that we know and so from this knowledge seek reconciliation. In this estrangement our quest is for a god who will satisfy our wants, which are so often frustrated by the various circumstances of the world, not the least of which are other people whose wants conflict with our own.

If the alternative thesis is the correct one, wherein God's action is determined by human merit, we could expect God at this point either to withdraw the creative word that called the world into being or to institute a sacrificial system to take care of any sins that are committed. Instead, Adam and Eve are sent out of the garden to the east of Eden, where life is hard and not as it was originally meant to be.

The consequences of the original sin become evident in Genesis 4, when Cain kills his brother Abel. As his defiant question to God, ". . . am I my brother's keeper?" (4:9) indicates, Cain has abandoned the purpose for which human beings were created and has turned to the opposite goal. The act of murder is the supreme expression of one's trying to be another's god. Individual acts of sin are not separate and unrelated moral lapses, as they would be in the alternative thesis—and as they would be in archery. They have their unity in the rejection of ultimate purpose. Again, though human beings reject God, God does not reject human beings but instead takes the appropriate steps to preserve them alive and eventually to restore them to their original purpose.

The received tradition of the flood, widespread in the ancient world, is interpreted by the biblical writers under the rubric of purpose. The conduct of God in the story is not that of a referee or judge who is meting out punishment on the basis of merit to players who have violated rules. It is more that of a coach who frantically calls time-out when virtually the entire team has turned to the wrong goal and is heading straight for hell. Since the purpose of the coach's judgment is always remedial, the last word is never destruction but is always renewal. To this end, after the flood God makes an everlasting covenant with every living creature (not just with human beings), promising never again to destroy all flesh by flood (9:8–17). Thus, the final word will not be the destruction of God's ultimate purpose for the creation but the restoration to it.

The source for the final episode in the account of the original sin (Gen. 11) is perhaps a received tradition about the origin of various languages. Again the biblical writers have taken the tradition and interpreted it under the rubric of ultimate purpose. Here the rebellion against God's purpose is seen among the *nations*, not just among *individuals*. All nations are plotting to build a tower to reach heaven, the abode of God, to take the place of God as the one who decides human purpose. God, the coach who remembers the purpose for which the nations were created, intervenes before the rebellion succeeds and separates the nations by confusing their language, thus making it impossible for them to understand one another (11:1–11). Thus the estrangement of nation from nation is the result of nations choosing to turn away from God's purpose.

Israel, God's Chosen Nation: Election and Predestination

The next major episode in the unfolding plot of the biblical narrative is God's election of Israel as the chosen people through the call of Abraham and Sarah, the ancestors of that nation. For those who accept the alternative thesis and some form of the synopsis that goes with it as the correct interpretation of the biblical material, there is no idea more vexing—indeed more unacceptable—than that of chosen, elected, even predestined, special people. How, they ask, can a God who is just and who therefore must be related to human beings on the basis of their righteousness or merit, exercise arbitrary preference for one nation and rejection of all others? Any such idea is patently a violation of justice. Since God's justice is an axiom not to be doubted, there are within the alternate thesis at least two ways to treat the matter. One is to say that Israel really was more righteous than the others, and that therefore God's choice of them was actually based on their merit. The other way is to downplay the entire notion of Israel as chosen, claiming that it is an aberration in an otherwise consistent biblical view of God—an aberration explainable as an almost universal tendency for nations to think of themselves as special in God's sight. But neither of these ways of dodging the issue does justice to the centrality of Israel as God's chosen people in the entire Bible. As we shall see, the rest of the plot hangs on this idea.

How, then, is this apparently unjust election of Israel, with its concomitant rejection of others, understood by the biblical writers? They certainly neither take it for granted nor accept it uncritically. For them it is so utterly and over-whelmingly astounding that it requires them to reject all conventional ideas of religion, God, justice, righteousness, and salvation—indeed, to reject the very rubric under which these ideas had been understood before—and to rede-fine them under another rubric! In "doing" their theology, therefore, they do not begin by accepting the conventional, received traditions about God's jus-tice as an axiom and then try to make Israel's election harmonize with them. Instead, they begin with God's unconditional love for them as shown in the exodus—a love that they know only too well is not based on their merit—and ask what all the conventional terms in religion must mean in the face of this one undeniable reality of their existence.

This idea, at least, is the claim of our thesis and its accompanying synop-sis. Let us now see if the biblical text bears it out. But a word of caution: We should not be surprised to find in the biblical text vestiges of the alternative thesis. It takes time for a revolutionary new thesis to ferret out all the features of the old thesis that are inconsistent with the new one. Simply think about how long it has taken—and is still taking—for scientists to ferret out of sci-entific theories all features that are not in harmony with the rubric of utility!

After the fall, when all humankind, individually and collectively, have rebelled against the goal or purpose for which they were created and are hell-bent for their own goals, YHWH (the LORD) calls Abraham (Abram), to accomplish through him (his descendants) the restoration of the fallen cre-ation to its intended purpose. That restoration (salvation), which gives mean-ing to everything that YHWH subsequently does, is stated at the outset as the justification for this election: In Abraham "all the families of the earth shall be blessed" (Gen. 12:3). For that end two preliminary promises are given. The first is that Abraham and his wife Sarah shall become the parents of a multi-tude (15:1–21:7), thereby forming a "critical mass" for a new community. The second is that their descendants shall possess a land (the promised land, 15:18–19), a land in which they can be a "pilot project," a nation of people who know YHWH to be God and therefore know their ultimate purpose to be to love one another as YHWH has loved them.

YHWH's special blessing on this nation is given so that the ultimate promise might be accomplished, that through it all nations shall be blessed—shall know YHWH to be God and so become a community of faithful loving-kindness. These promises are repeated several times in the stories of Israel's ancestors (22:17–18; 26:4). To have *faith* is to live one's life in the confidence that God *shall* keep these promises. Notice that the biblical writer gives the perplexing story of God's command to Abraham to sacrifice Isaac just this meaning (22:1–19): since Isaac is the last hope for God's promises to be fulfilled, his death would put an end to the promises. Although Abraham cannot understand how, if he obeys God, God can still keep the promises, he nevertheless obeys, believing that God *shall* be faithful to the promises. (See Paul's discussion of Abraham's faith in Romans 4.) It is these promises, with God acting to fulfill them, that constitute the basis for the rest of the biblical plot.

The first promise is fulfilled in the familiar stories of the ancestors (Abraham, Sarah, Isaac, Rebekah, Jacob, Rachel, Leah, Zilpah, Bilhah, and the twelve sons of Jacob, including Joseph), with the accompanying rejection of Hagar, Ishmael, and Esau. To read those stories under the alternative thesis, expecting to find in them any notion that God is in the business of rewarding good people with what they want and punishing bad people with what they do not want, will lead to disappointment. The ancestors are anything but ideal moral role models. The biblical writers seem to go out of their way to make it clear that those who are chosen and blessed by God are all morally flawed and are certainly no better—and often much worse—than those who are rejected. The stories bear witness to the writers' conviction that God is in the business of taking people who have rebelled against the Creator's purpose for them and restoring them to that purpose, and that the choice of Israel is to *that* end and to no other.

The theme that runs through the stories is this: Time after time it seems that a combination of human recalcitrance and natural forces will thwart the promises, but *God* always acts to fulfill them. The blessings that God grants to the ancestors are not rewards for their goodness; they are provisions to fulfill the purpose for which they have been chosen. This perhaps comes out most clearly in Genesis 24 when Joseph, now the second-in-command in Egypt, reveals his identity to his ten older brothers who had sold him into slavery there. What Joseph says in effect is, What you did, you meant for evil; but God meant it for good, to keep the promise, to save us all alive in this famine which would have otherwise killed us all (45:4–8).

In summary, the biblical writers have, in the light of the exodus, interpreted all the events of Israel's remembered past under the rubric of ultimate purpose; they have placed them in the putative world in which the ultimate telos of reflecting God's character of faithful loving-kindness explains every action of God and thus gives every episode of the story its *meaning*. (Notice that this is precisely parallel to the way in which present-day scientists constantly reinterpret the *scientific past* to bring it into accord with the latest scientific theory—all under the rubric of utility.) At the end of Genesis the first promise has been fulfilled; the stage is set for the second promise to begin.

When the narrative in the book of Exodus begins, generations have passed and the descendants of Jacob (whose other name was Israel) are still in Egypt but are now slaves of a pharaoh (a king) who does not remember Joseph. YHWH's objectives in the second promise are to create a nation out of this motley group of slaves, to let them know that YHWH and not an idol (or idols) is God, and to nurture and equip them for their vocation—to be the ones through whom YHWH will fulfill the third promise. Since the rest of the Hebrew Scripture is about this second promise, if our thesis and not the alternative thesis is correct, we should expect that here also all events will belong to the putative world constructed in accord with the telos of YHWH's ultimate purpose.

Let us consider briefly the received tradition—the political and religious setting in which YHWH begins to accomplish these objectives. In keeping with what the biblical writers regard as a universal political pattern, the pharaoh, as king of Egypt, is the absolute ruler of his realm, whose will defines the purpose of the nation and of all those in it. The very notion of a kingdom suggests that it is a place where the king's will is law and is to be obeyed. Therefore, as slaves in Egypt, the Israelites now have their (ultimate) purpose determined by Pharaoh, who is a mere human being, and a male as most monarchs then are. The Israelites' purpose is to make bricks. In having their purpose determined by a human being and not by YHWH, they are *oppressed*.

In such a monarchy, *religion* is understood to be a function of the political establishment to win the aid of the idols in accomplishing the king's will. Typically, the idols are not thought of as having any ultimate purpose for human beings; rather they are conceived of as personifications of various unpredictable powers in nature—powers that even kings cannot control. Therefore, the features of official religion—acts of obedience to laws, performance of rituals, offering of prayers, observance of special days or seasons, offering of sacrifices—are believed to be the things necessary to win these capricious powers to the service of the king's will by pleasing a sometimes arbitrary idol and placating the idol when it may be angry or displeased. Priests of the official cult, therefore, are servants of the king; their ultimate loyalty is to him and their responsibility is to guarantee that the idols will cooperate with the royal will.

It is in this situation that YHWH remembers the promise to the ancestors (Exod. 2:23–25); calls a very reluctant Moses who has long since fled Egypt; convinces him in a burning bush episode that YHWH, not an idol, is God (ch. 3); sends him to confront Pharaoh in a series of plagues; and empowers him to lead the exodus from Egypt to the promised land. In the hands of the biblical writers, the account of the plagues and the escape is not told in order to convince readers that if they want to control the powers of nature, they had better believe in YHWH and shun the idols. As in the stories of the ancestors, the point here is to assert that YHWH uses the forces of nature and overcomes the initial reluctance of Moses to accomplish YHWH's purpose for Israel, and subsequently for all nations. No merit of Moses or of the Israelites had anything to do with the events.

After the escape from Egypt, they reach Sinai, where YHWH gives them the law, usually called the Ten Commandments. Since they occupy such an important place in Israel's understanding of YHWH, and since they figure large in the Christian understanding of Jesus, it is important for us to examine them under our thesis and under the alternative thesis to see the different meaning they would have under each.

The Ten Commandments: Obedience versus Faith

The community of the biblical faith considers the law embodied in the Ten Commandments to be the ultimate moral or ethical standard. Before we begin a discussion of the law itself, let us therefore turn to that branch of philosophy sometimes called *normative ethics* so that we can acquire a fairly standard, clear, and unambiguous vocabulary with which to conduct that discussion.

Normative Ethics

In traditional philosophy the term *normative* suggests that ethical standards so designated, no matter how they are construed or formulated, are to be understood as unchanging, absolute, and final; their authority is neither dependent on nor altered by circumstances or consequences. If there are such ethical standards, they have a status in reality or being; they are a part of the "stuff" of reality just as surely as protons or quarks are a part of it. Some claim that their status in reality is above the status of all other things that may be real, but that is not our concern here. Such ethical standards, though they are real, are not necessarily obeyed. The reality of the standard and the actuality of the events of human behavior are related to each other by human responsibility. Therefore, ethical standards are quite different from scientific laws of nature.

As we saw in our discussion of the scientific method, scientific laws *describe* the events that happen when we organize experience under a paradigm. Therefore, if in science an event "breaks" a natural law, the law is subject to modification in any of a number of ways. In the language of normative ethics, an ethical law *prescribes* human behavior; it does not describe it, as does a scientific law, such as one in the science of psychology. Therefore, although the word *law* is used in both science and normative ethics, the word is used in two quite different senses that should not be confused. In the language we have repeatedly used, scientific laws have their place in a putative world developed under the rubric of utility; ethical normative laws have their place in a putative world organized under the rubric of ultimate purpose. Therefore, if our thesis is correct that the knowledge-claims of the biblical faith are to be understood under the rubric of ultimate purpose, the language of normative ethics may help us to sort out some often vexing issues.

Within normative ethics, the ultimate ethical standard has been construed mainly in two different ways, which we must carefully note. The first, and the one with which most of us are perhaps most familiar, thinks of the ultimate ethical standard as a set of commands about *specific kinds of acts* we are to perform or not to perform. A typical list might include murder, truth telling, stealing, obeying parents, committing adultery, performing rites, and cheating. The law will require us to perform some of these acts always and without exception, and the law will absolutely forbid us to perform others. The rightness or wrongness of any act depends solely on the very *form* of the act, not on its consequences or the circumstances in which it is performed. Therefore, a normative ethical system so construed is often called a *formalistic* system.

Many of us were introduced to ethics with instruction in this formalistic pattern, as our parents or guardians taught us "right from wrong." Therefore, for a great number of people this formalistic understanding of normative ethics is not only the received tradition but also the only "thinkable" position; for these people, even to question formalism is to threaten the very foundation of morality. Nevertheless, it has been challenged as an adequate way to construe an absolute ethical standard. Let me emphasize that the criticism we shall now turn to is *not* a denial of an ultimate ethical standard. It is a challenge to the view that the ultimate standard is a list of absolutely required and absolutely prohibited kinds of *acts*.

There are three main difficulties in formalism, quite apart from the difficulty of verifying what acts are required and what acts are prohibited. (The problem of verification of absolute standards is not unique to formalistic ethical systems, and our concern here is not with verification but with alternative ways of formulating ethical systems.) One difficulty is defining a required or forbidden act without ambiguity. For example, if murder is prohibited, when does an act of killing constitute murder and when does it not? One does not have to read the newspapers carefully to realize that even among those who believe that it is wrong to murder there is a widespread and strong difference about just what makes an act really an act of murder. Another difficulty is determining if the list of required and forbidden acts is complete. For example, is there an absolute eternal law that forbids cloning? Many of the issues at the center of contemporary ethical discussions, arguments, and bitter disagreements are about acts that are now possible for us to perform but had not even been conceived of only a few years ago. There is nothing *within* a given formalistic system either to indicate that it is a complete list of required and forbidden acts or to suggest how, when new possibilities arise, we are to make additions to the list. The third difficulty is the virtual impossibility of constructing a list of absolute commands that will never conflict. For example, if we are commanded to tell the truth always, and to obey our parents always, what are we to do when our parents command us to tell a lie? If each commandment in the list is in itself absolute, there is nothing within the system to guide us in such an ethical dilemma.

In the face of these difficulties, some ethicists have suggested a different way of construing the absolute ethical standard. In this view, the ultimate standard is not a list of acts, each of which is absolutely right or absolutely wrong by virtue of its form. Instead, it is an ultimate *telos*, which is absolutely and unconditionally *good*, and as such is the goal which any act, if it is to be judged a right act, must promote in an optimal way. In this view, the telos is often called the *intrinsic good*. A system of this sort, regardless of what specific telos it designates as the intrinsic good, is called a *teleological* system of normative ethics. Since the word "optimal" only vaguely suggests how an act and the telos are related, we shall examine it with the aid of an illustration.

Let us assume, solely for the purposes of illustration, that the one and only intrinsic good is *pleasure,* and that pleasure is quantifiable so that it is meaningful to talk about units of pleasure. (In our understanding of the biblical faith, the intrinsic good—the telos—is, of course, not pleasure but a community that images the character of God—faithful loving-kindness.) Since in our illustration pleasure is the opposite of pain, pain is the intrinsic evil, and it is also quantifiable. Every unit of pleasure has a value equal to that of every other unit of pleasure, regardless of who or what being experiences it, and for purposes of calculation one unit of pain cancels out one unit of pleasure. Every act that I am capable of performing has both immediate and long-range consequences, some of which are almost certainly an amount of pleasure and an amount of pain not only for myself but also for many other creatures who are now or will be in the future capable of experiencing pleasure and pain. Since the *right act* for me to perform at any time is the one that is *optimal* in producing the intrinsic good, it is that act, out of all acts that I could perform at that moment, which will produce the best balance of pleasure over pain in the long run. It is therefore conceivable that in some instances the right act for me to perform would actually produce more pain than pleasure, because every other possible act would produce an even less favorable balance of pleasure and pain. It is also conceivable that at some moment two or more acts that I could perform are equally optimal, in which case any one of them would be the right act for me to perform; or that at some time the right act for me to perform is one that gives *me* no pleasure at all.

Although such a teleological system has its own difficulties, as we shall soon see, it does have the conceptual advantage of avoiding the difficulties of formalistic systems that we noted previously. If it is granted that the intrinsic good is known, then it is always possible *in principle* for me to know what I should do. No area of possible ethical significance is excluded for lack of a formalistic rule. New occasions can indeed teach new duties, and time can make ancient right acts uncouth. And no two duties can conflict with each other. No matter what the situation is, I should always do an act that is optimal in producing the intrinsic good.

A teleological system of ethics is one in which the end (the intrinsic good) justifies (determines the rightness or wrongness of) the means (the acts). Since the expression "The end justifies the means" is one that many people, for example, politicians, use to brand as morally bankrupt their opponents, whom they accuse of espousing it, we need to examine it carefully. Ordinarily, to say that I believe the ends justify the means is to say that if I want something, no matter what it is, I believe that the mere fact of my wanting it justifies my employing any means necessary to get it, no matter what the other consequences of those means might be. Such a view is, of course, an invitation to ethical anarchy and is not at all what teleological ethical theory is about. Yet people who accept the received tradition of a formalistic ethical position commonly accuse anyone who accepts a teleological ethical theory of believing that the ends justify the means and therefore of being at best dangerously relativistic and at worst totally amoral. Those who accept a teleological position are indeed relativistic about formalistic rules, and they do indeed believe that the circumstances have an inescapable relevance in determining what is the right act to perform. But they are nonrelativistic about what they consider to be the ultimate ethical standard—the telos or the intrinsic good. In the illustration above, it is the telos *pleasure* (not just my pleasure) that is considered to be the absolute, intrinsic, nonrelativistic good—the ethical norm. (In our view of biblical ethics, the intrinsic ethical norm will be the community of faithful loving-kindness—God's ultimate telos for humanity.

Let us now consider some of the difficulties of the teleological view. If the consequences of an act, both immediate and long range, must be calculated before I can positively know what I ought to do, can I ever even approximate ethical certainty about what act I should perform in a specific circumstance? At any moment there are innumerable possible acts that I could perform—acts whose consequences I must figure out. The consequences of each of these possible acts depend on countless variables that I can never know and include amounts of pleasure and pain in countless present and future sentient beings. In comparison with figuring out what I should do in the next moment, predicting next year's weather is no problem at all. Although in principal I can know that there is a right act for me to perform, and I can also know why such an act would be right, I can never know what it is.

To meet this difficulty, the advocates of teleological ethical systems respond by saying, first of all, that just because our knowledge is less than perfect or certain, we should not give up acting on the best knowledge we have. Even in the field of ethics the possibility of predicting the consequences of our acts is not as remote as it seems. Just as in the field of civil engineering, the engineer does not have to know the properties of every subatomic particle in the universe before predictions can be made about the consequences of certain proposed design features of a bridge, so in ethics we do not have to know everything in the universe before we have a pretty good idea of what actions will tend to have optimal pleasure-pain balances within a reasonably short period of time in creatures who are somewhat like ourselves. The ethically good people, therefore, will not resort to an ethical system that does not take into account the consequences of an act in judging it to be a right act. They instead will act on the best knowledge they have at the time of the action, but will constantly be trying to improve such knowledge.

It is at this point that teleological ethicists take seriously the time-honored rules of established formalistic theories. In defending their own teleological system they believe it to be necessary to give a reasonable account *within the terms of their own system* of why formalistic systems have such a strong appeal. For a system that takes pleasure as the intrinsic good, such a defense might go like this: All human beings know experientially that pleasure is good and pain is evil. Therefore, if we have any moral sensitivity at all, we know that we ought to promote pleasure and strive to eradicate pain. Over long years of experience we have learned that certain kinds of acts *generally* tend to increase pleasure for all concerned. Among them might be acts of keeping promises made under oath, obeying parents and others in authority, and telling the truth on the witness stand. Other kinds of acts, we have learned, such as wanton killing and theft, generally tend to increase pain.

Eventually this knowledge will harden into a set of rules about what we should and should not do. As generations of parents teach generations of children "right from wrong," the justification for the rules—the telos—recedes into the background and eventually disappears. The rules come to be thought of as absolute ethical laws, embodying eternal verities, whereas the only eternal verity in this illustration would be that pleasure is the intrinsic good. Most formalistic rules, therefore, are certainly not nonsense. They are useful rules of thumb that embody the collected experience of generations for our benefit. Nevertheless, because they are rules of thumb, they are not above criticism and challenge. In circumstances where following them would clearly tend to promote a less favorable balance of pleasure over pain than would acts of violating them, we should violate them if we wish to be ethically responsible. It is always our duty to promote the intrinsic good by performing the act that to the best of our knowledge will do that.

Another questioned feature of teleological systems—one that is important for us to examine closely because it will illuminate a similar feature in the biblical law—is its alleged inability to give an adequate account of common, ordinary justice. In teleological systems the right acts focus on the *future* in the hope of bringing about the most favorable balance of the intrinsic good. Therefore, in our illustration one unit of pleasure experienced by the most incorrigible unrepentant criminal has the same value as one unit of pleasure experienced by the most law-abiding, public-spirited citizen. But *justice* is in a strikingly different way focused on the *past,* because it insists that pleasure be meted out on the basis of each person's merit. Justice would demand that as I try to maximize the intrinsic good, pleasure, I must not overlook the *fair distribution* of that pleasure. A world in which good guys do not finish first and bad guys do not finish last is not a just world! For no other reason than that evil people in the past have been evil and have caused others to suffer, they *deserve* to be punished—to suffer—and a just society will make them suffer. The books must be *balanced*. Revenge must be taken. Few moral convictions seem to be more widespread than this one of *retributive* justice. Critics of teleological ethics, therefore, hold up the formalistic law of justice as a touchstone by which to judge any system of ethics. Since teleological systems cannot insist on it as a formalistic principle, they are inadequate.

Advocates of teleological ethics sometimes respond to this criticism by pointing out that acts of *punishment,* but not acts of *revenge,* may at times be required and justified by the telos of the system. In fact, it may be one of the time-tested rules of thumb that the practice of rewarding good people with pleasure and punishing bad people with unpleasant experiences tends to bring about in the long run the most favorable balance of pleasure over pain. Punishment is a deterrent to those future acts of bad people that would, if actually performed, increase pain and reduce pleasure. Among good people, therefore, the sole motive for punishment is to achieve the telos, and they should be ready to deviate from the requirements of the formalistic law of justice in those instances in which it seems to be clear that the telos will not be served by following it. In a teleological system of ethics the desire for retributive justice, revenge, is not ethically admirable and the demand for it is not ethically justified. Much of the current debate in this country concerning the criminal justice system is between those who espouse a formalistic view of justice and those who espouse a teleological view. During the preparation of this chapter, several highly publicized criminal trials have generated many shrill demands for vengeance.

Revisiting the Ten Commandments

The discussion of philosophical normative ethics ends here, and we are now ready to return to the discussion of the Ten Commandments and to the question of whether the biblical writers' understanding of them better fits our thesis or the alternative thesis. As we do, I believe the vocabulary of normative ethics will make this discussion easier.

If the alternative thesis is the correct one, then the biblical writers should present the Ten Commandments as a list of formalistic laws, given to Israel as God's eternal and unalterable will, constituting the basis on which Israel could establish merit by obedience to them. As formalistic laws, their meaning, either individually or collectively, would not be derived from an ultimate telos that God has in mind for them, since by definition it is its *form,* not its *consequences,* that makes such a law designate a right act. If there is a telos or end connected with obedience to these laws, it would be only the fulfillment of Israel's own wants for itself, and if this were the case, then the commandments would be understood under the rubric of utility. Since God is just, giving to each person what he or she deserves and collectively to each nation what it deserves, it would follow that individual and national prosperity or lack thereof would be the indicator of individual or national righteousness. If God were just, good guys or nations would finish first. The sacrificial system would provide an alternative means of accumulating merit points when the law fails in its intended function of being the means for our earning them.

If we (a) take the alternative view, with its implicit implication that it is guided by the rubric of utility, as a hypothesis about the biblical faith, and if we (b) believe uncritically that every system of laws is by definition a formalistic system made up of individual independent imperatives, then we will no doubt understand the Ten Commandments (and by implication the biblical faith) as a system in which human beings are seeking to establish merit before God in order to be rewarded by God. But the difficulties of doing so are formidable. There is little evidence that Israel's prophets so understood the law. Let us consider just a few of the many biblical emphases that are at odds with the alternative thesis.

Israel is to *love* the law; it is to be bound to hand and forehead (Deut. 6:8) and written upon the heart (Jer. 31:33). The author of Psalm 1 calls the person "blessed" or "happy" whose "delight is in the law of the LORD" (vv. 1–2).

For the great ethical prophets the basic indicator that Israel is breaking the law of YHWH is not the suffering of lawbreakers (Israel), but the oppression of the poor, the sojourner, the widows, the orphans—those most likely to suffer when the nation forgets the purpose for which YHWH called it and instead thinks of YHWH as an idol.

Jesus, whose avowed intention is not "to abolish the law or the prophets . . . but to fulfill" (Matt. 5:17), epitomizes the law (Matt. 22:37–40) by citing two passages from the Hebrew Scripture. The first is from Deut. 6:4–5: "Hear, O Israel: The LORD is our God, the LORD alone. You shall love the LORD your God with all your heart, and with all your soul, and with all your might." The second is a part of Lev. 19:18, but it is helpful to quote all of verses 17 and 18: "You shall not hate in your heart anyone of your kin; you shall reprove your neighbor, or you will incur guilt yourself. You shall not take vengeance or bear a grudge against any of your people, but you shall love your neighbor as yourself: I am the LORD." The justification of all the formalistic-appearing rules or laws is the telos or ultimate purpose of human life: to know and love YHWH, and to reflect that knowledge and love in one's life with others in the community.

When Jesus is accused of breaking the law by plucking and eating heads of grain on the Sabbath, he replies, "But if you had known what this means, 'I desire mercy and not sacrifice,' you would not have condemned the guiltless" (Matt. 12:7). The passage is from Israel's prophet Hosea (6:6), where it is addressed to those who are very punctilious in their observance of sacrifice and other formalistic ceremonial obligations but have no concern for the oppressed neighbor. They are the people who regard performance of sacrifices and other rites as an alternative way of amassing merit before God, thereby making obedience to the moral law a secondary, and essentially unimportant, concern. Jesus could have quoted almost any other of Israel's great prophets—Isaiah, Amos, Jeremiah, or Micah, for example—for they all engage in polemics against those who in one way or another think that the commandment to love God trivializes and virtually makes nonbinding the commandment to love the neighbor as oneself. For these prophets, not loving the neighbor is the most telling evidence that one does not love God, or even understand who God is. This does not mean that these prophets believe ritual to be unimportant or nonobligatory. It means, rather, that ritual, including sacrifice, is something entirely other than an alternative way of acquiring merit; we will soon turn our attention to what it is understood to be according to our thesis.

Before we do, however, let us consider one more biblical writer whose writings make it difficult to hold the alternative thesis, although, ironically, he is often thought to be the virtual author of it—the apostle Paul. For Paul, the ultimate purpose of human life is to be conformed to the image of Christ, the one human being who perfectly knew God's character and the one whose life perfectly imaged or reflected that character. God not only made us for that purpose but works through all things, including the life of Christ, to bring it about. It is in this context that Paul uses the strongest language possible to state his assurance that God will fulfill in the creation this purpose, the word "predestined": "We know that all things work together for good for those who love God, who are called according to his purpose. For those whom he foreknew he also predestined to be conformed to the image of his Son, in order that he might be the firstborn within a large family. And those whom he predestined he also called . . ." (Rom. 8:28–30).

To be predestined does not mean that ultimately one's wishes will be fulfilled and that another's wishes will be denied, regardless of merit and simply because God has already decided that it be so. To add a doctrine of predestination to the alternative thesis is ludicrous. To mix the metaphor of archery a bit, not only would the playing field not be level but the officials would be absolutely arbitrary, utterly capricious, unreliable, and unconscionably unjust. But Paul is not involved in archery; he is involved in basketball, and God is not the referee but the coach, the very one who recruited Paul on the sandlot when he was headed for the wrong goal and promised to restore him to the goal for which he had been created in the first place. For Paul, who does all his theology in accord with this metaphor, God the coach is absolutely consistent, never departing from the divine character of faithful loving-kindness; God is utterly dependable, because faithful loving-kindness always keeps its promises; and God is scrupulously just, because justice is now defined by the telos and not by a formalistic rule.

To act *justly* is not to deal out rewards and punishments in accord with recipients' merit, but always to do the act that will lead to the realization of the telos. This is the context in which Paul understands the commandments and the ordinances of God that were entrusted to Israel at Sinai. They were never intended to be a set of formalistic rules, by obedience to which Israel could acquire merit (Paul's term is "righteousness of one's own")—a merit that would give them the right to expect from a just idol the advancement of their own wishes and the defeat of their enemies. These laws and ordinances truly are good and state God's purpose for Israel and so for all nations. They are *spiritual,* Paul's term for *oriented toward the right basket.* The difficulty, as Paul sees it, is that human beings are *of the flesh,* Paul's term for *oriented toward the wrong goal* (Rom. 7:14). As long as we are headed toward our own goal for our lives and not toward the goal for which we were created—the goal toward which the laws are oriented—we will always regard the laws not as the word of God that defines our purpose or telos, but as a list of rules by obedience to which we can earn the rewards that we desire.

As long as we are of the flesh, dribbling toward the wrong goal, the laws and ordinances are incapable of effecting in us their genuine meaning. For them to do that, we must first be turned around, reoriented, and enlightened about our true purpose. No amount of making perfect shots into the wrong basket will do this. For Paul, this is what Christ does: In Christ we virtually *die* as creatures going toward the wrong goal, and are raised as *new* creatures facing the correct goal—all so that we may "become obedient from the heart" (6:17). In Rom. 8:3–4 Paul epitomizes his view of the law with these words: "For God has done what the law, weakened by the flesh, could not do: by sending his own Son in the likeness of sinful flesh, and to deal with sin, he condemned sin in the flesh, so that the just requirement of the law might be fulfilled in us, who walk not according to the flesh but according to the Spirit."

In other places Paul refers to the work of Jesus as that of writing the law on the heart, the prophet Jeremiah's expression for what YHWH must and will do before Israel can become truly obedient and so fulfill the purpose of its election as YHWH's people (Jer. 31:31–34). Paul also, when summarizing the law by stating the telos at which each act is to be aimed, uses the passage in Lev. 19:18: "Owe no one anything, except to love one another; for the one who loves another has fulfilled the law. The commandments, 'You shall not commit adultery; You shall not murder; You shall not steal; You shall not covet'; and any other commandment, are summed up in this word, 'Love your neighbor as yourself.' Love does no wrong to a neighbor; therefore, love is the fulfilling of the law" (Rom. 13:8–10). I find nothing in Paul's writings to suggest that he considers the sacrifice of Christ to be an alternative source of merit for believers that would exempt them from their purpose of employing every talent they possess in pursuit of the telos that gives each law its meaning. Paul's theological understanding of the law therefore is in harmony, not at odds, with that found in Israel's great prophetic tradition.

Since the alternative thesis seems to fail the test of being an adequate explanation of the law as the biblical writers understand it, let us now put our thesis to the test. Our thesis demands that the Ten Commandments, like everything else that comes from YHWH, be a gift of YHWH's faithful lovingkindness, given for the purpose of restoring Israel to its proper telos and upholding it in that telos. We will test our thesis by examining the commandments collectively and individually to see if they conform to this requirement.

The Ten Commandments are found in two places: Exod. 20:1–17 and Deut. 5:6–21. They are traditionally divided into two tablets: the first, commandments 1–4, deals with obligations to God; the second, commandments 5–10, deals with obligations to others. We will discuss them accordingly.

Commandment 1: "[Y]ou shall have no other gods before me."

The introduction to the entire law makes it clear who the giver of this commandment is—YHWH, the God who delivered Israel from slavery in Egypt, a God who unlike the other gods or idols is not related to human beings by their merit, for Israel had certainly not merited such deliverance by its moral superiority to Egypt. Therefore everything about YHWH's relationship to them will be qualitatively different from the received tradition about the relationship of gods to their worshipers. If YHWH's goodness to them is not motivated by their merit, what is the explanation for it? That explanation must be in the character of YHWH, and must be in some purpose that YHWH has for them, and not vice versa. That purpose—ultimate purpose—is to image God's character. Therefore Israel cannot have many gods who are idols. Why? Idols, the conventional gods, are in the business of giving their worshipers what they wish for, in accordance with their merit. Therefore, within the received tradition of idolatry it makes perfectly good sense to worship as many idols as there are, to get all the help one can in realizing one's own wishes. But if God is not an idol—not in the business of meting out blessings on the basis of merit—but is the author of ultimate purpose, one can have only one God, since one can have only one ultimate purpose.

Commandment 2: "You shall not make for yourself an idol. . . ."

An idol is traditionally understood to be the personification of a natural power, which is often capricious and which the people would like to harness. But YHWH is not an available power to be harnessed for the worshipers' purposes. Those who conceive of their gods in this way and make images of their gods have replaced YHWH's purpose with their own and are heading for the wrong basket. YHWH is a jealous God who will not allow this among the Israelites but will punish those who show that they have begun to think of YHWH as an idol—as a utility. YHWH's jealousy is not a character flaw; it is an expression of absolute faithfulness to the promises. It is the faithfulness of my coach when I have turned to the wrong basket. Allowing me to continue in the wrong direction would be exhibiting a character flaw. YHWH's punishment—judgment —is not retributive justice, giving me what I have earned. It is faithful loving-kindness appropriate in the specific situation. It is YHWH's love so great that it will not fail Israel, even though Israel has failed YHWH.

Commandment 3: "You shall not make wrongful use of the name of the LORD your God. . . ."

In the broad culture of which Israel was a part, names had an importance that they have since lost; a name was in some mysterious way a reality itself that partook of the significance of the one who bore it. Specifically, an idol's name carried the natural power that the idol personified. Thus, speaking the idol's name in the appropriate ritualistic manner was believed to bind or control that power for the worshiper's use. Idolaters did not pray to "whom it may concern." They had to use the idol's *name* in order to make the prayer effective. It is this received tradition that lies behind the third commandment, which specifically forbids Israel to use the name YHWH in this manner. Israel is indeed to use YHWH's name, but the rightful use of it is completely different. Since the significance, or the character as we have called it, of the God who bears the name YHWH is faithful loving-kindness, which character gives Israel its ultimate purpose, the rightful use in rites and ceremonies is doubly important. First, it is always to remind the Israelites of who God is and therefore what their ultimate goal is, and second, and following from it, it is to instruct them concerning *what* they are to pray for. They have not used God's name rightfully if in prayer they have presented to God their own wish list and then have added to it the magic formula "in YHWH's name we pray," believing that because they have done so, YHWH is bound or obligated to grant their wishes.

Let us use our basketball metaphor to illustrate. Suppose that when I am driving toward the wrong basket I remember the coach's promise to help me whenever I am in need. Trusting in the promise (and assuming that I have some way of communicating with the coach), I pray, "O great coach, who keepest promises, help me to make this basket." What would the coach's answer to my prayer be? It would no doubt be cast in strong theological language, but its gist would be that he would not help me to achieve the opposite purpose from the one for which the promises were made. But if I remember what my purpose is and am pursuing the right goal, then when my petition is that he help me to attain that goal, he will do everything possible to help me.

Since the "Lord's Prayer," the prayer that Jesus taught his followers to pray (Matt. 6:7–13; Luke 11:1–4), is a perfect example of using the name of God rightfully, let us now examine it rather closely to elucidate further the significance of the Third Commandment. In this prayer virtually every salient point that distinguishes our thesis from the alternative thesis can be clearly seen. An examination of the prayer, therefore, should be an excellent test for both theses.

The first line, "Our Father in heaven" (Matt. 6:9), and the third line, "Your kingdom come" (v. 10), immediately raise the vexing issue of the regular use of two masculine titles for YHWH, *father* and *king*. The alternative thesis sheds no light on the question of why the biblical writers adopted this usage, a question that has been hotly debated for a generation and is still being debated. Among those who accept the alternative thesis two positions have been taken. One is that the titles reflect YHWH's eternal plan (will) that males be superior to females. They therefore imply a formalistic rule that we are to follow, and that rule needs no further justification. In following it we acquire merit; in violating it we incur the wrath of God. The other position within the alternative thesis is that the biblical writers either by intention or by default used the terms to perpetuate, and indeed to reinforce, the received tradition of the patriarchal society. Therefore they are not a part of the theological truth-claim of the biblical material but are an aberration of it. There is nothing to be learned from them, and they should be deliberately abandoned.

If, on the other hand, *our* thesis is adopted, the usage of these two masculine titles is eminently understandable, and although it does indeed arise out of the received tradition of male superiority, it is adopted *not to perpetuate* it but *to condemn* it. How is this so? We have already noted that in the political ethos of biblical times, it is the kings of the nations who by virtue of their power decide what the purpose of the nation and of its people is. For the biblical writers, in doing this the kings (since there are few monarchical queens) are usurping a prerogative that belongs only to YHWH. In Egypt Pharaoh the king has oppressed the Israelites by imposing upon them a purpose that is decidedly at odds with the purpose for which they were created. The gift of the promised land to the Israelites is not understood to be a release from bondage to the pharaoh so that they can now decide for themselves whatever they would like their purpose to be. Instead, the promised land is to be a realm in which no human being *whatsoever* presumes the right or authority to determine the purpose of any other human being. That ultimate purpose is to reflect YHWH's character as it has been revealed in the exodus—absolutely unmerited faithful loving-kindness. Since the title *king* in the received tradition denotes the one who determines their ultimate purpose, the Israelites are forbidden when they get to the promised land to have a human king, as the other nations do. Instead, *YHWH* is to be their king.

The expression, "YHWH is king," therefore, is not a bland *acceptance* of the status quo. It is a polemic shout in *defiance* of the status quo. In that expression the name *YHWH* is to be stressed and italicized, and it is to be understood to mean "*YHWH and not any human being, male or female,* determines the ultimate purpose of our lives." If we, instead, read the expression as if it meant,

"YHWH is our *king,* not our *queen,*" we completely miss the point and misuse the name of YHWH, thus violating the Third Commandment. Later in Israel's history when YHWH reluctantly permits Samuel to appoint Israel's first king, Saul, to save them from the Philistine threat of annihilation, it is with the strict understanding that Israel's kings are never to arrogate to themselves the prerogatives of YHWH. Kings or queens in Israel are to be no more than vice-regents, always ruling Israel in accord with YHWH's purpose for the chosen people. When Israel's human kings or queens do appropriate to themselves the divine prerogatives, as many do, then the prophets pronounce YHWH's judgment on them. But these prophets, always keeping an eye on YHWH's ultimate purpose, proclaim that in time YHWH will raise up a new king, who will rule not as he sees fit but only in perfect accord with YHWH's purpose.

In the Greek Scriptures, Jesus is believed to be that new king, the new anointed one, the Messiah, the Christ. The constant witness to him in these writings is that he came not to do his own will but the will of the one who sent him. The one who sent him is Israel's God, YHWH, whom Jesus almost always calls by the title *Father.* Why? The community of the Israelites in the time of Jesus (now mainly Israelites of the former kingdom of Judah, the Jews) is no longer a nation with its own king. But among the religious leaders of the community are some who, like the former kings of Israel, have arrogated to themselves the prerogative of YHWH to determine the purpose of the common folk. They apparently like to be called *father,* and they take their own traditions and impose them upon the poor as if these traditions were the very embodiment of God's plan, will, and purpose for all human life. In almost any patriarchal society, the title *father* or some similar one carries with it the connotation that the word of the father is law!

It is because few actual societies are organized as matriarchies that the word *mother* does not have quite the connotation of authority that *father* has. It is in the context of patriarchy that Jesus' use of the title *father* for Israel's God is to be understood. And here, as in the case of the title *King,* the usage is intended not to *sanction* the patriarchal institution but to *condemn* it. Thus in Matt. 23:9, after discussing the conduct of these religious leaders, Jesus says, "And call no one your father on earth, for you have one Father—the one in heaven." Jesus' use of the title is polemic. The statement "God is my Father" means "God alone, not any human being, male or female, has the authority to determine ultimate human purpose." Only in a matriarchal society would "God is my Mother" carry an analogous meaning, and then it would be equally polemic, *condemning* the matriarchal institution. (It should be noted that when biblical writers use female and male *metaphors,* in contrast to *titles,* for God, they are attributing to God in a superlative degree the admirable character traits found in women or men. Thus God's faithful loving-kindness is like that of a mother who will not desert her nursing child, only more so, or like that of a father who always welcomes home his prodigal son, only more so.)

With this usage of the titles *Father* and K*ing* in mind, let us return to the Lord's Prayer. To pray to our Father in heaven is not to pray to an idol who just happens to have the name YHWH. Therefore, the one praying does not ask that one's own kingdom come, that one's own will (or purposes) be done, but that the ultimate purpose of the Creator be realized in oneself and in all creatures on earth. These opening petitions get one's priorities straight and provide a context for all subsequent petitions. In our basketball metaphor, these petitions ask that the coach always keep us facing the proper basket. Then the petition for daily bread is prayed in the confidence that the Creator who made us for a purpose will give us what we need to be sustained as we pursue that purpose. The next petition, that in the end God's forgiveness of us be like our forgiveness of others, sounds at first as if it belongs in a prayer to an idol: "In obedience to your law, we have forgiven others; now as a *reward* for our obedience, you are obligated to forgive us, and give us what we want." But in its context, it is a petition asking God to sustain us in a life of treating others in accordance with the divine character of faithful loving-kindness, so at the end God will have made us fit to be people of *God's eternal kingdom.*

In the metaphor of basketball, it would be like the plea of a member of the scrub team who, when he gets a chance to play, prays to the coach, "Help me to be the player you have recruited me to be, so at the end of this season, you can judge me to be fit for the varsity next season." God's final forgiveness is not an act that finally releases us from pursuing God's purpose for us so that we are at last free to pursue our own interests. It is seen as the last and *completing* act of faithful loving-kindness that makes us fit for the *king*dom. The final petition, that we be kept from the time of trial and delivered from the evil one is prayed in the confidence that ultimately God will protect us from anybody or anything that tries to entice us to the wrong goal.

If the Lord's Prayer is a perfect example of using YHWH's name correctly in prayer, the Twenty-third Psalm is a perfect example of using it correctly in song. I will leave it to the reader to examine this familiar psalm under the alternative thesis and under our thesis.

Commandment 4: "Remember the sabbath day, and keep it holy."

The command to keep the sabbath holy is a command to remember that the Creator of the world is none other than YHWH, the God who delivered them from Egypt. Therefore, nothing is outside the scope of faithful loving-kindness. As Israel commemorates YHWH's resting on the seventh day, it remembers that Pharaoh gave them no day of rest, but YHWH did. Because it is their purpose to image YHWH, they are not to oppress others—including the animals—as Pharaoh oppressed Israel, but are to grant a similar rest to all (Deut. 5:12–15). Thus this commandment serves as a bridge to connect the commandments that state Israel's duties to YHWH with those that state Israel's responsibilities to the neighbor. Nothing is said explicitly in the commandments about the various rites, ceremonies, and celebrations that constitute Israel's cultic or ritual worship before YHWH, but they are spelled out in great detail in accompanying ordinances. To understand better why Israel's prophets regarded all the commandments to be a unified whole, so that breaking one was tantamount to breaking them all (a point of view hardly consistent with the alternative thesis), let us examine the act of worship in idolatry and in Israel, using the act of sacrifice as the focal point of the discussion.

In the worship of an idol, the act of sacrifice, along with all other cultic practices, was for the purpose of acquiring merit so that the beneficial relation between the worshipers and the source of power could be reestablished or maintained. In the act, the worshipers gave up to the idol something that they valued in order to get back from the idol something that they valued even more. Even today, this understanding of the word "sacrifice" seems to be almost universal. Consider what a "sacrifice" is in the game of baseball. Cultic worship as a whole, then, was understood under the rubric of utility; in the putative world of idolatry, sacrifice was something the worshipers engaged in to further their own agenda. When Israel revolted against idolatry, it kept much of the outward manifestation of idolatrous worship (the conservative tendency in all intellectual activity); but in adopting the rubric of ultimate purpose it radically altered the conceptual understanding of worship (the reforming or revolutionary tendency). If YHWH is at work in their history to restore the Israelites to their God-given purpose, then in their putative world everything that YHWH does is seen as a gift to them to further this purpose. The Ten Commandments as a whole constitute such a gift, and the very institution of worship is YHWH's gift to Israel to reestablish and uphold the nation in God's purpose for it. This being the case, the act of sacrifice must be drastically reinterpreted.

The sacrifice of the Passover lamb was commanded on the eve of Israel's departure from slavery in Egypt. When they finally get to the promised land they are to keep the feast each year without fail. Why? Is it so that YHWH will continue to give them whatever they want? Not at all! In keeping the Passover, the Israelites who did not themselves participate in the exodus will relive it in the feast and thus remember YHWH's unmerited, faithful lovingkindness. And in so doing they will know their ultimate purpose. The annual celebration is to uphold them in this purpose, for if they should forget YHWH's acts, they would surely lapse into idolatry again. The children are to see the preparations for this unusual meal, and as it is being eaten they will ask, "Papa, why are we doing this?" Then the father will smile and say, "I thought you would never ask" and proceed to recite the events of the exodus, ending perhaps with the admonition "Children, it is our God's gracious acts that make us who we are and give our life its ultimate purpose. Children, this is who we are."

In the Christian community the biblical writers understand Jesus to be the new Passover Lamb, in whose life and death the unmerited love of YHWH is seen; it is in the regular remembering of this sacrifice—this gift of YHWH—that the community is upheld in its purpose. In this putative world of the biblical faith, sacrifice is not an alternative means of acquiring merit so that worshipers, by appropriating it, can get from God whatever they dearly want; it is the gift of God to restore and uphold them in God's purpose. The command to remember it always and celebrate it regularly is also a gift of God to prevent the community from lapsing into idolatry. Worship in the biblical faith, therefore, is primarily an act of *remembering* the acts of YHWH by which the promises to Abraham and Sarah are fulfilled.

When the people of the biblical faith are admonished to praise, laud, exalt, adore, and magnify YHWH's holy name, the reason for their doing so is not that God is excessively vain and so is pleased with much fawning. It is that in so doing they will be upheld in the promises. In summarizing the first four commandments, the commandments about one's duty to God, we might use our basketball metaphor again. When the coach has recruited us, he gathers us together on the court and says, "I now want to teach you the most important thing there is for you to learn about basketball. If you forget it, nothing else is worth a thing. Whenever you are on the court, for God's sake remember which goal is yours."

Commandment 5: "Honor your father and your mother. . . ."

The last six commandments, those that are about one's duty to parents and neighbor, all follow systematically from the first four—that is, they follow from remembering what one's proper goal is. If we attempted to understand these commandments under the alternative thesis, there would be no systematic unity among these six or with the first four, since each of the ten would be a formalistic law, having no justification outside itself. So understood, any one could be broken without necessarily breaking any other.

The Fifth Commandment is not about a unilateral relationship between parents and children. The parents whom children are to honor are those who have the prior responsibility of teaching the children all the words about who YHWH is. In Deut. 6:6–7, the parents are commanded, "Keep these words that I am commanding you today in your heart. Recite them to your children and talk about them when you are at home and when you are away, when you lie down and when you rise." If when they get into the promised land the parents faithfully teach the children about YHWH, and if the children respond by honoring the teachings of the parents, then the purpose for which they have been given the land—to be the faithful pilot project through whom the third promise is to be fulfilled—will prosper and come to fruition.

On the other hand, if the parents fail to teach their children properly, then the nation will not be fit as the instrument for the third promise and YHWH will have to judge them severely to turn them back to their proper goal. This is what the business of punishing the children for the iniquity of their parents, found in the Second Commandment, is all about. If one generation of parents, by neglecting the parental responsibility of teaching the children, allows the entire nation to fall back into idolatry, then YHWH, in order to keep the promises, will have to deal with the nation in a judging manner for as many generations as it takes to turn it again to its proper goal.

Commandment 6: "You shall not murder."

The very antithesis of imaging God's faithful loving-kindness in one's relationship with another is to try to impose one's own will on another as the purpose of the other's life. Perhaps the most extreme attempt to do so is to murder the other. Therefore, in the community that remembers its goal, murder will have no place. In the Sermon on the Mount, in Matt. 5:21–26, Jesus puts this original meaning back into this law for those who had forgotten God's purpose for giving it to Israel and had come to think of it as a simple formalistic law: that is, by not murdering, they were doing all that this law required and so could count themselves righteous and therefore meritorious. Jesus says that if you are angry with another, the fundamental relationship with another that this law requires has ceased to exist.

Commandment 7: "You shall not commit adultery."

The salient aspect of YHWH's character behind this commandment is faithfulness to promises. If YHWH is faithful to promises, those who know that their purpose is to reflect YHWH's character will be faithful to their promises to one another. The biblical writers understand every act of YHWH to be one of faithful fulfillment of the promises to Abraham and Sarah, and that these promises can be counted on. Suppose that I, a member of Israel, make a promise to you, on which you bank your life, planning your life before God on the confidence that I will keep it. Then if I break that promise simply because keeping it does not suit my fancy, I have treated you like a *thing,* not a person, perhaps making it impossible for you to fulfill your own obligations to YHWH. In the cultural milieu in which Israel became a nation, women, along with orphans and foreigners, were particularly vulnerable to oppression. If husbands did not keep their marriage vows, wives, whose lives depended on those vows being kept, faced a bleak future, indeed. Therefore, in Israel you do not treat your wives like dirt. Jesus restores this original meaning to the law when he says that if any man looks at a woman (presumably even his own wife) with lust—that is, as a *thing* whose purpose is to fulfill his own wishes—he has already violated the relationship that this commandment is about (Matt. 5:27–28).

Commandment 8: "You shall not steal."

If we adopt the alternative thesis as the correct one by which to understand this commandment, then it becomes a claim based on the rubric of utility and not ultimate purpose. Accordingly, this law would entail a formalistic institution of private property, in which each individual has the right to decide the purposes for which he or she will use his or her privately owned property. The law against stealing would then simply forbid my doing anything to deprive another of the opportunity to exercise this right. If I obey the law, I am meritorious; if I disobey, I incur punishment.

There is little in the biblical writings to support this thesis, yet there is much to deny it explicitly and to support our thesis. Israel's prophets understand the land, and specifically the promised land, to belong to YHWH. It does not belong to the Israelites to use as they see fit. YHWH has provided it for them so that they can live as a community of faithful loving-kindness in accord with YHWH's purpose for them. When they enter the land they are to apportion it among the families and tribes so that there will be no poor—so that everyone will be free from the possibility of economic oppression. Stealing occurs whenever some Israelites, especially those who belong to the king's circle, arrogate to themselves YHWH's prerogative to determine their purpose, and so also arrogate to themselves YHWH's prerogative to determine the purpose of the promised land.

The prophet Isaiah describes these Israelite nobles who have become veritable pharaohs to their own people in this way: "Ah, you who join house to house, who add field to field, until there is room for no one but you, and you are left to live alone in the midst of the land!" (5:8). The prophet Micah (2:2) uses these words: "They covet fields, and seize them; houses, and take them away; they oppress householder and house, people and their inheritance."

This is the theme in virtually all of the great prophets, and they all pronounce YHWH's imminent judgment on the nation not because some Israelites have broken a rule about private property but because they have turned the nation away from YHWH's goal and toward their own. But YHWH, the good coach, will punish not as retribution but as a merciful action to restore to the proper goal. This commandment against stealing, like all the others, can be understood in the way that the biblical writers understand it, only within the putative world of the rubric of the ultimate purpose of humanity.

Commandment 9: "You shall not bear false witness against your neighbor."

Again, this is not simply a formalistic rule in the keeping of which one can become meritorious. If we follow our thesis, this law will also have its foundation in the ultimate purpose of human life. Therefore, instead of being a requirement to tell the truth about what your neighbor has *done,* especially if you are on the witness stand, it is a requirement to witness to the truth about who your neighbor *is* in the eyes of YHWH. If you and I are both Israelites, then the truth about you to which I am to bear witness in what I say and do is this: You are one whom YHWH loved so much that YHWH brought you out of bondage and into this land so that you and I can live together as a part of the community that reflects the divine image of faithful loving-kindness. This is the meaning that Jesus put back into the law in the story of the woman caught in the act of adultery (John 8:3–11). Jesus knew perfectly well what the law of Moses (the Ten Commandments) says about adultery and about telling the truth about one's neighbor. But he also knew that the law is about the truth concerning who she is in the eyes of God. When he refused to condemn her (v. 11) and told her to go away and sin no more, he was bearing true witness to the most important thing about her: she is one whom God so loves that God sent the only begotten Son to die for her, to restore her to the purpose for which she was created. If I claim to bear true witness to anyone, but do not do it in love, I am omitting what is the most important truth about that person.

Commandment 10: "You shall not covet. . . ."

This commandment is a fitting one for the close. In the Greek Scriptures covetousness is occasionally identified with idolatry (Col. 3:5), and as we have seen, the commandments as a unified body of law can be understood as a call for a relationship with YHWH that is entirely different from the relationship to an idol. In covetousness, my desire is always foremost and gives meaning to every religious concept. In the biblical faith YHWH's faithful loving-kindness is always foremost, gives meaning to all religious concepts, and determines the ultimate purpose of human life. In idolatry, I seek ways to get the gods to do my will. In the biblical faith, YHWH seeks to restore human beings to their purpose and, in the plot of the Bible, gives them the Ten Commandments to this end. In idolatry, justice and mercy are contradictories; no idol can be totally just and totally merciful. In the biblical faith they are the same—both are appropriate acts in their location in the plot to accomplish God's totally free and unmerited desire to save the world that has deserted the divine purpose. In idolatry the question of whether I am saved by works or by grace is always vexing, precisely because the question of the idol's justice and mercy is a vexing one. In the biblical faith, the law is not a means of earning merit but is itself a gift of grace to restore us to obedience, which *is* our salvation. Thus the very idea that since I have been saved by grace I can forget the law is not an issue to be seriously debated; it is a throwback to idolatry— a symptom of having forgotten the most important lesson in basketball: Remember which goal is yours.

Our discussion of the vexing problem of *faith versus obedience* as the means to salvation has shown that if we understand all the major terms under the rubric of ultimate purpose and not the rubric of utility, then the problem disappears. The question "Am I saved by faith or by works?" was a loaded question, based on the totally erroneous assumption that the biblical writings are explained by the alternative thesis. When the alternative thesis is replaced by our thesis, and when all the terms in the question are defined under the rubric of ultimate purpose, then the question disappears.

Chapter 9

Testing Our Thesis

From the Promised Land to the Suffering Servant

Treatment of the Enemy and Unjust Suffering

The two remaining vexing issues to be examined are (1) the apparent *unloving* treatment of the enemies by Israel during the conquest of the promised land and afterward, and (2) the apparent *unjust* distribution of suffering in the world. We will discuss these two issues together, since most of the suffering in the biblical narrative (not quite all) is that which is inflicted by and upon enemies. In this discussion we will follow the history of the Israelites from the time of the exodus, through their life as a nation (or as two nations), and into the era after they have lost their political independence and are again subjects of a foreign monarch. In the biblical plot, this is roughly the period of the second promise, during which Israel as the pilot project is being prepared by YHWH to be the instrument for the fulfillment of the third promise. Our thesis claims that all the events of this period are therefore to be read under the rubric of ultimate purpose, and that everything YHWH does is for no other reason than to bring about the promises to Abraham and Sarah to save the creation. It is important that we keep this in mind and also remember that in any intellectual activity there is always a reforming or revolutionary tendency.

In this period there is an ongoing theological critique of—consciousness-raising about—previous received traditions. That critique begins with the received traditions about the *enemy* and about *suffering* that are common in the putative world of idolatry, and it continues on with Israel's earlier revisions of those views in its own putative world of ultimate purpose. We should not expect to find consistency in details in the theological assessments of the enemy and of suffering, any more than we expect to find in the history of any scientific topic a consistency in details. The consistency we should find in science is always the consistency of understanding the experiences or phenomena *under the rubric of utility*. The consistency that I think we will find in the

157

biblical treatment of these topics is the consistency of *always attempting to understand the experiences of conflict with enemies and of suffering under the rubric of ultimate purpose.*

Let us take a simple example from science to clarify this point. From the dawn of civilization, human beings have sought knowledge about fire in order to harness the power that it exhibits. The knowledge or understanding thus sought would clearly be under the rubric of utility. In the history of the scientific study of fire, many theoretical understandings of it have been proposed, but many have also been, after a period of general acceptance, rejected. A topic in almost every elementary course in science is the phlogiston theory of fire. Why was that theory rejected? Was it because it was a nonscientific theory? Certainly not! It was rejected because it *was* a scientific theory, but when it was tested by experience under the rubric of utility, its utility was minimal and the unexpected side effects were too numerous—it predicted too few of the experiences that did occur, and it predicted too many experiences that did not occur. A new (revolutionary) theory had to be sought.

The "correct" theory of fire that I was taught, the one that succeeded the phlogiston theory (that fire was the rapid chemical combining of oxygen and the fuel) was hardly the last word. It proved inadequate to explain the fire that constitutes our sun, which under it was a colossal anomaly. Eventually that theory had to suffer its own revolution and be subsumed within a more inclusive theoretical system that could explain what it could not explain. The ongoing attempt to harness fire has produced several such theoretical revolutions, *all under the direction of the two strict taskmasters of science: the rubric of utility and experience as it occurs.*

Now let us take a similar simple illustration from biblical theology. Suppose under the rubric of ultimate purpose I theorize that suffering is an undeniable indication that the sufferers have headed for the wrong goal and that YHWH is calling them to repent. This explanation gives me not only permission but also the command from God to regard and treat all sufferers as sinners and perhaps to lecture them about the necessity of repenting and amending their ways. This "theory" of suffering (very common in the world today, I might add) works pretty well as long as the sufferers are my enemies. But when the sufferers include my righteous friends or, even worse, my righteous *self,* while my patently unrighteous enemies are enjoying unpredicted prosperity (prosperity that is inconsistent with my theorized meaning of suffering), then something has to give. I can either defiantly demand from God an explanation of this anomalous situation, or I can, on deeper reflection on the ultimate purpose of life, reform my view of the significance of suffering. This is the situation that both Job and Habakkuk wrestle with in the Hebrew

Scriptures. Their decision in the end is to keep their confidence in YHWH and to seek a deeper and more satisfying understanding of the experience suffering—an understanding that is to be directed by the two strict taskmasters of biblical theology: the ultimate purpose of life, which is to image faithful loving-kindness; and their experience that suffering seems to be distributed on some principle other than the measure of the victim's righteousness.

In the discussion of the enemy and of suffering that follows, the experiences that must be dealt with are these: the defeat of Pharaoh's army; Israel's repeated sufferings in the wilderness; the wars of conquest, in which the main enemies are the Canaanites; the enemies of Israel after it has become somewhat independent as a nation in the promised land, typical of which are the Assyrians; the Babylonian captivity after they suffer a catastrophic defeat and cease to be a political nation; and the events of the postexilic period. As these *experiences* are repeatedly examined *under the rubric of ultimate purpose,* Israel's great prophets hammer out the views of the enemy and of suffering that become part of the accepted, received tradition in the Greek Scriptures of the Christian community.

Let us begin with a brief discussion of the enemy and of suffering as they are understood in the culture of idolatry. Since idolatry is understood under the rubric of utility, it will impart to these topics their meaning. If I am a king, the enemy is by definition another nation whose king (or in rare instances, queen) has a purpose in mind for his (or her) nation that is incompatible with my purpose for my nation. If the incompatibility is of sufficient importance, we will lead our nations into war against each other, each one trying to attain his (or her) own goals. We will each instruct our priests to enlist our idols' full cooperation in the struggle. Often the price of the idols' cooperation is the slaughter of the enemy, including women and children. Failure to pay this price could result in the withdrawal of the idols' aid and therefore in defeat by the enemy. Such a defeat and its accompanying suffering, if less than total disaster, may be interpreted as evidence that the idols are displeased with some aspect of the cultic life.

If my nation suffers such a defeat, I may put to death those whom I hold responsible for the displeasure of the idols. If my nation is victorious, I have evidence that my idols are superior to the idols of my enemy, and I may slaughter the defeated king as a required sacrifice to my idols, or I may exact from the defeated king total obeisance to my idols. If I am defeated but escape slaughter, I may take the defeat as evidence that the enemy's idols are superior to my own and in that case, when I am in captivity, I will switch my allegiance to the idols of the enemy. In the case of either monarch, the success or suffering of the nation is determined by a relationship of merit between the human being and the idols. If you are meritorious, or righteous, you prosper; if you are not meritorious, you suffer. By your prosperity or suffering the world can know your righteousness or unrighteousness.

If we should adopt the alternative thesis for explaining the biblical faith, the understanding of suffering and of the enemy would be essentially the same as the one given in idolatry. Since in the alternative thesis there is no ultimate purpose by which to judge between me and someone I call my enemy, it is an incompatibility of another's wants and my own that makes us enemies. Unlike the two kings in idolatry, we are both appealing to the same God, and we both understand ourselves to be related to that God by our righteousness or our merit. Therefore if I win and you suffer, both we and all the world can see that I am more righteous than you. If our fortunes are reversed, you are the more righteous. If we should believe, as the alternative thesis suggests, that accepting in *faith* a sacrifice of another is an alternative way of appropriating merit to oneself, then my success and your suffering would indicate that my faith was stronger than yours.

When Israel's writers talk about their enemies and both the suffering of their enemies and themselves, they certainly do not do so under the requirements of this alternative thesis. In waging wars, Israel may adopt tactics that are part of the received tradition about how to fight a war (think for a moment about how virtually all nations in our own day fight wars in approximately the same way, regardless of what causes they claim to be championing). But in reaching an understanding of who the enemy is and of why it is Israel or the enemy that suffers, YHWH's ultimate purpose for human beings and YHWH's promises to Abraham and Sarah for accomplishing that purpose in all nations consistently inform that understanding. Furthermore, because the roles that Israel and the enemy nations play in the fulfillment of these promises are quite different, the explanations of Israel's suffering and the enemy's suffering may be quite different. As we shall see, the Egyptians, the Canaanites, and the Assyrians, though they are all enemies, by no means play the same role in the biblical plot. Therefore the sufferings that they themselves undergo or inflict on Israel do not have the same meaning in the plot.

Let us now consider the experience of the exodus, when the Egyptians are the enemy and they suffer ignominious defeat at the Red Sea. This central revelatory event in Israel's history is so overwhelming that they have to reinterpret everything in their history, including enemies and suffering, under a new rubric to understand it. (Keep in mind Figure 1.)

For our guide here we will use the book of Deuteronomy, one of the two great biblical accounts of these events. In all probability, the book's form that we have now was the culmination of generations of theological contemplation of these events under the rubric of ultimate purpose. If we read Deuteronomy under the rubric of utility, as the alternative thesis suggests that we do, with God in the role of the referee in archery, meting out blessings and curses in accord with merit, it will be a confusing and ultimately dreary book. On the other hand, if we read it under the rubric of ultimate purpose, as our thesis suggests we should, God becomes the faithful coach who recruited Israel and now threatens Israel with curses if it strays from that purpose, shouting, "Damn you, turn around," but also promising to help them fulfill their purpose when they do turn around. If we read it in this way, it turns out to have an exemplary consistency and an excitingly fresh insight into what has so often been seen as a most vexing period in the biblical plot.

According to Deuteronomy, at the time of the exodus *all* nations and peoples stand guilty before YHWH, not because they are deficient in merit but because they have all deserted YHWH's purpose for human life and have turned to their individual goals. The explanation for Egypt's defeat and Israel's triumph cannot be that the Israelites are either more powerful or more righteous, so that God is rewarding each according to its measure of merit. The explanation, rather, is that YHWH has promised Abraham and Sarah to restore all nations to the "right basket" through their descendants and is grooming Israel for that task. All of the plagues on Egypt and the hardened heart of Pharaoh are used by YHWH to make sure that when the Israelites are released, they cannot possibly explain their good fortune by conventional religious reasoning: "Things are going so well for us that we must be doing something right!" The only possible explanation for them is that since YHWH loves them utterly without any regard to their merit, this is a God who is entirely different from the idols, a God whose character is overflowing unmerited love. The only rubric that can comprehend such an overwhelming experience is the one of ultimate purpose: We must have been delivered so that we can live our lives in accord with this character. Consequently, Egypt's suffering to grant us this deliverance is not to be understood simply as YHWH's giving them what they deserve; it is YHWH's using Egypt *at this point in the plot of history* to accomplish the promises. There is no doubt of Egypt's total unworthiness before YHWH. But there is also no doubt of Israel's total unworthiness (Deut.7:7–11).

When the Israelites are free from Egypt and have received the Ten Commandments and ordinances as gifts from God to uphold them in their purpose, they occasionally have a quite different kind of enemy—not some other nation but some force of nature that wreaks havoc on them. They are constantly tempted by the hardships of life in the wilderness to return to Egypt and to idolatry. After all, idolatry does have some very nice features. According to that belief, if we are righteous, the idols will give us good things. In effect, the wrong basket lures them away from the goal that YHWH has recruited them for. Time after time in the wilderness they suffer various tragedies. How is their own suffering after they are safely in the wilderness, in contrast to the earlier suffering of Egyptians, to be explained? Under the rubric of purpose, this cannot be understood as retributive justice, as it would be under the alternative thesis. It is always YHWH's purpose for Israel that provides the explanation: When they forget YHWH and go after the idols of their Egyptian days, YHWH will sometimes use the forces of nature to jar them into *remembrance* of who they are.

After forty years in the wilderness, the Israelites begin the conquest of Canaan, the promised land. Now they have different enemies, and according to Deuteronomy, enemies with a different role from that of the Egyptians. The Israelites are never to think that they are morally superior to the Canaanites whom they are replacing in the land. The two peoples are equally unrighteous. It is YHWH's promise to Abraham and Sarah that makes this conquest of the land, with its concomitant suffering of the Canaanites and of the Israelites, understandable. In the plot, the Canaanites are ardent worshipers of the idol Baal, so much so that virtually every feature of their life that might be attractive to the Israelites is bound up in their understanding of their idol. The Israelites are what might be called new converts to a diametrically opposed understanding of life's ultimate purpose. If in the land the Israelites mingle with the Canaanites, have any traffic with them, or even worse, intermarry with them, the temptation will be irresistible to turn back to idolatry, either by worshiping Baal or by thinking of YHWH as just another idol who can be worshiped alongside Baal. In this early stage of their life in independence from Egypt, they need time and "space" to think through the implications of their new understanding of the purpose of their national life without outside influences. So as, over generations, the writers of the Hebrew Scriptures contemplated this conquest with its accompanying slaughter, this was the understanding that they gave it. In YHWH's long-range plan to save all nations, this conquest was a strategic move to save alive and intact those who had been chosen for the task. Merit had nothing at all to do with the choice of Israel or the ousting of the occupants (Deut. 9:4–7; 12:29–32).

We might take as a model for the conquest of the promised land the history of the present women's liberation movement. In the early days of that movement a relatively small number of women had a new vision of what life should be like, a vision that would have vast—indeed destructive—implications for life as it was then lived. It would take time and concentrated study to think through all those implications. They needed time to arrive at a clear idea of which features of the old way of life could be fitted into the new way and which could not. It was therefore deemed necessary for those dedicated to this view to have consciousness-raising groups in which only those who were dedicated to the new view participated—not only to strengthen their dedication to the view but also to sort out the behavioral implications of the view without the carping of those who were still on the other side.

In those days those of us who were on the other side (mostly men) felt not only that we were excluded but also that we were hated. When we accompanied "the girls" on social occasions, we couldn't understand their sudden change of behavior. Hadn't we always put the "dears" on pedestals? Hadn't we always paid for the food and entertainment? Hadn't we always opened the doors for them and carried the heavy bags? Hadn't we always made the really tough decisions so that they would not have to worry their pretty little heads about such boring details? Why, then, did they hate us so? What in the world did they want?

It wasn't until later that we began to listen to what they were saying and to get some inkling of what the movement was all about. It was about a new understanding of what it meant to be a person. They did not hate us; they wanted us to have that new understanding, too. But in those days, when the territory still belonged to men in an unchallenged way (when male supremacy was the unexamined received tradition), if the women compromised with us in even the most trivial of those practices that demeaned personhood, no matter how pleasant they might otherwise be, then both they and the men would be lost. The biblical writers think of the conquest of Canaan as such a consciousness-raising period.

After the conquest of the land, when Israel is more or less in tenuous possession of it, new enemies arise who have still a different role to play in the plot. The enemy nations are numerous, but the great nation Assyria, with its capital Nineveh, is now the epitome of the enemy. This is the period during which Israel is first led by judges. The era of the judges is followed by the monarchical period, which is itself divided into three subperiods. First, there is the united monarchy, when all twelve tribes become politically united under three kings in order. Of the three kings of this period—Saul, David, and Solomon—David is remembered as the one who united them under the kingship of YHWH, making Zion at Jerusalem, with the ark of the covenant (containing the Ten Commandments) the center of their national political and religious life.

Second is the subperiod of the divided monarchy. Most of the tribes in the northern part of the land rebel against Solomon and establish themselves as a separate kingdom. They make Samaria their capital, and they retain the name

Israel. (This multiple use of the word *Israel* can lead to confusion if one is not careful.) The people of the southern part of the land, mainly those of the tribe of Judah, retain the monarchy of the Davidic line, with Jerusalem, where Solomon had built the temple, as their capital. This segment of the divided monarchy is the kingdom of Judah. The relations between Israel and Judah range from hostility at one extreme to guarded friendship on the other when their unity under YHWH's purpose is remembered and longed for again.

Third is the subperiod of the kingdom of Judah alone. The northern kingdom of Israel falls to the Assyrians, who devastate its land and take into captivity a large part of the population, who now disappear from the pages of biblical literature except in memory of their past unity with Judah and in hope that YHWH will reunite all tribes again in accordance with the promise to Abraham and Sarah. These Israelite captives are known as the ten lost tribes of Israel. Although Judah suffers greatly under the political and military dominance of the Assyrians, it survives and continues as a monarchy with kings in the line of David. But Judah at last suffers a fate similar to that of Israel when the Babylonians, who had "replaced" Assyria as the enemy, defeat Judah; lay waste Jerusalem, its walls and the temple; terminate the kingship; and lead much of the population away into captivity, thus ending the monarchy and beginning the period called the Babylonian captivity.

This long period of Israel's life as an independent nation is also the period of some of Israel's greatest prophets, whose biblical writings are profound theological commentaries on the events of the times and so are our main source concerning the theological meaning of the enemy and of suffering during this period. Since we have mentioned prophets before but have not given much information about them, it will be helpful for the purposes of this chapter and our thesis to do so now.

The Hebrew word that is usually translated as *prophet* does not have as its primary meaning one who foretells the future. Rather, it designates one who speaks for another. Our slang term *mouthpiece* and our more proper term *spokesperson* come close to suggesting what the prophet's role is. The true prophet speaks the word of God. But beyond that, we need to interpret that function within our rubric. The prophets play a role under the rubric of the ultimate purpose (of YHWH) for human life that is analogous to the role that theoretical scientists play under the rubric of utility. The scientists' first, foremost, and unswerving loyalty or allegiance is to the rubric. Then *under that rubric* they aim to construct a putative world that will make consistent intelligible sense of our total experience. The prophets' first, foremost, and unswerving commitment is to the conviction that YHWH's character is faithful loving-kindness, that ultimate human purpose is to image that character, and that YHWH will bring that purpose to fruition in all nations according to the promises to Israel's ancestors. Then *under this quite different rubric* they aim to construct a putative world that will make consistent intelligible sense of Israel's total experience up to the latest moment. Because their intellectual tasks, though under different rubrics, are similar, there are parallels between the two that will help us to understand the role of the prophets in this period. Let us consider a few of these.

One parallel is that both scientists and prophets intend for their knowledge claims to be understood and adopted by the people to whom they are addressed. Scientists do not intend for their theories, no matter how strange they may seem at first, to be occult mysteries that only initiates into a secret inner circle can decode and understand. Likewise, prophets intend for all Israelites who remember the exodus not only to hear and understand but also to obey when they thunder out, "Thus says YHWH." If some people do not heed the word, it is not because it is esoteric and available only to the privileged few but because they have hardened their hearts to it. The second parallel is that, in accord with our thesis, the *meaning* of knowledge-claims is not to be sought in some mysterious correspondence between linguistic entities and a metaphysical "reality." The meaning is in what they *do*. Scientific knowledge-claims guide our conduct in getting results that we want efficiently with a minimum of unwanted side effects. Biblical prophetic knowledge-claims have their meaning in calling rulers and peoples to repentance and to living in accord with their ultimate purpose.

This brings us to a third parallel, which is that sometimes events predicted by scientific knowledge-claims and by prophetic knowledge-claims do not come about, but for somewhat different reasons. (Remember, all scientific theories are prediction devices, and scientists, no less than prophets, are in the business of foretelling something of the future.) In the case of science, the reasons for the failure of predictions to come true range from dirty test tubes to theories that are in need of revision. In the case of biblical prophecy, it may be that the intended outcome of a predicted disaster is realized by the mere threat of it, making the disaster superfluous. Those puzzling passages where God (speaking in this case to Jeremiah) claims to repent of promised evil are explained in this way:

> At one moment I may declare concerning a nation or a kingdom, that I will pluck up and break down and destroy it, but if that nation, concerning which I have spoken, turns from its evil, I will change my mind about the disaster that I intended to bring on it. And at another moment I may declare concerning a nation or a kingdom that I will build and plant it, but if it does evil in my sight, not listening to my voice, then I will change my mind about the good that I had intended to do to it. (Jer. 18:7–10)

For the prophets, the promises of God to restore the creation to its original purpose are not subject to any repentance or mind changing. But the tactics employed with both Israel and the enemy to bring about the promises are always to be understood as appropriate at any particular point in the plot.

The fourth parallel is one we have already discussed but should mention again now. In science, when a new paradigm or theory replaces an older one, the conservative tendency is at work so that many of the terms of the older theory are repeated in the new one, but with new meanings. We therefore must be on guard lest we think the recent user of terms is using them to preserve the old theory. When the biblical writers reject the religion of idolatry and adopt a different rubric to speak of YHWH, they do not invent a new language from scratch but use most of the old terms *with revised definitions*. One such term is *vengeance*. Whereas in idolatry the term refers to the idol's giving unrighteous people what they deserve on the basis of merit with perhaps a little more thrown in for good measure, in the rubric of ultimate purpose the same term refers to YHWH's acts of punishment that are appropriate for fulfilling the ultimate telos. Such acts of vengeance, therefore, are expressions of faithful loving-kindness.

In the period we are now entering, the pattern is this, with variations from time to time: After the people are in possession of the land given to them so that they can live in accord with YHWH's purpose, they forget the promises, the exodus, and the covenant at Sinai. They think of the land as one in which they can live for their own purposes, and they think of YHWH as an idol who will bless them in their self-generated purposes if they are righteous by keeping all the ritual requirements. They oppress the poor just as surely as Pharaoh oppressed them in Egypt. The rituals, which were gifts from YHWH to remind them constantly of YHWH's faithful loving-kindness, are now performed lavishly to harness the power of a god who is now nothing but another idol. This is the situation in the kingdom of Judah at the time of the prophet Isaiah.

During his service in the temple Isaiah has a vision of God and realizes that not only he himself but all of the people have turned from their proper goal and are headed enthusiastically for the wrong basket (Isa. 6). Now the Israelites themselves are the enemy of YHWH (Isa. 1:24):

> Therefore says the Sovereign, the Lord of hosts, the Mighty One of Israel:
> Ah, I will pour out my wrath on my enemies,
> and avenge myself on my foes!

The instrument of YHWH's vengeance will be that hated evil empire, Assyria.

> Ah, Assyria, the rod of my anger—
> the club in their hands is my fury!

Against a godless nation I send him,
  and against the people of my wrath I command him,
to take spoil and seize plunder,
  and to tread them down like the mire of the streets.

(Isa. 10:5–6)

Although now Israel, the chosen people of the promise, are made to suffer at the hands of God's chosen instruments for this task, the comparative merit of Israel and the Assyrians has nothing to do with the explanation of the suffering. The Assyrians are just as sinful as Israel, pursuing their own wrong basket with equal vigor. They have no intention or awareness of doing YHWH's will. They are out after all the spoils of battle they can gather (10:7–11).

The explanation is that YHWH is using punishment to restore Israel to its telos:

I will turn my hand against you;
  I will smelt away your dross as with lye
  and remove all your alloy.
And I will restore your judges as at the first,
  and your counselors as at the beginning.
Afterward you shall be called the city of righteousness,
  the faithful city.

(Isa. 1:25–26)

Punishment is remedial, never the last word. Israel will be restored to be the nation through whom all nations know YHWH and are themselves restored to the purpose for which they too were created. Therefore, in due time, after YHWH has accomplished the punishment of Israel with the Assyrians, they, too, shall have to pass through the purifying fire of YHWH's wrath, along with all of the other nations (10:12–19). But with them, also, punishment will not be the last word. The purified and restored Israel will then be the judging and purifying instrument by which the whole earth will be filled with the knowledge of YHWH (11:1–9).

We will postpone for a short while the discussion of *how* Israel is to accomplish this judging and purifying of the nations, because in answering that question the prophets introduce an entirely new understanding of suffering and the enemy. Meanwhile, the other great prophets, before and after Isaiah—Amos, Hosea, Micah, Jeremiah, Ezekiel—exhibit this same understanding: Israel turns from YHWH, and YHWH uses enemy nations as instruments of divine "vengeance" on Israel to restore it to its purpose. For these prophets it is the basketball metaphor, not the archery metaphor, that is useful for illuminating YHWH's vengeance.

As the monarchical period advances, it begins to occur to some of Israel's prophets and other writers that the widely accepted explanation for Israel's suffering at the hands of the enemy (as it was explained in the previous paragraph) is not totally adequate. It seems to serve well for some instances but not for all. Sometimes when Israel is *headed for the right goal* and the enemy is *headed for the wrong goal* the enemy still pummels Israel unmercifully. To borrow language from modern science, the writers complain that too many anomalies are arising if we attempt to comprehend all experience under the prevailing paradigm. These writers, while remaining committed to the rubric of ultimate purpose, demand to know from God why in these instances the righteous are suffering while the unrighteous are prospering (Habakkuk and Job). Clearly, if we are to remain under the rubric, a new paradigm for suffering is needed.

An example of that new paradigm to explain this anomalous suffering is provided by the great unnamed prophet of the Babylonian captivity, whose writings are a part of the book of Isaiah, beginning at about chapter 40. For this reason, and because he or she is clearly influenced by Isaiah's language and thought, many scholars dub this anonymous prophet Deutero-Isaiah. The captivity was an utterly devastating event for Israel. Virtually every tangible bit of evidence that they were the people chosen for God's purpose was gone—the promised land, the temple and the required sacrifices, the Davidic monarchy. How could YHWH possibly be keeping the promises to Abraham and Sarah? This was as impossible to understand as the death of Isaac would have been for Abraham, and in this case Israel *is* "dead" whereas Isaac was spared. Many of the captives simply abandoned their faith and blended into the Gentile–non-Israelite world.

Deutero-Isaiah, who is *absolutely* committed to the rubric (Isaiah 40), must come up with a new paradigm that will explain how YHWH is fulfilling the promise that Israel will be the nation through whom all nations shall be restored to YHWH's purpose while letting those same unrighteous nations defeat Israel when Israel, though certainly not perfect, was certainly facing the proper goal. This understanding had to be in accord with YHWH's character of unchanging faithful loving-kindness. Deutero-Isaiah, who in my opinion ranks in his discipline with Newton and Einstein in theirs, produced the paradigm of the *suffering servant* that is later used in the Greek Scriptures to explain the death of Jesus, the one whom Christians believe to be Israel's promised new David, the new anointed one.

Deutero-Isaiah's answer to the question "How can the suffering of the righteous at the hands of the unrighteous possibly bring about God's telos?" is this: If Israel, YHWH's servant nation, understands its purpose and lives in perfect accord with that purpose in the midst of the other nations (where YHWH has strategically placed it), then the difference between Israel and the other nations will certainly not pass unnoticed. As the Israelites worship their God—not to control God's power but to learn God's purpose for them—and as they exhibit that purpose by a life of compassion for the oppressed rather than one in which they strive to dominate and oppress others, the nations will see that they and the Israelites have utterly incompatible views of the ultimate significance of human existence. In the language of the basketball metaphor, it will be glaringly obvious to them that they and Israel are going toward different goals. Furthermore, because these views are incompatible, the other nations will see Israel's view, if allowed to go unchallenged, as a threat to everything that they hold to be right. They will see Israel, therefore, not only as wrong but as damned wrong. There is not room in this basketball game for both teams to win, so Israel must lose. Accordingly, the nations will inflict on Israel the most devastating suffering of which they are capable. This is precisely what the Babylonians have done, and as they and other nations contemplate Israel's total and humiliating defeat, they will judge it to be a complete vindication of idolatry over this strange and potentially dangerous faith of Israel.

But now, says Deutero-Isaiah, YHWH will do the impossible! Across the impassable wilderness that separates Babylonia from the ruins of Jerusalem, YHWH will figuratively bulldoze a superhighway and, in the presence of the kings of the nations, will restore the captives to the promised land. The kings will be so startled at this strange turn of events that they shall shut their mouths. They shall have to reassess everything that they had ever thought about the significance of life. If Israel's God YHWH has vindicated Israel, then it is they, the nations, who had turned to the wrong goal, who had gone astray. The punishment and suffering that they had inflicted on Israel was not divine vengeance for Israel's sin: YHWH is now using that punishment and suffering to save the nations, to turn them to the same goal that Israel is facing, and to heal their wounds (Isa. 52:13–53:12). Furthermore, the prophet says elsewhere (ch. 45) that YHWH will accomplish this deliverance of Israel, which will save the Gentile nations through Cyrus, the king of the Persians. Notice that in this account of suffering, as in all the previous ones in the Hebrew Scriptures, suffering is not seen as YHWH's meting out punishment in proportion to one's righteous merit or lack thereof. It is instead understood to be the appropriate act of YHWH for keeping the promises to restore all creation to its original purpose.

When Cyrus allows the Israelites to return to their land, they do so not as a restored kingdom of Judah but as a community of faith within the Persian Empire. Cyrus, unlike former tyrants whom Israel had known, is benevolent and allows them considerable freedom in the practice of their religious rites. But events do not happen as Deutero-Isaiah had expected. When the enemy nations do not turn to YHWH, the returnees are left to ponder again the meaning of their existence. They experience the tension of being in the world but not of the world. Some in this Jewish community (for they now think of themselves as the remnant of Israel living in the land of Judah) believe that they can only be completely restored as the united Israel under YHWH's purpose by isolating themselves as much as possible from "the nations," for in their view it was the influence of those nations that led them astray and ultimately into captivity. But others of the Jewish community—keeping their unique understanding of the ultimate purpose of all nations under YHWH—believe that they belong in the midst of the enemy nations as God's prophets or spokespersons. How else can they fulfill their own unique task within the promises? The book of Jonah is a prophetic sermon directed at this issue.

In the book of Jonah, the prophet is the epitome of Israel in this tension. The city of Nineveh, the capital of the once great Assyria, is the epitome of the enemy and all that that term has meant throughout Israel's monarchical history. The plot of this short book parallels Israel's own history thus far. Its gist is this: YHWH elects Jonah for an important task—to proclaim YHWH's judgment against Nineveh. But Jonah rebels against YHWH's purpose for his life and flees in the opposite direction (Nineveh is to the east of Judah; Tarshish is as far west as you can go in the known world of that day), claiming even as he is in rebellion that he worships YHWH, the creator of all that is. YHWH, true to the divine character of faithful loving-kindness, will not allow Jonah to be other than what he was elected to be; even though Jonah has deserted YHWH, YHWH will not desert Jonah. With that jealous love, YHWH uses the forces of nature, a beast of the deep, and even the prayers of idolatrous sailors to stop Jonah in his tracks and return him to his proper goal. Now back on track, facing the right basket, Jonah goes—but reluctantly—to Nineveh and proclaims YHWH's gracious and restoring words of judgment against it. Jonah preaches his eight-word sermon of hellfire and damnation: "Forty days more, and Nineveh shall be overthrown!" (Jonah 3:4).

Just as Jonah had suspected, the whole city, from the king to the cows, repents. Jonah is so angry that he wants to die:

> "O LORD! Is not this what I said while I was still in my own country? That is why I fled to Tarshish at the beginning; for I knew that you are a gracious God and merciful, slow to anger, and abounding in steadfast love, and ready to relent from punishing. And now, O LORD, please take my life from me, for it is better for me to die than to live." (4:2–3)

In the end, YHWH gently chides Jonah by reminding him of the everlasting promises that he (Jonah), as a prophet of Israel, should know by heart, the promises that are not just for Israel but for all nations and all creation, including the cows: "'And should I not be concerned about Nineveh, that great city, in which there are more than a hundred and twenty thousand persons who do not know their right hand from their left [do not know which is their right basket], and also many animals?'" (4:11).

The understanding of who the enemies are and what punishment is for is clear: The enemies are those whom YHWH loves so much that YHWH has chosen and nurtured Israel to be the instrument of divine redeeming love to them. Therefore, if Israel thinks that it can keep its faith pure by isolating itself from the enemies, Israel has already lost its faith and become exactly like the enemies. For YHWH's people, their so-called enemies are in reality their neighbors, and punishment is not something that idolatrous "justice" requires in order to balance unrighteousness with an equal amount of suffering. YHWH's justice, vengeance, judgment, and punishment are entirely different. Their sole purpose is to restore those who do not know their right hand from their left. If an eight-word sermon will do the job or if the suffering of the righteous servant will do it, 'tis enough. One can well imagine that Jesus had the book of Jonah in mind when in the Sermon on the Mount (Matt. 5:43–48) he repeated its message:

> "You have heard that it was said, 'You shall love your neighbor and hate your enemy.' But I say to you, Love your enemies and pray for those who persecute you, so that you may be children of your Father in heaven; for he makes his sun rise on the evil and on the good, and sends rain on the righteous and on the unrighteous. For if you love those who love you, what reward do you have? Do not even the tax collectors do the same? And if you greet only your brothers and sisters, what more are you doing than others? Do not even the Gentiles do the same? Be perfect, therefore, as your heavenly Father is perfect."

Monotheism and the Doctrine of the Trinity

In testing the thesis of this chapter by biblical theological material, the last topic I wish to discuss is the doctrine of the Trinity. Although the word itself does not appear in the Greek Scriptures and there is no examination of the specific idea there, Christian thinkers have believed the doctrine to be implicit in those Scriptures. From early times in the Christian community the Trinitarian formula of God the Father, God the Son, and God the Holy Spirit has been considered by most parts of that community to be a necessary foundation for all subsequent theological statements. The Trinity, more than any other doctrine, comes closest to uniting the Christian church in spite of its many divisions. I introduce it now not because it is a *vexing* problem, like suffering or law, that seems to cast doubt on our thesis but because it is to many people a *perplexing* topic that seems to be so lacking in meaning that belief or non-belief in it is totally irrelevant to our thesis. In keeping with our pattern of discussion thus far, we will attempt to establish its relevance to our thesis by following the biblical plot.

As the scriptural account of the last period in the history of the Israelites (now the Jews) nears its close, the increasingly important issue for theological contemplation is how (not whether) YHWH will fulfill the promise that through Israel all the nations shall be restored to YHWH's ultimate purpose for them. The Greek Scriptures are the theological works of writers who assert that that promise has begun to be fulfilled through Jesus of Nazareth, who is none other than the promised messiah of Israel. The Greek Scriptures of the Christians, therefore, claim to be about YHWH's fulfilling the third promise to Abraham and Sarah: These writers accept the Hebrew Scriptures of Israel to be the authentic Word of God, and to be the only context within which Jesus, as the Savior of the world, can be understood. Therefore they tell the story of Jesus in such a way as to attribute to him all the messianic titles and tasks that are a part of Israel's hope.

Jesus is the Son of God who does what a good son should do—he perfectly obeys the one who truly has the prerogative to determine the purpose of his life. He is the Christ. (The English word *christ* is derived from the Greek word that means "anointed"; the English word *messiah* is derived from the Hebrew word that means "anointed." Thus *anointed, messiah,* and *christ* mean the same thing, and when capitalized, they designate the one officially chosen and appointed by YHWH to be the new King David, who will do for all nations what David did for the twelve tribes of Israel.) Jesus is the Word of God (Ten Commandments, God's ultimate purpose for humanity) incarnate, made flesh, who has come to restore and establish the law, not to destroy it. He is the light of the world, the light to the nations of Deutero-Isaiah. He is the suffering servant. He has come to write the law on the heart. For the writers of the Greek Scriptures, the entire vocation of the chosen people is now focused in Israel's messiah, who, because he is perfect in his knowledge of and obedience to YHWH's ultimate purpose for all creation, is capable of being the effective suffering servant. His death on the cross, therefore, for human life is the perfect sacrifice for the sin of the world. He is the new Passover sacrifice, in remembrance of whom all nations are to be restored and upheld in their purpose to love others as YHWH has loved them.

If the alternative thesis were the correct one by which to understand the biblical writings, we should expect the following: (1) After Jesus has been proclaimed to be the perfectly obedient one, his sacrifice for the sins of the world is effective precisely because he was perfect in every way. (2) The Greek Scriptures would then go on to say that because Jesus has made the perfect sacrifice for us—that is, because he has provided us with an infinite and inexhaustible supply of merit to make up for our deficiencies, which result from our disobedience to the laws—then we really do not need to worry ourselves with the law anymore. (3) Grace has replaced the law as the source of merit and is therefore the means for our getting from God the fulfillment of our wants and desires here and hereafter. In other words, we should expect that the Greek Scriptures would express very strongly a theological position known as *antinomianism.* The word means "against law," and the theological position states that because we are saved by the merits of Jesus, we no longer need to do works of the law, such as feeding the hungry, clothing the naked, ending the oppression of the weak by the powerful, or loving the enemy and doing good to those who would wrongfully use us. At best, such works are merely our saying to God, "I really do appreciate what you have done for me. Therefore, please accept these few tokens of my appreciation." At worst, such works are a sheer denial of grace and are an indication that those who do them have not really accepted Jesus as personal Savior.

But there is not a trace of antinomianism in the Greek Scriptures. If anything, those Scriptures are adamantly *anti*-antinomian. In them Jesus is always admonishing his disciples to follow him. In Matt. 7:21 he says, "'Not everyone who says to me, "Lord, Lord," will enter the kingdom of heaven, but only the one who does the will of my Father in heaven.'" In the parable of the last judgment in Matthew 25, the question that will be asked at that time is about how you treated the least of Jesus' family: the hungry, the thirsty, the naked, the sick, the stranger, the prisoner. For how you treated them is the only evidence that you really had taken Jesus as Lord and Savior. In Luke 6:46 Jesus asks, "'Why do you call me "Lord, Lord," and do not do what I tell you?'" In John 15:16–17, Jesus tells his disciples, "'You did not choose me but I chose you. And I appointed you to go and bear fruit, fruit that will last, so that the Father will give you whatever you ask him in my name. I am giving you these commands so that you may love one another.'"

Modern antinomians often claim that their theological position is based squarely on the writings of the apostle Paul, but in fact Paul holds antinomianism to be beneath contempt. In Rom. 3:8 he writes the following about those who are accusing him of it: "And why not say (as some people slander us by saying that we say), 'Let us do evil so that good may come'? Their condemnation is deserved!" Then in Romans 6 Paul gives a sustained argument explaining why God's grace does not allow us even to ask, "Should we continue in sin in order that grace may abound?" It should not surprise us to find that Paul's argument is based on the metaphor of basketball, for Paul is an inveterate basketball player. These and other passages from Jesus and Paul demonstrate that the alternative thesis, which is based on the rubric of utility, requires something from the biblical literature that is not there.

On the other hand, if we adopt our thesis, which is based on the rubric of ultimate purpose, we find in the Greek Scriptures exactly what our study of the Hebrew Scriptures has led us to expect: The sacrificial death of Jesus on the cross for our salvation has nothing to do with transferring his merit to our account so that we can get what we want whether we deserve it or not. It has everything to do with what YHWH is doing to restore us to the purpose for which we were created.

We are now in a position to understand the *meaning* of the doctrine of the Trinity. As we begin, we must keep in mind our claim from the beginning that in both science and theology, the *meaning* of a term is a function of what the term *does*. The meaning of a term is not determined by its correspondence to some metaphysical entity that we can presumably know apart from experience. The choice of terms to be used in theories, therefore, is not based on our non-experiential knowledge of what a term *must* mean but on whether or not the term as it is defined within the theory will function with all other terms in such a way as to do what we want a theory to do. In science we want a theory to serve as an accurate and reliable prediction device, so that actions guided by that theory will have the results we want without too many unpredicted and unwanted side effects. If a theory in science is not doing its job as effectively as we want it to, we may be able to improve its efficacy by changing the definition of a term in some way. Although the term may be one that we have inherited in a received tradition, we do not change its definition because we have some intuitive knowledge of what it can or cannot mean. Sometimes, therefore, a new theory will contain a familiar term but with an utterly bizarre twist.

Let us look at two familiar examples. Nothing can seem more intuitively certain than this: Any given physical body, no matter how large or small it is, is either at rest or in motion, and if it is in motion, it is either traveling in a straight line or it is not traveling in a straight line. Another example is this: Any particular particle, no matter how small or large, has at any moment a discrete location in space and a discrete velocity. How do we know these two statements to be true? Does common sense tell us that things just have to be this way? Fairly recently some scientists have found it advantageous either to discard these common-sense notions or to redefine them in such uncommon ways that many of us find the resulting theories to be so incomprehensible that we shake our heads in utter perplexity. How could there possibly be a world that these new theories describe? But if the purpose of science is not to copy linguistically a world that we intuitively know must be but instead to provide us with theories (tools) of maximum utility, then if we ask scientists why they came up with such screwball theories, their answer would be, "The rubric of utility forced us to. Nothing else we could think up does the job as well."

Similarly in theology we do not have common-sense notions of what words such as *god, spirit,* and *divine* must mean. We may indeed inherit them in a received tradition, but we may have to redefine them and use them as the rubric dictates, not as common sense dictates. Now what does the rubric of the ultimate purpose of human life demand of those who are theologians in the biblical mode? Or to put the question in a different way, What are theological statements supposed to *do*? As we have already stressed, the task of biblical theology is always to shape our language about God so that nothing we say about God will ever give us permission to hate or oppress anyone, even our worst enemies. It will instead require us to understand all our talents and possessions to be gifts of God for the living of a community life of faithful loving-kindness. If we ask, then, What does the doctrine of the Trinity *do*? the answer is that it aims to make sure that I never hate you, and that I always regard you with faithful loving-kindness. Let us develop this idea further.

To confess one God is to acknowledge that God is the giver of ultimate purpose, and since I can have only one ultimate purpose, I can have only one God. I cannot have two ultimate loyalties. This one God I call *Father* only in recognition of the tradition that we discussed in the section on the Third Commandment, which forbids the wrongful use of the name of YHWH. That tradition, because of the historical circumstance that human "fathers" were usurping the prerogative of the Creator to determine the ultimate purpose of others' lives, asserts that only God has that prerogative, and that it is God's *character*, not some human being's *wishes*, that gives me that purpose.

To confess fully my faith, I must state where the character of this one God is experienced. Guided by the twin taskmasters of experience and the rubric of ultimate purpose, I confess that it is in the witness of the Hebrew and Greek Scriptures as that witness is perfected in Jesus. I confess him to be God the Son, meaning that in his life I experience totally unmerited faithful loving-kindness that has claimed my life. Thus, if anybody or anything else claims to be a revelation of God's character or will but is contrary to what is seen in the life of Jesus, and thus is not faithful loving-kindness, it is not a revelation of the Trinitarian God.

A God whose character is faithful loving-kindness is a God who is active in the creation to restore those who have turned away from their purpose. This is not a passive God who is sought by creatures in order to harness divine power for their own purposes. This is a God whose gifts are freely given to establish and uphold creatures in their ultimate purpose. Because the God whose character is revealed in Jesus is not a God whom we choose but a God who chooses us, I confess my faith in God the Holy Spirit. I choose the word *Spirit* not because I have some instinctive understanding of what the word really means but because the biblical writers, inheriting it in some received tradition, redefined and adapted it to speak of this indispensable *seeking* aspect of faithful loving-kindness. In the biblical language, the gifts of the Spirit are the talents and abilities that enable our love for others to be expressed in tangible ways. Because we are to love others, we are to pray for gifts of the Spirit to enable us to do so effectively. Consequently, any gift that does not serve my ultimate purpose but simply helps me to get whatever I want is not a gift from the Holy Spirit. The oneness of the Father, the Son, and the Holy Spirit is a oneness in the character of faithful loving-kindness.

If, as so many have tried to do, we try to give some meaning to this doctrine under the alternative thesis and its rubric of utility, where God is construed as a power that we can control for our own desires, the doctrine of the Trinity will almost certainly either become a disguised polytheism, or will be regarded as a mystery that we are required to believe if we want to go to heaven.

I now consider the thesis of part 3 to be sufficiently tested and sustained for us to think of it no longer as a hypothesis that needs to be justified. We may now regard it as an established principle in the light of which we can analyze other topics. What we have done in part 3 is similar to what we did in part 2 for our thesis concerning science. In part 4, with the use of these two established theses, we will analyze three topics that are at or near the center of the science versus religion controversy: creation stories, miracles, and an authoritative canon.

PART 4 Creation, Miracle, and Canon
in Science and in Theology

Chapter 10

Principles of Understanding
Applied to Three Vexing Topics

*T*he purpose of this chapter is to examine three of the most vexing topics that arise whenever science and the biblical faith are discussed. I have delayed introducing them in a serious way until now for a reason that I shall try to make clear. I shall begin to do so with an anecdote.

I once worked for an agency whose activities were inherently hazardous. Whenever new workers were oriented to their jobs, they were instructed in the safety rules that had to be observed. In addition, each month all staff members, regardless of how long we had worked there, were reinstructed in those rules that most of us had been over many times—what to do when a client appeared to be acting irrationally, where the fire extinguishers were located and which ones were to be used for which type of fire, where the escape routes were on each floor. Why this initiation and then repetition? If in the daily routine of our work we should forget the rules and then a crisis should arise, we would either do the wrong thing or waste moments—even minutes—trying to recall what we should do; in either case a tragedy could happen.

Intellectual activity, though necessary, is also inherently hazardous. In scientific intellectual activity if we are not alert *initially* and *constantly thereafter* to the two strict taskmasters, experience and the rubric of utility, then the results could indeed be some tragic unwanted and unexpected side effects. Similarly, in the intellectual activity of biblical theology, if we should have a lapse of attention to its two taskmasters, experience and the rubric of ultimate purpose of human life, we could end up with the tragic belief that God not only permits but even demands us to hate others.

Since intellectual activity is inherently hazardous, I did not want us to start the most hazardous task of examining the three topics of this chapter until we were well acquainted with the "safety precautions." I know of no other topics we are more prone to argue about on the basis of *unexamined* premises, received traditions, and ambiguous definitions than these three—and I do not exempt myself from this judgment. Therefore, let us consider the first three parts of this book to have been our *first* instructions in the safety rules. We must now keep them in mind *constantly,* for the consequences of not doing so could be unfortunate.

Even those of us who have heard the rules many times are subject to serious—even tragic—lapses of memory when we are distracted by the routine tasks of work. To see an example of how difficult it is to avoid such a lapse, turn to Figure 1 on p. 11. First look at it as a picture of an older woman, concentrating on doing so until there is no uncertainty in your mind about it. Now concentrate on it as a picture of a younger woman, saying to yourself over and over again, "I will not lapse and let my mind's eye see it as the older woman." If your ability to be single-minded is so great that you do not toggle back into seeing the picture as an old woman even for a split second, you are much better at it than I am; you will have to pardon the rest of us, who are ordinary mortals, while we go back over the rules.

The structure of this chapter, therefore, is first to go over the rules or principles that we are now to keep in mind as we discuss the three topics; and second, to ask how each of these topics is to be understood *within* each discipline, science and biblical theology.

The Rules or Principles

These rules or principles are simply the salient points of the thesis that we have developed and tested in the first three chapters. In this chapter, however, we are no longer attempting to test their appropriateness for science and theology. Here we are assuming their appropriateness to have been established and now are bringing them to bear on our understanding of the yet-to-be-discussed topics. This shift from hypothesis to established principle is similar to that shift in scientific inquiry when a new theory is considered sufficiently confirmed for it then to be used as an undisputed premise in solving other problems. (Of course, no principle here is ever completely confirmed beyond all dispute as long as experience continues to occur.)

The following rules or principles are similar to the Ten Commandments in theology in that they form a systematic whole. In both cases, if you violate one, you have violated all. Whereas the systematic unity in the Ten Commandments is provided by the ultimate purpose of human life, and therefore is a teleological unity, here the unity is provided by the thesis that knowledge is formed by understanding experience under a rubric. It is therefore a methodological unity. Because the principles are a systematic whole, no attempt is made here to formulate them as if they were mutually exclusive and totally exhaustive. Our only purpose is to help us to keep them in mind throughout our hazardous work.

Principle 1: Experience is primary. It simply *occurs*. It is not itself problematic.

Principle 2: Both science and theology are human intellectual activities that begin with experience as it occurs and attempt to understand that experience under the guidance of a rubric. The rubric of science is that of utility. The rubric of theology in the biblical mode is that of the ultimate purpose of human life.

Principle 3: The knowledge-claims or truth-claims made by science and by theology are about different putative worlds postulated by use of the different rubrics. Putative worlds do not just occur. They are problematic and are always subject to modification. Putative worlds do not make experience problematic. Ongoing experience makes any formulation of a putative world problematic.

Principle 4: Facts are *within* a putative world. For this reason they too are problematic and are subject to change as long as experience continues to occur. We have chosen to use the word "happen" to speak about facts or events, just as we have chosen to use the word "occur" to speak about experience. Therefore events *happen* within a putative world.

Principle 5: The questions "What really *occurred*?" and "What really *happened*?" are two quite different questions and ought not to be confused.

Principle 6: In the putative world of science, formed under the rubric of utility, the events of that world are ideally connected by *mechanistic laws,* so that any event is completely explained by previous events and those laws. In the putative world of ultimate purpose, all significant human events are ideally explained *teleologically* as the result of responsible conscious decision. In that world all of God's acts are understood to be the appropriate ones in their circumstances to bring about the telos of a world that images faithful loving-kindness.

Principle 7: The work of a scientist can be thought of as seeking to "discover" the laws of nature. But the work of a theologian in the biblical mode is not to be thought of as seeking to find the ultimate purpose of life. It begins with the overwhelming conviction that the purpose of life is to mirror the character of God, which is faithful loving-kindness. The putative world of biblical theology is one in which God, not the human being, is the *searcher* and *finder*.

Principle 8: Many key words and terms are defined *within* a given putative world and may have a quite different meaning within another putative world.

Principle 9: Almost all intellectual activity begins with a received tradition as one facet of *occurring experience*, with its laws, definitions, concepts of "stuff," and so forth. In trying to understand any new truth-claim, it is help-ful to inquire about the received tradition out of which it grew and which it may have modified.

Principle 10: The position of metaphysical realism with its correspondence theory of truth is untenable.

Principle 11: The meaning of a statement, therefore, is in what it *does*.

Principle 12: Neither rubric with its resultant putative world is the correct, or right, or proper one.

Because both rubrics with their putative worlds are essential for those of the biblical faith for the living out of that faith, their concern for integrity in employing these two rubrics correspond to their desire to be obedient to the two divisions of the Ten Commandments: love God and love the neighbor, divisions that cannot be separated. The rubric of ultimate purpose concen-trates solely on the ultimate purpose of imaging YHWH's character of faith-ful loving-kindness. But precisely because that purpose is to be lived out in the everyday world of neighbors (including enemies), who have needs and who are oppressed, the rubric of utility is needed to provide the knowledge of how to meet those needs and ease oppression with as few unwanted side effects as possible. If we keep in mind our discussion of means and ends in part 1, the cogency of James 2:15–16 is clear: "If a brother or sister is naked and lacks daily food, and one of you says to them, 'Go in peace; keep warm and eat your fill,' and yet you do not supply their bodily needs, what is the good of that?"

Three Vexing Topics

Creation

Many of the cultures of the world have their own accounts of creation. For those who are born into a particular culture, its creation account is a facet of their total experience and thus a part of the received tradition within which they attempt to understand all new experiences. As we have already noted, because Israel as a community of faith had its origins in the cultural milieu of idolatry, every aspect of its received tradition had its significance within the idolatrous understanding of life. Then when the Israelites experienced YHWH's love as totally unrelated to their merit, and therefore as totally different from an idol's love, it was necessary for them to redefine virtually every aspect of the received tradition. They did not do so by starting from scratch and in effect inventing a new world. They retained many outward forms of the old tradi-tion but drastically altered their understanding of them.

Now everything had to be subsumed under the telos of faithful loving-kindness, and the events of their lives had to be put into a teleological framework in which YHWH was accomplishing that telos. Thus a sacrifice was no longer defined as something of value that they gave to God to get back from God something that they valued even more. It was now something that God gave to them to establish and uphold them in their ultimate purpose. Likewise wars had to be understood in a new way, and as the result of long critical thinking about them, Israel came to understand the "enemy" as those equally loved by God and those for whose sake (for whose telos) Israel might be called on to be a suffering servant.

A significant part of Israel's received tradition from idolatry was a collection of creation accounts, which attributed events in their prehistory to idols, whose behavior was *not* motivated by faithful loving-kindness. To use the language of the thesis of this book, the accounts in the received traditions were organized under the rubric of utility rather than ultimate purpose, and they often presented the idols as capricious powers who could be brought to the aid of human self-devised agendas by various religious acts and rites.

Israel could not fit its new and revolutionary understanding of God into these received creation accounts simply by substituting the name YHWH for the names of the idols. The conservative tendency in critical intellectual thought had to give way to the revolutionary tendency. Something drastic was required. The framework for the accounts had to be made *teleological* rather than *mechanistic;* the ultimate purpose of human life—to *image* YHWH's character of faithful loving-kindness—had to be clear in the beginning if YHWH is indeed a God whose character does not change; the world and all within it had to be good and for YHWH's good purpose. As we have already seen, the creation accounts in Genesis do just these things and are indeed the result of critical theological reflection on Israel's experience of YHWH's love in the exodus. To put it another way, when the Israelite writers constructed their putative world, they had to be sure that nothing they said about its creation could be construed as giving them permission—or worse, commanding them—fundamentally to hate others.

But as revolutionary as Israel's theological thinkers were, they did not *completely* abandon the received tradition; they retained any features of it that were compatible with their understanding of YHWH. One modern specialized discipline within the field of biblical theology is the study of ancient Near Eastern documents in order to determine insofar as possible the sources for the biblical accounts of creation. Several such significant documents are well known; these predate the biblical material, and their literary kinship to the biblical accounts is striking. The purpose of studying these documents is, of course, not to debunk the Bible by pointing out that its accounts of creation are not original. Nor is it to establish that Israel's faith, on the one hand, and idolatry, on the other, are essentially the same because there is literary dependence between the two. The purpose is to determine how the Israelite writers modified the received tradition so as to remake it into a polemic *against* idolatry rather than a *support of* it. It is an intellectual mistake of great magnitude to assume that literary dependence between two documents indicates that the two documents have the same meaning. The meaning of each document is discerned within its putative world, not independently of it.

If we take seriously our thesis that the meaning of a truth-claim is not in its correspondence to some presumed objective metaphysical reality that we would have to know in some nonexperiential way, but instead is in what it *does,* then we can say this about the biblical creation accounts: They have an essential place in the plot of the biblical narrative, which is an attempt to make sense out of Israel's experience under the rubric of ultimate purpose of human life. This plot says that YHWH, the God whose character is faithful loving-kindness, created human beings within a good creation to image the divine character; but when human beings turned from that purpose, YHWH with a jealous love promised to restore them to it and is keeping the promise to the end. The creation accounts have their meaning within the entire plot, not independently of it. In their context they signal a tremendous intellectual shift away from idolatry, a shift that is not a mere paradigm shift within the same rubric but a complete change of rubric.

If we ask why the biblical writers included creation narratives at all, a suitable answer might be that without them the teleological structure of their putative world would have been flawed; without them the systematic unity required of rational intellectual activity would have been lacking. If in that putative world the plot line is about what God is doing to restore the world to its original purpose, the stories of the creation and fall are there to state what the original purpose was, from which all have deviated. To consider the stories of the origins to be unimportant would be comparable to considering a murder to be unimportant in the plot of a murder mystery. Without the murder, we would not know what the detective is doing or why. Likewise in the Bible, without the creation narratives we would lack a crucial clue about what God is doing and why. To use the metaphor of basketball again, if the coach had not recruited me for a purpose, then his calling out, "God damn you; turn around" would make no sense at all; it would be mere profanity.

When Israel turned from idolatry to the worship of YHWH, it did not conclude that utility was henceforth unimportant. Instead, the Israelite writers shifted the basis for understanding utility. In idolatry, the basis was construed to be in great part the capricious, often clashing, whims of the various idols, and the method of bringing those powerful whims under control for human utility was religious practice. But to the biblical writers the basis of utility is the faithful constancy of YHWH's loving-kindness. The goodness of the creation in Genesis 1, echoed in the promise given by YHWH after the flood that seedtime and harvest, cold and heat, winter and summer, and day and night shall not perish from the earth, is a theological assertion that YHWH, far from being an idol whose whims can be controlled by human beings, is a God of purpose, whose providential care for all creatures—including the beasts—is within that purpose. YHWH is the God who makes the sun to shine and the rain to fall on the good and the evil alike. Religious practice is not a means for human beings to alter this regularity in the furtherance of their own private interests, though YHWH may use the forces of nature to accomplish the divine purpose. What we have called the knowledge of *means,* formulated under the rubric of utility, is not privileged knowledge available by some special revelation only to Israel. For the biblical writers, it is available to all, whether or not they know YHWH, because YHWH's purpose includes all within it.

Therefore, theological knowledge-claims in the book of Genesis do not include what we would call today scientific knowledge-claims. Israelite intellectual activity, on the principle that the squeaky wheel gets the grease, is focused on the question of purpose, for it is this question, and not the question of utility, that underlies its revolt against idolatry. Because modern science as we have discussed it is formulated under the rubric of utility, if we attempt to make the Genesis stories into accounts of prehistory that should be taught as alternative scientific theories because they come from the Bible as the inspired word of God, we completely ignore what the writers of those stories are at pains to do—to get YHWH out of the utility business entirely. In other words, if we should read those stories under the rubric of utility (which we would have to do if we consider them to be alternate scientific theories), we would find it virtually impossible to read them under the rubric of ultimate purpose. (Try to look at Figure 1 as a younger woman and an older woman at the same time.)

Reading Genesis is indeed a hazardous intellectual task. If we should for a moment forget that it was written under the rubric of purpose and instead should lapse into reading it under the rubric of utility, we would fail to notice what it was intended to *do.* Failing to notice its intended purpose (by forgetting the "safety regulations"), we could make two serious and potentially tragic mistakes: (1) We could continue to hate our enemies and assume that God's help is available to us for defeating them. (2) By insisting that Genesis be taught as science, we could diminish the utility of scientific knowledge and increase the possibility of unintended side effects. In other words we could make the mistake of throwing out the baby and keeping the bathwater.

Let us now turn our attention to creation accounts in modern science. As time passed, the Genesis stories themselves became the received tradition about the origin of the world. For the community of the biblical faith this caused no trouble as long as they were read under the rubric of ultimate purpose and were understood in a teleological context. But unfortunately, just as in biblical times the constant temptation was to change YHWH into an idol, so it has also been the temptation for the community of the biblical faith ever since. To realize this, simply consider how much of contemporary religion that goes under the name of Christianity seems to have little concern about having unmerited compassion for the oppressed of the world and instead seems to be a sharply focused program to get Jesus to further the personal agenda of the worshiper. In other words, the temptation is simply the *original* one—to shift from the rubric of ultimate purpose to the rubric of utility when thinking about God.

One characteristic of this constant temptation is that it is subtle. We do not suddenly decide one morning to cease thinking of YHWH as the one who gives life its ultimate purpose and to begin thinking of God as the answer to the question of utility. If one rubric has been dominant and its putative world has proved to be satisfactory for its function over a long period of time, it is almost inevitable that we will begin to think of that putative world as "real" in the sense that metaphysical realism understands that word. Then if we should imperceptibly shift the question and therefore the rubric, we would continue to think of that putative world as the appropriate one for the new question—until it proved to be inadequate. *It is rare in a culture that there is a constant overt awareness of which rubric dominates its intellectual life and therefore guides in the formulation of its putative world.*

At the end of the Middle Ages, when in Western culture modern science arose as a serious critical intellectual activity, it did not invent a new putative world from scratch but began with a received tradition concerning the origin and structure of the world that was nearly two thousand years old, a received tradition of which the book of Genesis was an important part. What we can perceive today with much greater clarity than it could have been perceived at the time is that a gigantic *shift in rubric* was taking place, a shift from the rubric of ultimate purpose of human life to the rubric of utility, and it was taking place with a received tradition that had had its beginning in a gigantic rubric shift in the opposite direction. In other words, modern science was beginning with a received putative world constructed to answer the question that modern science was not asking. (Keep in mind that within the thesis of this book, there is nothing wrong with asking either question; both are important.) In the two-thousand-year interval between the shifts, the Bible had taken on authority not just in matters of ultimate purpose but in matters of utility as well, so that to believe in the Bible was to assume it to be the ultimate "truth" as the word "truth" is understood in metaphysical realism. Consequently, by the beginning of modern science, to doubt any part of the Bible on the grounds that it did not agree with knowledge based on experience formulated under the rubric of utility would be seen as doubting everything in it.

In many ways, then, the modern scientific revolution against the received tradition of the Genesis creation accounts is just the reverse of Israel's revolution against the received tradition of idolatry (though I am in no way suggesting that it was a return to idolatry, as we shall see). Significantly, the leaders of this scientific revolution were asking what seemed to many of them to be a new question, or at least one that the intellectual tradition of the past had not been interested in developing a method to answer—the question of utility, with its answers in the form of useful knowledge. To be sure, the category of utility had not been totally ignored in the past; but what we have previously called the Aristotelian method seemed to them to be not only sterile in producing new knowledge to deal with this question but sometimes positively prolific in producing knowledge-claims that were just plain wrong.

As interest spread in discovering new knowledge that would be useful in fulfilling human wants, the early modern scientists did not look at knowledge-claims about the ultimate purpose of human life to be unimportant or even nonsensical. Many—perhaps most—considered the received tradition of the Bible and church theology to be adequate in this regard. But on the principle that the squeaky wheel gets the grease, in this intellectual revolution it was the question of useful knowledge that demanded attention. Therefore, much of the so-called conflict between science and religion from the end of the Middle Ages to the present day has been the result of an ongoing critical appraisal of the received tradition of the book of Genesis under the rubric of utility. That critical appraisal exhibits the conservative tendency characteristic of all intellectual activity by accepting those aspects of the received tradition that appear to be compatible with experience comprehended under the rubric of utility. But it also exhibits the revolutionary tendency by rejecting those parts of it that appear not to be compatible.

An example of this conservative tendency is the acceptance by the early scientists—sometimes tacit and sometimes expressed—of the claim of Genesis that the world is orderly because of the character of the Creator. Although mere sense experience provided considerable grounds for saying that total reality is chaotic, these early scientists, as they sought knowledge that had utility, did not go back to the capricious idols that Israel had rejected, attributing the chaotic aspects of the world to their capricious behavior and trying to base utility on various ways of controlling these idols. Instead, they began with the conviction that there is a law-like order behind the apparent chaos of nature that can be discovered by what has become known as the scientific method, and no small number of these scientists believed that in "discovering" these laws they were discovering the very thoughts of God. (Einstein's remark, noted earlier, that he could not believe God played dice with the universe, can be construed as a late expression of this conservative tendency.)

In the early days of modern science, then, the conservative tendency in human intellectual activity operating implicitly under the rubric of utility found the idea of the mind of God and the idea of universal deterministic natural laws to be quite compatible. But since then all has not been that easy. As scientists have been able to devise or discover more and more comprehensive laws or theories of nature, and have constructed the putative world of utility based on experience and these laws, the revolutionary tendency toward the received tradition has been increasingly prominent. Many aspects of the developing scientific putative world, especially those pertaining to the events of prehistoric times, are in significant, prima facie disagreement with the corresponding events in the putative world of biblical theology as expressed in Genesis and elsewhere in the biblical literature. The age of the universe, the order and manner of coming into being of parts of the universe, and the origin of the various species of plants and animals are three such aspects.

As we have noted several times before, this prima facie disagreement would be serious indeed if we accepted the view of metaphysical realism that understood "truth" to be a correspondence of verbal knowledge-claims, on the one hand, with a mysterious metaphysical reality that we would have to know apart from experience, on the other. In that case one or the other or perhaps both sets of creation accounts would have to be false. But we have rejected the view of metaphysical realism and have adopted the view of putative realism, which understands meaning and truth to be functions of what knowledge-claims *do*. So now we must ask, within this understanding, why science, based as it is on the rubric of utility, must develop creation stories. What do these knowledge-claims *do*? To put it a different way, what contribution do scientific accounts of human prehistory make to the maximizing of utility?

To begin our rather long answer to this question, let us remind ourselves of something that should be obvious but often seems to be overlooked. In constructing knowledge-claims about the past, in science as well as in theology, we never go back to have *experience* of the past. All of our knowledge-claims about the past are developed from present experience and the appropriate rubric. So we must keep in mind that just as the biblical writers developed their accounts of creation and early times on the basis of their current experiences and the rubric of the ultimate purpose of human life, so scientists have developed their accounts of the origins of the universe and of the species on the basis of present experience and the rubric of utility. Scientists today do not have more *experience* of prehistoric times than the ancient Israelites had. Both groups had or have no such experience whatsoever. What distinguishes the modern scientists from the biblical writers as they develop knowledge of prehistoric times is that the modern scientists have more *present* experience because they deliberately go about having it in a guided way and they operate under a different rubric. (It would also be well if we kept in mind that *within* the putative world of modern science, billions of years elapsed *before any experience whatsoever occurred.* This would pose an interesting difficulty if one assumed that all knowledge is based on experience and also that the knowledge so based is *eternal* truth.)

Let us now continue with the question of why science must develop knowledge-claims about the origin of the universe and of the many species of experiencing beings in it. It is certainly not to make valid knowledge-claims about the ultimate purpose of human life or lack thereof (even though some individual scientists who are explicitly or implicitly metaphysical realists claim that evolutionary biology has proved that life has no purpose). The shift to the rubric of utility is precisely for the purpose of asking and answering a different question. Similarly, it is not merely to satisfy our curiosity about our origins, although curiosity may play a part in all intellectual activity. Mere curiosity would not explain why the scientific method rather than the teleological method was chosen. Prima facie, a teleological rather than a mechanistic explanation of origins is much more satisfying to curiosity. *The answer to the question of why science must develop knowledge-claims about origins must therefore lie in the rubric of utility itself.*

That rubric, as we have noted, is not so much a factual presupposition about innate orderliness or determinacy of the universe as it is an imperative to produce knowledge-claims that will maximize utility and therefore to construct a putative world in which all events ideally can be explained on the basis of mechanistic laws. It has been in the attempt to follow this imperative relentlessly, regardless of its implications for the received tradition, that scientific knowledge-claims about origins have been made.

If science is to be a serious intellectual activity, it is the imperative of its rubric to maximize utility that requires it to produce a putative world that will describe that world's *past and its future* in a way that will be quite distinctive. If knowledge-claims about that world are to be useful in instructing us concerning what we must do to satisfy our wants, then that world must be composed ideally of stuff that moves in accordance with mechanistic, deterministic laws. Therefore science must alter the received tradition of the world by removing from it all traces of explanations that connect events by conscious purposes and seek to replace such explanations with those that employ nonconscious, deterministic laws. The justification for doing so is not that scientists have some mysterious insight into the deterministic nature of ultimate reality. The justification is that a putative world operating on such deterministic laws is one that tends to maximize utility. A putative world in which events are explained on the basis of conscious, responsible decisions or purposes is one over which human control is seriously limited—one in which utility is anything but maximized. Teleological explanations have no utility value. So it is the rubric of utility that challenges the received tradition in the way that events are connected. The reason that scientific theories about the world do not make knowledge-claims about an ultimate purpose for the creation or about any grand design is that the scientific method has been invented by human beings to do something quite different.

Moreover, if the rubric is obeyed, it is almost inevitable that scientists will have to change more than just the *way* that events are connected. They will also have to change the very *events* themselves, as those events are construed from experience. Why is this so? We have discussed this in part 2, but it is well to repeat it here. In the attempt to construct a deterministic putative world, we are concerned not only with the formulation of the laws but also with the nature of the "stuff" of the world that constitutes the events that happen in accordance with these laws. We have characterized the scientific method as a spiral-like process, in which we are constantly trying to get a good "fit" between experiences, on the one hand, and a putative world of stuff, events, and laws, on the other. What do we do when experience tells us that the fit is not so good? We certainly do not throw up our hands in surrender and say that the world is chaotic after all. We employ one or more of the several procedures or techniques in the scientific method to improve the fit. Each time we do so, we remake the world we now experience into one that is made up of events somewhat different from the events of the world that we experienced earlier as chaotic. In other words, each time within science that we have a paradigm shift or a revolution, we have an altered putative world with an altered set of events or facts.

Facts and events are theory laden. In this constant effort to improve the fit and thus maximize utility, it is the rubric and not the received tradition concerning the facts that is the judge of our success. In other words, as long as experience continues to occur, not only are the laws subject to alteration but also the events of the world, *including the events of the past.* It would be tempting to say that by this diligent application of the scientific method what is really happening is that we are getting closer and closer to the "real" truth about the "real" world and its past. But the only ground on which we could claim that this is happening is the acceptance of metaphysical realism with its correspondence theory of truth. Because of the conceptual difficulty with metaphysical realism, a difficulty that we have already examined, it is much more satisfying to say that by this diligent application of the scientific method we are increasing utility. In the language of instrumentalism or pragmatism, we are constructing better tools.

One very important implication of this method is that the received tradition concerning the basis of the order in the world—the mind of God—is now irrelevant to the doing of science. In the early days of modern science, when it was still assumed that the method enables us to *discover* the laws of the universe, and when the laws so discovered (like Newton's Laws) seemed to have a necessity about them that any rational mind could recognize, it was possible not only to assert the compatibility of the scientific method and the mind of God but to go further and claim that the orderly rational, necessary laws "discovered" by the scientific method constituted evidence for the existence of God. But as older, intuitively satisfying laws gave way to newer, less intuitively satisfying laws, it became clearer that the basis for the possibility of doing science—for maximizing utility—was not some fundamental objective order in an ultimately real metaphysical world but was the method itself, which simply demands that when present knowledge-claims result in too many unpredicted experiences, we must try to do better. And one possible way to do better is to invent a new law or theory.

We are now ready to answer the question of why scientists must construct a putative world with its accounts of creation and evolution. How does this activity contribute to maximizing utility, which it must do if the billions of dollars spent on research in these fields are to be justified? The answer lies in an appreciation of the first characteristic of any serious intellectual activity— the attempt to produce systematic knowledge-claims of the broadest generality. In science this attempt has been focused on the development of universal deterministic theories, which will organize all experience into a *universe*—a universal putative world. The advantage of systematic knowledge over piece-meal knowledge is incalculable. Systematic knowledge allows the direct evidence in support of any particular law to be indirect evidence for all other particular laws within the system.

To appreciate this advantage, try to imagine how science would be carried on if in the field of medicine every disease were treated as an isolated phenomenon, with its causes and cures unrelated to those of any other disease! Almost weekly I read about breakthroughs in the field of genetics that enable us to understand heretofore-puzzling disorders and begin to produce cures for them. Such tremendous increases in utility—and I consider the ability to cure diseases a utility—would be unthinkable without the systematizing of biological knowledge that has been going on for centuries and that has been supported by billions of dollars. In the various areas of engineering, virtually none of the conveniences that make modern life possible would be imaginable without the development of systematized knowledge in the physical sciences, a development that had its roots in the work of the early astronomers and has continued almost unbroken since then.

Systematizing, therefore, is not just an amusing pastime for inhabitants of scientific ivory towers. We have already noted that among practicing scientists there are some whose work is focused on the solution of pressing problems. It is easy to see that their activity is in response to the question of how we can get what we want. At the other end of the spectrum are those whose work is focused on bringing all knowledge into one theoretical system. At times it is difficult to see that their work has anything to do with any of the practical problems of everyday life. I once heard an anecdote about an eminent physicist who, when asked what good his theoretical contributions were, thought for a while and then said, "Well, they've made me a good living." It is the systematic body of theoretical deterministic knowledge that greatly enhances our ability to solve the pressing problems at the other end of the spectrum.

Therefore, at any given stage in the development of a scientific theory that purports to be universal in its scope, be it cosmology in physics or evolution in biology, that theory has *implications for the past.* Those implications are arrived at by logical deduction, just as the implications for the future are. The theory, as a hypothesis, serves as one set of premises, and the present facts (remember that facts are not just experiences but emerge from experiences interpreted by the theory) serve as another set. Then it is possible to predict consequences for the future and to test the hypothesis by those consequences, or (to use a pretentious-sounding word) to *retrodict* the antecedents of the present facts, and to test the hypothesis by those antecedents. But there is a significant difference here. Whereas we can have experiences of the consequences, since they are yet to come, we cannot have experiences of the antecedents, since they are already in the past—and some of those antecedents ostensibly occurred before there were any experiencing beings whatsoever. But all is not lost. What we can have is experience of the evidence that those antecedents did happen. For example, an evolutionary theory may predict that I will experience *in the future* certain objects that, when interpreted by the theory, count as fossil evidence that certain events happened in the past. Then the finding or not finding of such evidence counts for or against the theory.

Constructing theories of the past, and therefore constructing putative worlds that include events stretching back into the prehistoric past, is an important part of the scientific method that constantly and single-mindedly in obedience to its rubric seeks to maximize utility by constructing deterministic, mechanistic theories of broadest generality. It should not be unexpected that at any time the putative world of science would be strikingly different from the putative world of the ultimate purpose of human life, simply because the scientific method and the method of theology in the biblical mode have been designed by human beings to do quite different things. *If on the grounds that the putative world of science is incompatible with the putative world of Genesis we should claim that the former is wrong and that the teaching of it should be forbidden or challenged or suppressed, we would be guilty of ignoring a great segment of the evidence that is significant in developing universal deterministic theories of potentially great utility.*

On the other hand, we should avoid making the opposite claim, the claim that because the two putative worlds are incompatible, the putative world of ultimate purpose is the wrong one. Let us examine this mistake. Because the scientific method has been successful in doing what it was invented to do, it has taken on the aura of being the correct method for determining the answer to *any* question. Consequently, its putative world has come to be thought of as the "real" world in the sense that the word "real" is understood in metaphysical realism. What has happened in this period of the ascendancy of the scientific method is just the reverse of what happened during the period of the ascendancy of biblical theology in Western culture. The result is that it is now not uncommon, in the heat of the science versus religion controversy, to hear partisans of science make pronouncements about the ultimate purpose of human life based on premises from the current scientific putative world.

The argument, with variations, goes something like this: "In science, it is no longer necessary to assume the existence of an intelligent omnipotent lawmaker in order to account for the apparent orderliness of the universe. We can get along very well without God. Likewise, we do not need to postulate an ultimate purpose or resort to teleological explanations to account for the origin or development of the species. Therefore, we can conclude that not only is human life without ultimate purpose but that the universe as a whole is without purpose. All events, including human actions, are the result of inexorable mechanistic causes." We should constantly remind ourselves, however, as we engage in hazardous intellectual activity, that we cannot argue in a logically valid way from the contents of one putative world to conclusions about the contents of another putative world. Granted, it is not only possible but imperative if the rubric of utility is taken seriously to construct the scientific putative world with deterministic laws and thus with no hint of teleology or purposive acts. But one should conclude regarding such a putative world that it has no bearing on teleological acts aimed at accomplishing ultimate purposes in some other putative world.

The logical positivists earlier in the last century were scrupulous in denying that their method could be validly used to conclude that there was no God or that there were no ethical truths. They instead said that the terms *God* and *ethical truths* were literally meaningless and that any sentences purporting to state anything factual about them were not statements at all and had no truth-value whatsoever; they were neither true nor false because they made no truth-claims. The difference between the position of the positivists and the thesis of this book is that whereas they made no acknowledgment of any method other than their own for constructing putative worlds and truth-claims, our thesis does. We would thus alter slightly the positivists' judgment and say that the terms *ultimate purpose* and *teleological action* are meaningless within the putative world of science and that *within that putative world* no knowledge-claims can be made about them. Because science can and does speak with deserved authority about its own putative world, it is unfortunate and sometimes quite dangerous when its authority is invoked to make pronouncements about the contents of a putative world constructed to speak to the question of the ultimate purpose of human life.

In the heat of science-versus-religion debates on origins it is more than just a bit ironic to hear certain supporters of the religious side making claims about what should and should not be included in the scientific putative world *on the basis of their religious position,* and to hear certain supporters of the science side making claims about what should and should not be included in the putative world of theology *on the basis of their scientific position.* This book aims to provide an understanding of the competence and limitations that are put upon each discipline by its rubric, so that those working in one discipline can do their work with knowledge, respect, and appreciation for what others are doing in their respective disciplines. Each putative world is an *instrument* or *tool* that does the task for which it was fashioned.

Miracles

As we begin the discussion of this second vexing topic we need to keep in mind Principle 8: *Many key words and terms are defined* within *a given putative world and may have a quite different meaning within another putative world.* If we should forget this principle for even a moment, we might easily assume that everyone knows what the word *miracle* means and that the only question to be discussed is whether or not miracles have ever happened. But within the intellectual history that we have discussed thus far, the word has had several meanings. That simple question is thus really several questions, with perhaps different answers depending on which meaning of the word is intended. The common assumption that words have real, permanent meanings is relatively harmless in a culture that is living comfortably with a received tradition of long and good standing. Since the received tradition, as an expression of the putative world of the culture, gives the words their meanings, the longer a received tradition has been the dominant one, the more likely it is that people in that culture will use a word in the same way and therefore the stronger will be the assumption that a word does have a real meaning. But when received traditions are being challenged, when paradigm shifts within a discipline or shifts in dominant rubrics are creating new putative worlds, the assumption that words have real, permanent definitions is anything but harmless. It becomes a formidable barrier to understanding and communication and may bring about heated but essentially empty disputes.

Clearly, then, we should (a) begin with the definition that our own culture—our received tradition—gives to the word *miracle*, (b) next discuss the features of the culture that gave rise to that definition, and (c) then ask if that definition is suitable in the present understanding (the present putative world) of science, and if it was the definition implicit in the putative world of the biblical writers when they discussed those events that we today refer to as "miracles." The answer in both cases, as we shall see, is no. In arriving at that answer we shall discover that the two rubrics, the rubric of utility in science and the rubric of ultimate purpose in biblical theology, determine the word's distinctively different meanings in each intellectual discipline.

The Definition of Miracle *in Our Received Tradition*

Over the past forty years every time I have heard or read the word *miracle*, I have made it a point to ask myself how the speaker or writer is using the word. In the vast majority of cases, the implicit definition is something like this: The word *miracle* means "an event that breaks the natural laws of science." And almost always that usage carries with it the implication that *if* a bona fide miracle does indeed *happen* (remember that we use the word "happen," not the word "occur," when we are speaking of events), then that event constitutes valid confirmation of the existence of God. This same definition is implicitly used by members of two groups that we can call the believers and the skeptics. The believers say that bona fide miracles have indeed happened and that therefore belief in God is justified. The skeptics say that no bona fide miracles have happened and that therefore, at least on these grounds, there is no justification for believing in God. The attitude of the skeptic is, "Show me a real miracle, and then I will believe!" This morning before I began to write this paragraph I looked up the word *miracle* in the dictionary I use most often, just to make sure that my reading of the received tradition was a fairly accurate one. Much to my relief, the first definition for the word was essentially in agreement with my reading of the received tradition. (Remember that a dictionary is a repository of the received tradition.)

The Source of the Definition

If this definition is almost (but not quite) universal in ordinary discourse in our own culture, we should now seek its origin. It seems to have arisen in the early days of modern science when, as we have already noted, many scientists were making two significant assumptions: (1) that they were *discovering* (not inventing) the laws of nature and (2) that in discovering these laws they were discovering the thoughts of God. The first assumption was given credence by the fact that two significant systems of deterministic knowledge-claims of the very broadest generality had been devised. The first system was not a new one but was the old one of Euclidean geometry. The axioms of that system possessed a clarity that made it easy to declare them to be self-evident truths, from which all the laws of space could be derived and by which they were explained. The other system was a new one, one that could be thought of as the ultimate flowering of the scientific method, namely, Newtonian mechanics, whose basic principles seemed to be comparably self-evident and from which all laws of the universe could be derived. In the light of such convincing achievements it was difficult to doubt that science had indeed *discovered* the fundamental laws of the universe—laws that had a status in reality just as secure as the status of the "stuff" of the universe and that deterministically governed all the movement of that "stuff" in real Euclidean space. The second assumption, that in discovering the laws of nature the scientists were discovering the thoughts of God, was an adaptation of the biblical received tradition that the order of the universe derives from the character of the Creator.

From the understanding of science inherent in these two assumptions a new putative world was emerging within the terms and categories of which all experience—past, present, and future—had to be comprehended. And this new, emerging putative world was being constructed under the rubric of utility. How, then, are the biblical stories that are called miracles to be comprehended and included in this new putative world? As this question was dealt with, the now-common definition of *miracle* emerged.

Since the stories of these events were part of the received tradition that had come to be thought of as "true" in the sense of that word in metaphysical realism, they could not simply be dismissed or ignored. But because the rubric under which the new putative world was being constructed had gradually and imperceptibly become the rubric of utility (the rubric that required all events to happen in accord with natural law), and because so many of these events did not seem to fit this requirement, they had to be given a special status. Since God is the omnipotent author of the natural laws, God, and only God, can also break them. Since we can and do know the natural laws, and since we can recognize when an event breaks these laws, we can know by the happening of such an event that there exists one who is capable of breaking the natural laws, namely, God.

Hence the word *miracle* had a new definition: "an event that breaks the natural law and thus proves the existence of God." This definition was widely accepted by scientists and theologians alike, as it became part of the new received tradition. But we must not think that this process was a conscious one, one that came about because the thinkers of the time recognized that an old definition was no longer adequate. Because the change in the rubric had happened so gradually but decisively, it was simply assumed that this definition (which we in the twenty-first century can see to be a new one) had been the one that the biblical writers had used in their time. Indeed, that there might have been a different definition in biblical times was an idea that could hardly have been entertained by most. Consider Figure 1 again. If I have always seen it as a young woman and have never even heard of anyone's seeing it otherwise, it will hardly occur to me that other people might see it otherwise.

The new definition of *miracle* gave rise to a number of investigations or research projects that were devised to demonstrate whether or not some of the alleged biblical miracles really were in fact miracles. The claim of the skeptics, that these alleged miracles were events that could be explained by natural law if we knew all the facts, is behind the often-heard jibe that God exists to account for the events that science has not yet explained. The apparent success in giving scientific explanations for many biblical miracles drove many believers into a defensive posture, which is still in evidence today.

Contemporary Science and "Miracles"

We must now ask if this common definition of the word *miracle* is one that is cogent within the understanding of the scientific method today. The answer is no because developments in science have made that first assumption—that by the scientific method we *discover* objectively preexisting laws of nature—no longer tenable. Specifically, these developments have led to the replacement of Euclidean geometry and Newtonian mechanics—the two systems that gave the assumption its credence—by systems of geometry and mechanics whose fundamental principles are at significant points quite different from those of Euclid and Newton. These new principles lack the clarity of the Euclidean and Newtonian principles that had led generations of thinkers to declare them to be self-evident, indubitable, necessary, and therefore objective and eternal truths. As long as those systems were the prevailing ones in scientific thought, it was just those "truths" that made it seem unthinkable to doubt metaphysical realism and its correspondence theory of truth. If the question were asked, "How do we know that these truths of science, which are confirmed by our experience, do indeed correspond to the real, objective truths of ultimate reality?" the answer would be, "They are so clearly and self-evidently true that even God could not think them to be otherwise." As long as those systems were the prevailing ones, it was difficult *not* to believe that scientists were discovering—indeed had discovered—the laws of nature.

Why, then, during the first part of the twentieth century did the scientific community reluctantly give up Newton and Euclid and embrace Einstein? Certainly it was not because it had some nonexperiential knowledge of an eternal truth and had finally come to see that Einstein's theories corresponded to it. Its reluctance to accept the change was precisely because in order to accept the change, any claim to possess such certain knowledge of eternal truth would have to be given up, and the scientific community as a whole would not give it up gladly. It was the *rubric of utility* that finally gave the stamp of approval to the new system. Of the two systems of mechanistic theories, it was Einstein's rather than Newton's that proved to have the greater utility. To put it a little more precisely, when experience as it occurs is transformed into facts under the guidance of Einstein's theory, his theory does a better job of explaining those facts than Newton's theory does for the facts generated from experience under the guidance of his theory. Or to put it another way, when Einstein modifies the putative world of science, experience shows it to be an improvement over the version of the scientific putative world as Newton had constructed it.

The replacement of Newtonian theory by Einsteinian theory, when considered *within* the intellectual discipline of science, is simply a paradigm shift, but of course a very important one. However, when considered in a broader intellectual context, its implications are not about *which* scientific theory is to be accepted, but about how *any* scientific theory is to be understood as a knowledge-claim. It is in this broader context that the shift constitutes a formidable challenge to long-held assumptions of the received tradition about what knowledge is. Let us see what it does to the received definition of "miracles."

Einstein's theory is better than Newton's not because between the two theories it does the better job of explaining the *same set of events that make up the world*, for as we have seen in our discussion of the scientific method, there are no independent events and facts that exist outside a theory to explain them. Events *happen* and facts emerge as statements with meaning and truth-value only when experience, which *occurs,* is interpreted under the guidance of a theory. As long as Newton prevailed, it was easy to believe that events, on the one hand, and laws of nature, on the other, were not so intertwined but could be independently known. Thus the rather linear view of the scientific method was easy to accept: First, experience tells us what the events of the world are (which we express linguistically as *facts*); then on the basis of logic, we move from the facts to the universals, called laws, which govern the facts; we recognize these laws to be true, even though they have been logically derived from only a fraction of all the facts, because on the basis of their clarity and undeniability they are necessarily, eternally, and objectively true.

The new theories of space and mechanics, however, by *denying the undeniable* principles and replacing them with bizarre principles, predicted an equally bizarre set of events—a set of events that experience, interpreted by these bizarre principles, saw *happen.* It became increasingly apparent that events, on the one hand, and laws or theories, on the other, are not so neatly separable into independent objects of knowledge. The linear notion of the scientific method was no longer tenable. The belief that scientists were *discovering* the truth could no longer be supported by saying that the laws and theories produced by the scientific method have the indelible mark of necessary eternal truth. The correspondence theory of truth accordingly lost the possibility of identifying anything at all that scientific truth could correspond *with*, and so became meaningless along with metaphysical realism.

And what about miracles? All of the presuppositions of the received tradition concerning the nature of scientific knowledge—the presuppositions on which the definition of the word *miracle* had been based—are gone. The very notion that events are the kinds of things that can break a natural law, and the notion that natural law is the kind of thing that can be broken by events, are both meaningless, because now it is understood that law and events develop together in a method that is circular or spiral-like rather than linear. If in the course of time anomalies (events unpredicted by the theory) emerge among the events developed under the guidance of a theory, the conclusion that the event has "broken" the natural law does not entail the conclusion that there must exist some power that can hold the law in abeyance for a time. Under the rubric of utility, an anomaly entails the conclusion that scientific work is not completed and that it may be advisable in the future to amend the theory or law in order to eliminate the anomaly and maximize utility. In other words, a new paradigm shift may be called for.

Strictly speaking, science does not prove or confirm that events called "miracles" do or do not happen. Rather, we should say that within the language of the intellectual discipline of modern science the word *miracle*, as it is defined by the received tradition that began in the early days of science, now simply has no meaning. We should specifically note that we are required to say this by the rubric of utility and not by scientific facts. Human beings have deliberately devised the intellectual program called the scientific method in order to produce knowledge-claims that maximize utility. To attempt to make a place in the scientific putative world for miracles, defined as "events that break the natural law," would, if successful, be an invitation to disaster, since it would introduce into the scientific method some rubric other than the one of utility, thus increasing the possibility that knowledge-claims produced by that amended method would be unreliable. Even if such an attempt is unsuccessful, it has the unfortunate result of diverting the energies of scientists from proper tasks to the task of combating a frivolous attack. And, as we shall next see, such an attempt, though often launched as an effort to "get God back into science," does no service to the biblical faith. The fact that even in academic circles debates are still waged on the assumption that the word *miracle* means "an event that breaks the natural law" indicates that in the educated sector of our society there is a serious culture lag in the areas of science and theology, a lag that should be seriously addressed by academic faculties before it does more harm than it has already done.

The Biblical Writers and "Miracles"

I have already suggested several times that when the biblical writers told of events that traditionally have been called miracles, they did not understand them to be events that broke the natural law and thus proved the existence of God. There are two rather obvious reasons for this. The first is that in biblical times the understanding of natural law that underlies this definition of *miracle* was simply not a part of their intellectual repertory. As we have seen in the previous section, the developments in science that made that understanding of natural law plausible did not happen until about the end of the Middle Ages, when the interest in knowledge that has utility was increasing. To be sure, the biblical writers were aware of orderliness in the world, but they attributed that orderliness to the faithfulness of the God who had promised to restore the world to the purpose for which it had been created. Therefore, that orderliness could not be separated from that promise. The second rather obvious reason is that in the stories as they are told, more often than not the people who witnessed the miracles did not become believers but became hostile, claiming that the events were the work of Satan or a demon. Specifically, in the Gospels in the Greek Scriptures the very people who in one way or another deserted Jesus in the end included many who had observed the events. This should not surprise us if we keep in mind the principles at the beginning of this chapter.

On the basis of what we have claimed about the biblical faith in part 3, let us offer a different definition for the word *miracle*, a definition in keeping with the rubric of the ultimate purpose and with a putative world in which God is the principal actor, at work to restore the world to its original purpose. *For the biblical writers, the word* miracle *means "an event which the faithful understand to be a sign that God is keeping the promises."* The meaning of the event is therefore to be found by noticing the place that it occupies in the total plot of the Bible. The major part of that plot, as we have seen, is God's restoring the creation to its original purpose by keeping the promises made to Abraham and Sarah. Since God's character is faithful loving-kindness, every act of God has its meaning totally exhausted in its being the appropriate act in the circumstances to keep the promises. The biblical miracles, understood by the biblical writers as mighty acts of God, are no exception; their meanings, too, is totally exhausted in their being acts by which God is keeping the promises and is thus bringing about the restoration (salvation) of the creation.

The question that we are most prone to ask about miracles today—"Did they *really* break the laws of nature?"—is the wrong question on two counts. First, it is based on a conception of the laws of nature that has no cogency in the current understanding of science; it is therefore not a genuine question at all but a meaningless collection of words. Second, it asks a question that would be equally meaningless to the biblical writers. Whether or not an event allegedly breaks an alleged natural law has nothing to do with its meaning as a teleological act of God. To discover its meaning we need to look at its place in the plot. When we do this, events become understandable.

Let us begin by considering Matt. 11:2–6. In Matthew's account of Jesus' ministry, after Jesus had performed many acts that we call miracles, John the Baptist, who was in prison, sent some of his own disciples to ask Jesus if he was "the one who is to come," or if they should "wait for another." The expression "the one who is to come" stands for the expected messiah, whose task is to fulfill the promises. Jesus does not say yes or no, but this: "Go and tell John what you hear and see: the blind receive their sight, the lame walk, the lepers are cleansed, the deaf hear, the dead are raised, and the poor have good news brought to them. And blessed is anyone who takes no offense at me." The significance of this answer to John's question lies not in any claim that the acts had broken natural law but in the character of the acts themselves as a part of the plot. They were the acts that Israel in the Hebrew Scriptures had expected to accompany the coming of the messianic age, precisely because the various conditions mentioned—blindness, lameness, deafness, illness, poverty, death—were understood to be those that characterized that fallen human state in which human beings had rebelled against God's purpose for their lives, turning to their own way.

The prophet in Isa. 35:5–6 had expressed his faith that YHWH would keep the promise to restore the creation to its proper telos with these words: "Then the eyes of the blind shall be opened, and the ears of the deaf unstopped; then the lame shall leap like a deer, and the tongue of the speechless sing for joy." The events that are called the healing miracles, therefore, have no meaning outside the rubric of purpose. They are, like everything that God does, acts of totally unmerited grace, explained and understood solely as acts motivated by God's promise to restore human beings to the purpose for which they were created—to reflect God's character of unmerited faithful loving-kindness to all others. Therefore, if John the Baptist and his disciples share the biblical faith, they will see and hear Jesus' acts as authentic acts of the messiah, who is fulfilling the telos.

When we read the accounts of the miracles under this rubric as acts in the putative world of the biblical faith, we can also understand why the poor heard the good news gladly but the proud rejected him. What is the significance of Jesus' words at the end of the passage from Matthew, "And blessed is anyone who takes no offense at me"? Why would anyone take offense at someone who made the blind to see, the deaf to hear, the lame to walk, and the lepers clean? If these events had no other significance than that they were remarkable acts exhibiting the power of God, it would be hard to say why anyone would object. And indeed, in the Gospel accounts, much of the early response to Jesus is portrayed as the crowd's adulation of a wonder-worker. Apparently many in the throngs that followed him thought of him as one who possessed powers that could enable them to advance the fulfillment of their own agendas—they went after him to get their own bellies filled. But what became increasingly clear was that these acts were not performed for the benefit of meritorious people on the basis of their merit but for those who knew they had no merit.

To the proud, who thought of religion as a practice of strict requirements in order to bring the power of God to the support of their own agendas, this was offensive indeed. The implications of a God whose acts on our behalf are not somehow controlled by our own merit are what Israel had realized in the exodus—the implications that had led Israel to switch from the rubric of utility to the rubric of purpose in constructing its putative world. But now the religiously proud who had forgotten this and had turned YHWH into an idol, saw Jesus' acts of kindness unmotivated by the recipient's religious righteousness as an offense to "good" religion. To use our analogy of basketball, and perhaps stretching it a bit, if when I have turned to the wrong basket I become so enamored of it that I refuse to accept the coach's goal for me, the call to me to turn around will be bad news indeed.

On the other hand, for those who remembered the received tradition of the biblical faith of the prophets, these same acts that had offended many were seen as sure indications that in Jesus, God was indeed inaugurating the messianic age—the age when human beings are restored to true obedience. For the poor and humble, then, these signs, though not motivated by individual acts of meritorious human obedience, are a call to repentance and true obedience, a call to follow Jesus as the one who loves others the way God loves. The *faith* that is almost always associated with the miracles of Jesus in the biblical narratives is not, as it is so often thought to be today, a self-generated belief that is strong enough to coerce God to break the natural law in order to further the believer's own agenda. It is rather profound confidence that God is keeping the promise to fulfill in the believer, and ultimately in all creation, God's own agenda.

One further aspect of the cultural milieu in which the biblical faith emerged will shed light on the way that the biblical writers discuss the marvelous events. In that world there were many people, sometimes referred to as magicians in the Bible, who possessed the ability to do marvelous deeds. In the received tradition this ability was understood under what we have called the rubric of utility. Their powers were for hire. In the stories of the plagues that preceded the exodus, Pharaoh had in his service such magicians, whose task, along with that of his priests, was to see that Pharaoh's will be done. In those stories the magicians could almost match Moses, who is acting for YHWH, in doing the various marvelous deeds. It is highly improbable that the writers of these stories understood these deeds to be events that proved the existence of God by breaking natural law. What distinguishes Moses' marvelous deeds is that they are understood completely under the rubric of the ultimate purpose of human life. YHWH's power, unlike the power that the magicians had, was not for sale. It was for YHWH's and YHWH's purpose alone, to keep the promises to Abraham and Sarah to restore all nations to be a community of faithful loving-kindness.

After they were in the promised land, the Israelites were to remember that YHWH had delivered them from bondage by these many marvelous deeds. Why were they to do so? Was it so that anytime they wanted something, they could count on YHWH to perform similar marvelous deeds on their behalf?

Certainly not! It was when the Israelites were treating others oppressively, just as Pharaoh had treated them oppressively, that the prophets called them to the remembrance of these deeds. Consistently through the biblical literature there is a prohibition against magic—the practice of doing marvelous works for some agenda other than YHWH's.

In chapter 8 of the book of Acts there is a story with the same point. In the early days of the church after the resurrection of Jesus the proclamation of the good news by the disciples and apostles was accompanied by signs and miracles that were understood by the biblical writers to be gifts of the Holy Spirit for the very purpose of fulfilling God's promise to include the Gentiles in the restored community. In Samaria a magician by the name of Simon, who had won a considerable reputation as a wonder-worker who possessed the power of God, heard the preaching of the good news, saw the signs and wonders, and was baptized. Later when the apostles Peter and John came and laid hands on them, the new converts themselves received the gifts of the Spirit. When Simon saw this, he offered the apostles money so that he too could have the power to give the Spirit to anyone whom he laid his hands on. Simon was most severely reprimanded and called to repent. He was attempting to understand these signs and wonders and miracles under the rubric of utility, thus making the God of the biblical faith into an idol. Marvelous acts, therefore, are a part of the putative world that Israel inherited as its received tradition. The biblical writers did not reject them completely (just as they did not reject sacrifice completely); but in keeping them as part of the putative world of ultimate purpose, they had to understand them as acts performed by God to keep the promises. Any attempt to interpret them otherwise, such as that they demonstrate a power of God available to properly religious human beings for their private agendas, is to be condemned.

It is not our purpose in this chapter to analyze all scriptural miracles, but simply to explicate our thesis as one within which we are to understand them. But we should briefly discuss the accounts of Jesus' birth and resurrection before we conclude this section. It is especially in discussing these two accounts that I believe we are most prone to forget all the principles in the early part of this chapter and revert to the position of metaphysical realism. In most of the arguments on this topic that I have listened to and participated in during the last four decades, the participants have eventually raised the question, But what *really, really, really* happened? For me, it takes all my powers of concentration not to toggle back into the putative world created under the rubric of utility, to take that world as the really, really real world, and then to assume that the events of that world are the ones that really happened. In other words, the view of metaphysical realism is reasserting itself, along with its correspondence theory of truth, and I am tempted to think that the scientific method is the one by which to discover that truth.

If the thesis of this book has cogency, however, and I think it does, then that question is a heavily loaded one that implicitly denies everything in our thesis and therefore in our principles. On the basis of our thesis the question has no answer, not because we don't know enough to answer it, but because it really isn't a question. To *deal* with the question, rather than to answer it, I must say that the accounts of Jesus' birth and resurrection are events in the putative world of biblical theology, a putative world formed under the rubric of the ultimate purpose of human life, in response to the overwhelming experience of being loved without regard to merit or righteousness. That putative world under that rubric, must therefore give an account of all experience, not just the experience of being loved. That experience also includes the received tradition, which cannot be ignored but may be accepted or modified. Any *thing* or *event* whose existence or happening I can assert as a knowledge-claim is a thing or an event in a putative world and, as such, is problematical. As we have seen, there is in the biblical literature an ongoing modification of the putative world as it becomes clear that certain aspects of it do not fit given experience as it is understood under the rubric. In the putative world of the biblical faith, if that lack of fit becomes evident then it must be corrected. The putative world needs correction when it can be inferred from it that God does something other than fulfill God's promises and that God's ultimate purpose for human beings is something other than that we love one another without regard to the merit of the one loved.

Therefore, when we consider the accounts of the virgin birth of Jesus and of his resurrection, the first question to ask is not "Did they really happen?" Rather we should ask what these accounts meant to the biblical writers. They did not tell the stories as if they were about events that had obvious, self-contained, individually complete meanings in themselves, on the basis of which a theological system could be built. On the contrary, the biblical writers, in keeping with our assertion that the first aim of any intellectual activity is to be systematic, see the significance of these events only within the context of a plot that has a meaning and gives meaning to all events in it. For them, the Christian faith is not believing in a virgin birth and in a bodily resurrection of a man named Jesus, as if there were some virtue in believing in them. Rather, as the Apostles' Creed of the early church reflects, the Christian faith is believing in Jesus the Christ, who was among other things born of the Virgin Mary and was raised from the dead. It is the place that Jesus occupies in the entire biblical plot that is the object of the Christian faith. Let us briefly recall what that place is.

For the first disciples, their experience of Jesus—the given, occurring, non-problematical experience—was one of completely unmerited love. This was the meaning-giving experience in the light of which everything had to be understood. It is an experience that they comprehend within their received tradition of the Israelite community of faith and its Hebrew Scriptures. Jesus, then, is the Messiah, the one in whom the character of the Creator, YHWH, is fully revealed; and the one in whom the purpose for the creation and for human beings is revealed. Jesus is also the one in whom the life of true obedience is lived; in whom God's promises to Abraham and Sarah are being fulfilled; and by whom they themselves have been turned from their own agendas to God's purpose. Jesus as Messiah thus embodies God's eternal and unchanging will and reveals what God's creation must ultimately be conformed to.

For the biblical writers of the Greek Scriptures, this is who Jesus *really* is in their putative world of ultimate purpose. Therefore, everything that they say about him and ascribe to him must assert this and nothing must contradict it by suggesting that he requires from his followers anything but the imaging of God's love in their relationships with others in the human community of all peoples and nations. In this context the biblical writers tell the stories of Jesus' birth and resurrection. Thus Matthew and Luke say that his birth comes by action of the Holy Spirit, who in the putative world of the biblical faith is understood to be God acting to empower people to true obedience. In doing so, they relate his birth to an expectation in the Hebrew prophets (the received tradition) that one in the Davidic line as heir to the messianic title shall be born of a virgin or young woman. In Luke, Mary understands the significance of her yet-to-be-born son to be that he will fulfill God's promises to Abraham. In the Gospel of John, where there is no birth narrative, Jesus is called the eternal Word of God made flesh to dwell among us so that all who believe in his name will receive God's power to become children of God (those who truly and joyfully do the will of God). In the Epistles, where there also is no birth narrative, he is called the Wisdom of God, in contrast to the wisdom of the world, and the one in whom the fullness of God dwells bodily.

The stories of the resurrection are perhaps best illuminated by the experience of Saul, who after his conversion (his being turned around to the proper goal) became known as Paul, the Apostle to the Gentiles. For Paul, the experience on the Damascus road was one that he could call no less that the experience of dying and rising to newness of life. It was an experience that changed him from being a persecutor of his fellow Jews who called Jesus the Messiah, to his being perhaps the most influential apostle in the early church. It is this experience of being totally overwhelmed by unmerited love that requires the early disciples to interpret their other postcrucifixion experiences as experiences of the living Christ, still actively fulfilling the messianic task. In the putative world of the biblical faith, the living Christ is reality. To deny it would give us permission to deny that in him the eternal will of God is known, and therefore it would give us permission not to act toward others with unmerited loving-kindness.

If the miracle stories were about events in the world of metaphysical realism, then the scientific evaluation and theological evaluation would indeed be in serious conflict. It is when we are fully aware of the function that rubrics have in constructing putative worlds, and when we recognize the specific rubric under which each of these intellectual activities is carried out, that the conflict disappears.

Canon

In the heat of a discussion about the appropriate theory for understanding and explaining the diversity of species of plants and animals in the world, few things are more irritating to most modern scientists than the claim of the so-called creation scientists that no scientific theory contradicting the biblical account in Genesis is acceptable *because the Bible is the authoritative inspired word of God and contains no errors of fact.* To these modern scientists the notion of an authoritative canon, one that contains no errors of fact, comes close to being a contradiction in terms. Keeping in mind all the principles of our thesis, let us try to come to an understanding of what the community of the biblical faith might mean when it calls the Bible the canon.

I shall begin with an anecdote. Many have observed, and my own observations confirm it, that science has its own collection of classic texts that together make up something close to a canon. In the disputes about science and religion that are a feature of most academic communities, those arguing on the science side, be they professors or sophomores, are as capable of buttressing their arguments by references to their canon as those defending the religion side are of buttressing their arguments with citations from the Bible. The science canon consists of works by or about such greats as Kepler, Galileo, Newton, Darwin, and Einstein.

Let us ask why these venerable scientists, most of whom flourished a century and a half ago or more, are so often cited. In most cases it is certainly not because their works represent the state of the art in scientific knowledge. Most of their theories are so outdated that any institution using their works as texts for learning the current theories in their various areas would be in danger of having its accreditation seriously questioned. No, we cite them as authorities because they exemplify important aspects of what it is to *do* science. And one of the most important assertions of our thesis concerning science is this: To do science is to follow faithfully the rubric of utility, even if doing so requires one to take a revolutionary stance against a received tradition. The scientific method has been developed to maximize the production of knowledge that maximizes utility. The science canon, therefore, is not authoritative about the *content* of scientific knowledge; it is authoritative, at least implicitly, about the rubric to which scientists must pledge their ultimate and unswerving intellectual loyalty. To do science is indeed a hazardous undertaking. To claim to be doing scientific work, but at the same time not following this rubric, is heresy and invites disaster. In recent years there have been a few cases of scientists being "excommunicated" from the scientific community because they made knowledge-claims that were not founded on a scrupulous following of the rubric. The *original sin* in science is to desert the rubric of utility.

By analogy, the Bible is the canon for the community of the biblical faith, authoritative in matters of faith and practice. The knowledge-claims of this community are about the ultimate purpose of human life, which is to image faithful loving-kindness in our relationships with all others. The method of theology in the biblical mode begins with utter and unswerving loyalty to this purpose, and under the rubric of the ultimate purpose of human life it strives to make knowledge-claims about a world in which this purpose prevails. It makes knowledge-claims about this world for two reasons: (1) to witness to the world what its faith is, as a part of its own role in God's bringing this purpose about, and (2) to guide its own practice as it seeks to love others as God has loved all. For the community of the biblical faith the Bible is a record of the early community as it struggled to be faithful to that purpose. It is through its witness that God continues to fulfill the promise in the generations that have followed.

When the community of faith reads the Scriptures today under the rubric of purpose, it understands what is required to be faithful to the ultimate purpose when it encounters new and strange received traditions. To take the Bible as one's guide to practice is to turn from any attempt to make God into a utility and to understand every aspect of it as an assertion of God's faithfulness in the promise to restore us to our purpose. The unwillingness of the community to deny its faith and to deny the authority of the Bible is its unwillingness to say to anyone, "The Creator of the universe gives me permission to hate you and to ignore your oppression by anyone." To engage in theology in the biblical mode is indeed a hazardous undertaking. To commit heresy—to engage in it under any rubric other than the rubric of the ultimate purpose of human life—is not only to invite disaster but almost to ensure it. It is shattering to think of the hatred and oppression of others that has been and is now being done on the grounds that the biblical God commands it. The *original sin* in doing theology is to desert the rubric of ultimate purpose.

Once again, in dealing with a vexing intellectual issue that plays an important part in the discussions of scientific and theological knowledge-claims, it is in paying strict attention to the two rubrics that the issue becomes tractable.

The purpose of this work has been to present and defend a thesis that sheds light on the issues involved in the present debate in the United States concerning science and the biblical faith. With this chapter the attempt to accomplish that purpose is completed.

Index of Biblical Citations

Index of Subjects and Names